I0213073

Ponder

Pray

Practice

366 Daily Devotions
for Thinking Christians

by Robert F. Simms

Unless otherwise marked, all scriptures from
the King James Version of the Bible.

ISBN: 978-0-9834642-2-8
Published in the United States by
Robert F. Simms
Greer, South Carolina

For my wife, Dee
who has for many years
quietly pursued the discipline
of daily morning devotions
and with every passing year
has shown more of Christ
in her life.

Introduction

The daily devotional thoughts in this book have been designed for the Christian who wants something to chew on spiritually each day. Each little spiritual meal focuses on a challenging Bible verse, what it means and how it may be applied in a Christian's life. The short prayer suggestions included with each devotional thought are intended to act as starters for the Christian's daily conversation with God.

Devotional books exist in wide variety, just as people's personal preferences differ widely. This volume is aimed at the Christian who enjoys thinking. The purpose of a daily time of devotion is not to engage the Christian in technical theological studies but to draw his heart and mind into fellowship with God. Yet nothing inspires the Christian's private worship like pondering the great truths of the Bible. While the great truths are often stated simply, they are expressions of deep and profound matters that Christians of the ages have pondered and found to contain still greater depths.

May the thoughts stimulated by these daily readings impel the Christian reader to informed discipleship, as he or she is prompted to love the Lord with heart, soul, mind and strength.

Robert Simms

In the beginning, God …

How to begin

Most Christians will buy several Bibles for their personal use during their lifetimes. There is something special about a new Bible. Perhaps it lies in its being a new binding for an ancient message, reminding us that the Bible never grows old. How appropriate to open a new Bible and read first the opening words in its text. How fitting to open any Bible on the first day of a new calendar year, and remind ourselves of its opening truth: "In the beginning, God…" There is more to the verse than that, but these words are enough for a volume of thought or writing. The Bible does not begin with an argument for the existence of God. It assumes God from the beginning and backward into timeless eternity. When all that we know began, God was.

In the beginning, God—historically, theologically, dynamically, personally. God started the universe and thus flung the galaxies and collected the solar systems. We are well advised to begin with God when we speculate about the origins of the universe and life. It makes a world of difference. A world that just "happened" is a world with no point, full of people with no purpose. But a world with God as creator is a world with a plan, with people put here purposefully.

In the beginning, God. It also means that when you plan your life, you are best advised to begin with God. Do not simply take God into consideration. Turn your whole life over to him, seek him for every decision, find his will, his master plan for everything. There are many ways to guarantee failure in your life, but only one way to guarantee true success, whether you get rich and famous or not. That one way is to put God in the beginning of everything. In the beginning, God. In the personal account of each day's history of your life, this should be the first verse and the overarching theme: it all begins with God.

Father, you were the beginning of all things. May you be the beginning of good things and of all life for us today. Amen.

January 2 **Scripture Reading: Genesis 1:3**

And God said, Let there be light: and there was light.

Light for the world

In Genesis, the first creative act of God was to bring light into the world. That statement accords well with every theory of origins, including the astrophysicist's theory of the explosion of energy into matter in the Big Bang. In light of that creative event (pun intended), it is significant that Jesus said, "I am the light of the world." In the Bible, the mention of light frequently holds more than technical import. Light is truth, good, morality, knowledge, understanding, righteousness, glory. Light is everything that comes from God, and darkness is to be without God or to be against God.

We make use of this comparison continually. We say, "Shed some light on this subject." "I saw the light." "What he said really turned on the light for me." "You light up my life." We use the concept casually, but we understand intimately what light means. First of all, we *like* the light. No one who can see likes to be trapped without light. But even those who are unsighted do not like to be "in the dark" of too little information and understanding. Therefore, when it comes to the light of God, we should seek to know him. In this way we will have light in our lives, instead of the darkness of ignorance and lostness.

Second, we *reflect* the light. Jesus not only said, "I am the light of the world," but also, "You are the light of the world." Then he instructed us who know the light of life in the Son of God not to hide that light as it shines into our own hearts, but to let it pass through and radiate to dispel the darkness around us. The Christian reflects Christ the light, and becomes light to the world himself . The truth of God, the goodness of God, the morality and virtue of Christ, the knowledge of God, the righteousness of our Savior, the glory of God, are to shine through us to people we know and meet. Let the light of God in you help someone else to come to know Jesus Christ, so their lights will be turned on, too.

Father, this little light of mine, I'm going to let it shine, for you. Amen.

God divided the light from the darkness.

The day of dividing

"I save things," he said. "You are a pack rat," said his wife. He countered, "You never know when you are going to need something." He scrapped broken appliances, toys and do-dads. He took apart things others had thrown out, picked up nuts and bolts from parking lots, and otherwise collected mechanisms and parts. He put all these things in cans or boxes until some future date when he could sit down and sort them out, classify them, and put them where they belonged in his many parts drawers and shelves. Every once in a while, he took all the miscellaneous, unsorted junk and performed this routine upon it. Naturally, there were things he threw out. Not all parts of a thing are reusable, and some things he knew, when he put them in bins, he would end up throwing out. But the time for discarding had not yet come. Everything he gathered over time would have its day. Eventually, he would decide what stayed, and what had to go.

The day of judgment will be like that. God will separate what stays with him in his presence, in the glory of heaven, from what will have to go away from him into darkness. Genesis 1:4 says that in the beginning God separated light from darkness. This was part of the creative act, but it was a grand statement at the beginning of the history of this age that it will come to an end by the same act, in spiritual terms. The light will be separated from the darkness. People of the light will be divided from people of the darkness. When God remakes all things, heaven is described as having no night, but instead being eternally in the light of God's day.

Until judgment, God allows much evil to continue, intermingled with good. Sometimes this troubles us, but the time is coming when God will put everything in its place. You who are of the light, take heart.

Father, when you divide all things, may we through Christ be among those you keep forever. Amen.

This is the land that shall fall unto you for an inheritance, even the land of Canaan with the coasts thereof…

Living within God's boundaries

Ever since Israel became a nation again in 1948, it has been involved in conflict. In 1967, Egypt threatened from the south. In 1984 Syrian and Lebanese forces encroached along the north. In the 90s, Iraq lobbed missiles into Israel from the northeast. On the southeast, Saudi Arabia is the continual source of terrorism directed at Israel.

God's own geographical survey in Numbers 34:2 gives the land of Canaan to Israel. The chapter lays out boundaries that include even more land on the north, east and south than is presently possessed by Israel. The argument is over whose holy book to believe, if any at all.

In 2003, an Israeli official proposed that Jerusalem be administered by Jews, Muslims and Christians, with the U.N. Secretary General as Mayor, and that the city be known as the "Capital of the World." The irony of the suggestion should not be lost on Christians. The New Testament teaches that the lingering problems of this world will not be solved until all governments, even democracies, are put down and Christ returns to rule. Until then, conflict will continue.

Every human being lives out a similar struggle over whose will to obey, whose word to believe, which master to serve. But struggle in the soul can be solved in this life. We have only to surrender our rule to Christ and to live within the boundaries of God's loving will. He will bring peace to the troubled turf of our lives and guide us into fulfillment and joy. The factions that lay claim to the fringes or even the heart of what rightfully belongs to God will be conquered, when Christ becomes Lord of all.

Father, while the world is embroiled in struggle, let the peace of God rule in our hearts through Christ Jesus. Amen.

So then every one of us shall give account of himself to God.

Living as if it matters

Some mature adult quipped in the poem, "My get-up-and-go has got up and went:"

I get up each morning and dust off my wits,
Open the paper, and read the Obits.
If I'm not there, I know I'm not dead,
So I eat a good breakfast and go back to bed!

Each day's obituaries give notice that one more person's life opportunity has come to a close. All that is left is what will be said of their time here. What will people say of you? Some say they don't care. Others do care—not for their own sake, but for the sake of their descendants. They care for the sake of the people they know, the Lord they serve and the claims they have made. We deceive ourselves if we say we don't care what people think of us. Virtually all of us do.

What God says of us matters most, of course. But the truth will be known not only to God, but to people around us. Is your life now building a record that will find you held in admiration and respect? Will you be sorry near your end that you did not do something more or something different, or that you did much that was wrong? Will you have disappointed many people, failed many missions, omitted many things that should have been accomplished? The Bible says we will all give account of ourselves to God.

Obituaries typically feature the bare facts. In fact, usually they do not tell how a person died, but just that he did, and then list the survivors, give an address, and tell where a service will be held memorializing his or her life—if there is one. We may want to know more, like what kind of people they were, what they accomplished, what kind of character they had. We should wonder what our obituaries will say, if someone who knows us were to write them. We should determine then to live as if it mattered, because it does.

Father, we live not to die but to serve and love you. But grant that when we die we will have prepared long before, by living for Christ. Amen.

Let your speech be alway with grace, seasoned with salt, that ye may know how ye ought to answer every man.

Salting our speech

Did you ever say something you wished you had not? Something you wished you could draw back out of the air and "unsay?" Did you ever say something one way when you wished you had said it another? Sometimes it is good to write out what you feel, then decide whether or not you ought to say it that way. Those who have done that may discover that simply writing their feelings helps to release them, and they don't actually have to have the confrontation with another person they were tempted to have. Even if you don't have the opportunity or time to write it out, you can almost always afford to think twice. You might not be hurtful, spiteful, resentful, or ugly if you think twice.

Paul was getting at this when he wrote that grace should always typify our conversation, and that our speech should be seasoned with salt. The grace he speaks of is the attitude we take of giving the benefit of the doubt, preferring to believe the best when we may suspect the worst, responding kindly to mean and thoughtless initiatives from others. The salt we season speech with is that spirit of Christ that has a way of changing our natural impulses into something better.

Many cooks who prefer fresh vegetables prepare their own greens. Apparently large quantities of leafy green material cook down in big pots into much smaller amounts. But simply boiling them is not enough. Most people would not much care for the taste of greens cooked without salt. But with the right amount of this ancient and fundamental seasoning, greens are a delight. Salt cuts the raw taste and brings out the flavor.

Words are the same. They often need to be salted heavily to remove the raw effect. When we rethink what we first thought, what then we say is more like we ought.

Father, keep watch over our tongues, that they make not fools out of us or enemies out of others. Amen.

O man, who art thou that repliest against God?

Why me?

A minister visiting a church member in the hospital met a man who said that ever since his retirement on disability he visited the sick, helping them deal with their responses to physical problems. He had a tract in his hand titled, "Why, me?" He and the minister talked about the experience of Job, who asked this question long ago. Paul had some words for it, too. He asked why people who were puzzled over God's ways dared to talk back to him. The Bible contains many passages that deal with various aspects of the purpose for God's allowance of suffering. Sometimes, however, we go so far in demanding an answer of God, or of accusing him of being unfair, that we need to hear the limitation placed on our "right to know." There *is* a point beyond which we cannot know, or we have no ability to understand.

We have often misquoted Alfred Tennyson by saying, "Ours is not to reason why…" The original is from *The Charge of the Light Brigade,* and says, "Someone had blundered: Theirs not to make reply, Theirs not to reason why, Theirs but to do and die." He was speaking of soldiers, whose discipline is solely to obey orders. He was not speaking of the general public. In a sense, however, we are soldiers, soldiers of Christ if we are Christians. Though God does not forbid our wondering why life is as it is, he instructs us that the answer may be beyond our understanding, anyway, and he says that understanding why is not the most important thing.

Job asked "why" for forty chapters, and then God said, 'Enough!' and drew close to him in an encounter inspiring awe. Then Job realized that what was most important was not to feel the self-sufficiency of knowing why, but to feel the presence of God, and walk with him through it all. This priority has not changed for each of us.

Father, help us to be content to walk with you, to know you through the Savior, your Son Jesus. Amen.

No man, when he hath lighted a candle, putteth it in a secret place, neither under a bushel , but on a candlestick, that they which come in may see the light.

Useful illumination

Most of us are familiar with Jesus' saying about not putting a candle under a bushel. Most often we have gathered the lesson that Christians should not attempt to hide their faith, but share it. There is another interesting meaning in those words. It is quite possible, while not technically hiding your witness, for it to be doing no good anyway, because it isn't seen by anyone who needs it. Some people intentionally practice piety in obscurity to avoid confronting people with the gospel, while satisfying themselves they have done their duty. Others may be quite vocal or demonstrative about their faith, but only inside church buildings or at events where no lost persons are. In other settings they may be as indistinguishable from the rest of the world as any unsaved person on the street.

Those who are full of exemplary piety and praise only when by themselves or in family groups are like the tree in the forest that falls while no one is around. The classic physics question is, does it make a sound? A better question might be, does it matter? And people who are such brave witnesses in a crowd of Christians are like key chain lights on a sunny day. You can't tell if they are on or not. Their witness is not much needed where there is ample light already.

Many a person remembers from childhood years that his father or mother would go up and down the household halls turning off lights and asking if anybody was using them. Not only does unused lighting cost money, but it simply doesn't make sense to burn lights when they are doing no one any good. This is what Jesus is saying: the point of light is to dispel darkness. The Christian shares with Christ the mission of being light to the world. Where does your light shine?

Father, grant us light, and grant our little worlds to profit from it. Amen.

Thy money perish with thee, because thou hast thought that the gift of God may be purchased with money.

God cannot be bought

Most of us at some time in our lives have tried to avoid someone's demands on us by appeasing them. In relationships where demands are small, bribes are traded off willingly and happily. We call it, "give and take." But in other cases buying someone off is more sinister. You shouldn't buy off a policeman to get out of a ticket, bribe a judge to get out of a sentence, or make a deal with an official to get around a law. We all know these things, of course. How come, then, so many people try to buy off God?

Some Christians who do not attend church because they have a problem with a fellow member will send their offerings in by mail, as if that were their sole responsibility, or as if it would make up for their not being personally involved. Other people, who do go to church but who do not do much otherwise, use the same tactic—depending on their money to purchase their good standing. Or, as a variation on the practice, they may make a large donation to a pet cause to avoid guilt for not giving regularly to the budget. Or, they may even be involved in practically everything, trying to control the church, and their financial gifts, time and energy are ways of *buying* the influence they seek.

None of this is right, but how many of us are guilty of it at some time? It is no small matter. The Apostle Peter dealt with such a man and pulled no punches when he prophesied he would perish with his money for thinking he could buy off God. If God grants us a favor, it will be because of his desire to bless us, not our deserving anything at all. It will be out of his grace, not our gratuities. God cannot be bought by any means.

Father, if we are tempted today to evade our responsibilities, help us to resist. Amen.

January 10 **Scripture Reading: 1 Corinthians 3:9**

Ye are God's husbandry, ye are God's building.

Keep building

At a crossroads near a country church in upstate South Carolina there is a building under construction on the corner. It is just a cinder block wall about three feet high. Observers going by day by day will notice that it never gets any higher. In fact, the building has been under construction for years. There are never any laborers there. The grass has grown tall inside the enclosure and all around it. Perhaps "under construction" is a mistaken description. Whoever started it years ago also gave up years ago. Did they run out of money, or time, or motivation? Who knows.

Buildings never completed seem unusual to us, because we expect them to be finished, even if not on schedule. What a waste of time, money and material if they are not. But we have learned not to think too much about lives not finished because we see them so often: half-completed maturity, half-baked plans, half-traveled pilgrimages—not just in a state of flux, not caught in transit, but frozen, even abandoned. What happened? Was it failure and discouragement? Sin and disgrace? Opposition and resignation? Or just distraction and procrastination? The reasons are as varied as the lives involved.

Many Christians have lives that have experienced interruption like that—starting a life professing to follow Christ, and then walking off and leaving it unfinished. Many of our personal ventures also wind up on the scrap heap, taking precious time and energy and expenditure of life with them, never to be regained or profited from. When Paul calls us "God's building," his first reference is to the church, but each of us is under construction in the same way, and by the same means. God is the builder, and we are the carpenter's helpers. It should be our unflagging intention and our constant attempt to be completed. How will you ever know what you could have been unless you become it?

Father, lay another block on our low, unfinished walls today, and let us step back with you to see some progress in our lives. Amen.

Now we have received, not the spirit of the world, but the spirit which is of God; that we might know the things that are freely given to us of God.

The focus of our attention

How long did you spend deciding what to wear today? How long did you take fixing your hair? How long do you spend on your *image?* Modern Americans are enamored of this idea of "image," and most people would like to be what they regard as sophisticated—whatever they think that is. People tend to adopt a style that is considered desirable by their culture, and they seek the admiration and perhaps even the envy of those around them. This is what the Bible calls the "spirit of the world." It is the attitude of a worldly person, whose life is not centered and built around what God wants for him or her.

Paul writes that the purpose of our being given the Spirit who is from God is that we might come to fully know the salvation and life of godly potential he has given us. The Christian is one who, by accepting the personal Lordship of Christ, has received the Holy Spirit of God, whose personal leading in us is to do the will of God. The Christian on the right track is primarily interested in the Lord and in the Lord's plan. It is a matter of focus.

Those who have used SLR cameras, whether the old film type or the new digital models, know what selective focus means. Looking through the lens of the camera set to a moderate to wide aperture, if you focus on an object two feet away, the horizon is a blur. But if you focus on the sky, the objects close by become fuzzy and unimportant in the picture. It is similar with God, said Helen Lemmel: "Turn your eyes upon Jesus: look full in his wonderful face; and the things of earth will grow strangely dim, in the light of his glory and grace."

Father, if we know Jesus, we should concentrate on him, not on attaining any sort of image in the world—just the likeness of Christ. Give us grace and freedom to do that today. Amen.

God is faithful, who will not suffer you to be tempted above that ye are able; but will with the temptation also make a way to escape, that ye may be able to bear it.

Escaping temptation

Paul assured us that God will enable us to "bear it."What is "it"? Through the years, many good folks under the pressure of great sorrow or trouble, have taken comfort from this verse, saying, "God will not put on us any more than we can bear." The Bible teaches God comforts and helps us, but this verse is about temptation. God's promise is to give us a way to "bear temptation"—in other words, to encounter it but not give in to it.

This is a reminder to all of us who have let things keep us from doing God's will. For instance, many people fall prey to the least temptation to forsake Christ's church. If it rains, they don't attend worship, but they would go to work in the rain. A television program wins over a church visitation, but they wouldn't miss a big party for a TV show. Opportunity presents itself for their giving a verbal witness to a friend, but they let the fear of rejection or embarrassment prevail. It comes down to what is important. Sadly, to many Christians, Christ and his church are simply not as important as other things. They have not pre-determined that Christ shall have first place. The temptation was not too much for them; they simply did not take God's provision of escape—which is his power to say no to themselves.

If we fall prey to the least temptations, how shall we resist the great ones? Someone who continues and worsens in this way of forsaking Christ soon virtually proves he is no Christian at all. The old, anonymous hymn says, "I love thee, I love thee, I love thee my Lord, I love thee my Savior, I love thee my God, I love thee, I love thee, and that thou doest know—but how *much* I love thee, my actions will show." Are your actions those of a reborn person, escaping temptation in order to serve Christ with all your heart?

Father, let our lives tell on ourselves, and let us be proud of it. Amen.

Whether therefore ye eat, or drink, or whatsoever ye do, do all to the glory of God.

Let everything glorify God

Are you glorifying God right now? How about just before you picked up this book? Will you be glorifying God when you finish this page and go on to your next activity? These are not frivolous questions, though they may seem odd. The scripture clearly says no matter what we do, we should do it to God's glory. We don't find it difficult to understand how to apply this principle to major decisions or actions, but Christians have sometimes been curious about how it applies to mundane, everyday activities.

Put simply, the Bible means every action of ours is to be evaluated in the light of the glory of God. Will this action fit in with a life that lifts up Christ, that demonstrates God's plan, that fulfils God's purpose? Will it in any way defeat God's desires for me? It isn't that every movement of our hands or every blink of our eyes will cause people to think of God. It is more that everything we do should be in harmony with an overall lifestyle of surrender to the Lordship of Christ, and in keeping with his Spirit's leadership. In other words, no action or inaction of ours should conflict with what God wants of us.

This certainly means having some hard and fast moral rules—like not taking drugs, not cursing, not engaging in immorality, not abusing people, and so on. It also means, however, evaluating every neutral, otherwise harmless activity, to see if it is what God wants of us at that moment. Going fishing is great, but does it displace a responsibility you owe to Christ or his church at that time? On the other hand, going to church is usually good, but occasionally it turns out to be a way of substituting for our larger responsibility to be engaged in witness to people who are unsaved and unchurched. Innocent things can turn sinful when they are put in the wrong place or done at the wrong time in your life. Make sure everything glorifies God, instead of just satisfying you.

Father, in this world where every man is out for himself, make us people who live for you. Amen.

The things that I purpose, do I purpose according to the flesh, that with me there should be yea yea, and nay nay? But as God is true, our word toward you was not yea and nay.

Standing for something

It is said that politicians believe what will get them elected. They may say one thing to one group, and another thing to another group, depending on the character of the group. We are so hard on politicians! Do we ourselves ever say one thing here and another thing there? Of course, we do. Our doing so is the result, most often, not of intentional lying but of uncertain feelings. If you don't know what you believe, you may sway this way today and that way tomorrow, depending on what you *feel*. The Bible says we should *know* the truth, not float around in a vague *feeling* about it.

Paul told the Corinthians he had not said "yes" and "no" in the same breath about anything. He presented a firm, convinced message, no wishy washy one, and he spoke from conviction on every doctrine, or he did not speak. He did not soften the gospel for those most hostile to it or tread lightly over sin where it was most rampant. He put out the word, and he let it stand unaffected by his surroundings.

In a land where toleration of viewpoints has been elevated to the point of a religion of its own, Christians often believe they have no right to be too convinced or too confident of anything, and certainly not to "offend" others with their certainty. That's not what God says. We are to speak the truth—in love, of course—but speak it. We are to pray for boldness to stand firm in the gospel and to speak for Christ confidently. Whoever coined this phrase struck gold: "He who will not stand for something, will fall for anything." We should both know the truth and be unafraid to speak it, as led.

Father, you said we could know the truth, and you have revealed it. May we care enough to learn it, and teach it to others. Amen.

The eyes of your understanding being enlightened; that ye may know what is the hope of his calling, and what the riches of the glory of his inheritance in the saints.

Grasping our inheritance

It was a story repeated too many times in courtrooms: sisters squaring off with each other over their father's possessions barely a month after his death. Families feuded over furniture, cars and land and asked a judge to make them winners in their sad game of grabbing for things they would not possess more than a few years themselves.

This world is full of stories of people who couldn't wait for someone to die so they could get hold of a large inheritance. Even Jesus told a story about a young man who insisted his father give him his share before he died. It's just one way in which humanity has demonstrated the sinful quality of greed. Considering how eager we are to get what's coming to us, we may easily miss what God has provided for every Christian, the great inheritance of his blessing in Jesus. This is why Paul prayed for the Ephesians that they might be enlightened and discover what we Christians have inherited in Jesus Christ.

He was talking about that extra dimension of life that most people never enter. It is a life consumed by its ultimate goals, life enriched by a grasp on all spiritual blessings, and life empowered by a living Spirit of God. Paul knew what it was like, because he lived it. He wanted it for each of us. He wanted us to know the freedom of forgiveness and the power of fullness.

Some of those who come to Christ, are baptized, and join the church never really live that life. Because it does not come by some ceremony, or ritual, or even by a one-time act of commitment, genuine though that act may be. It comes by daily searching, seeking the face of the Lord, and daily acceptance of his Lordship in your life. It comes by inviting the Lord of fullness and glory to take control of, as well as take residence in, your life. Today, pray to experience the great dimension of life, the confidence, blessing, and power of the Savior, Jesus Christ.

Father, through the name of Jesus who died for our sins, forgive us, and through the name of Jesus who rose from the dead for our salvation, fill us with the joy and victory of your Spirit. Amen.

January 16 **Scripture Reading: 1 Thessalonians 5:2,4**

For yourselves know perfectly that the day of the Lord so cometh as a thief in the night...But ye, brethren, are not in darkness, that that day should overtake you as a thief.

No surprise

According to a California religious broadcaster, May 11, 2011, was supposed to be the day the church was taken out of the world and the clock began ticking down to global destruction five months later. We're all still here.

Do you know when the Lord is coming? You are probably answering in your mind, "No one does." To be technical, that's true. We are all quite familiar with passages like the above verse, and others that tell us no one knows the day or the hour when the Son will return (Mark 13:32). What people have ignored, though, are verses like the rest of Paul's comments to the Thessalonians: that believers are not among those who will be surprised by the Lord's return. He said bluntly that their being children of the light and the day would prepare them.

The Christian who is living close to the Lord will have an ability to understand the times and seasons, far over and above that of the non-believer or even the believing but faithless Christian. Paul's statement that "brethren" will not be surprised may imply that near the time of the Lord's return, Christians will know it—not the day and the hour, but its palpable nearness. This is when they will "look up, for [their] redemption draweth nigh" (Luke 21:28). Paul comes short of saying that guessing a date will be possible, but he clearly says that one walking with the Lord will sense the imminence of Christ's return, and will be ready.

This is why signs of the second coming are given to us. If we were not to have *some* idea, the signs would have been useless deception on God's part. Jesus is coming back to the earth—what if it were today? Would you be ready? The Christian, who by the grace of God is born again to life eternal, is ready as to the matter of salvation. It is also important to be ready as to our condition, through surrender, commitment, and fruit-bearing lives.

Father, send Christ soon, to take us from this wicked world to live with you forever in glory, and may we be ready, in every way. Amen.

For bodily exercise profiteth little: but godliness is profitable unto all things, having promise of the life that now is, and of that which is to come.

Doing spiritual exercises

We have all noticed how many people have gotten serious about exercise. Among men there have always been a few who lifted weights, sometimes just to build visible muscles, whether they needed them or not. But for some time now women have been getting in on the act in increasing numbers. For some people, weight training, aerobics and the like have a practical value—weight loss, or athletic competition, for instance. But for many others the fascination with gymnasiums, extensive running or exercise machines, is more like a theatrical display, an expression of individuality or accomplishment. No doubt for some it is little more than the show of one's body to attract the opposite sex. The television and magazine ads show healthy young specimens of both sexes using weight machines and reminding us all that without pain, there is no gain.

All this paints the picture in American culture that people are extremely interested in the vanity of physique. Being healthy is one thing; getting enough exercise is one thing; being a specimen of some physical ideal is another, and it is consuming too many people's time and concentration.

Paul told Timothy that physical exercise is of "little value"—which meant *a* little, or *some* value, but that godliness has as much greater value in everything, because it equips you both for this world and the next. We should be wary of the idea of spending most of our time developing our bodies, especially if we do not spend enough time developing our spirits. How many toned, tanned and physically tuned bodies are inhabited by weak, puny, flabby spirits? Ephesians 6:10 says, "Be strong in the Lord!"

Is your relationship with God adequately exercised? Do you pray enough? Do you read the word of God enough, worship or sing enough? Do you love enough? Do your spiritual exercises! They last.

Father, help us to be sufficiently concerned with our spiritual strength today, so that we can run the race and fight the good fight of faith. Amen.

This is a faithful saying, and worthy of all acceptation, that Christ Jesus came into the world to save sinners.

Jesus' willing death

When we think of the life of Jesus, we often mention his ministry of healing or his teaching golden truths. We often emphasize his example of love, his fulfilment of ancient laws. We speak of his unveiling of enigmas, and fulfilling prophecies. But Jesus came for one chief purpose: to save sinners, like you and me.

The case was reported a few years ago of a little girl who had come down with a serious illness and was in need of blood, or she would die. It was necessary to give her blood not only of the same type, but from someone in her family. Her little brother was the only one who fit the description. He was just a lad, and the doctor asked him, "Would you be willing to give blood so that your sister could live?" He thought just a moment, and with a look of determination answered, "For my sister? Sure." As he lay on the donor table, watching the procedure, he looked unusually somber. The doctor soon appeared, and the little boy said to him, "Will it hurt?" The doctor didn't understand, since now the blood had already been withdrawn, and he asked, "Will what hurt?" The little boy answered, "Will it hurt when I die?" It wasn't until then that the doctor realized that the boy thought that when he gave his blood, he would die. He had been willing to do that for his sister.

Do you realize that Christ was willing to give his life that we might be healed of the sickness of sin? He died in our place, and the cross frees us from sin's power. When we internalize that and feel the compassion of his heart, then we will begin to live in thanksgiving and imitate his compassion toward others. We will be willing to die, if only to our competing desires of the moment, so that others may find life in Christ. We will be willing to die perhaps to our more extensive plans for our lives, in order to pursue lives that will bless others more fully because we are serving God more faithfully. But dying to self enables us to live for Christ, and such a life is joy.

Father, it is astounding that Jesus would die for us. We know it must have hurt—in ways more profound than we can understand. Thank you for taking the hurt in our place. Amen.

This know also, that in the last days perilous times shall come. For men shall be lovers of their own selves, covetous…

Avoiding the love of ourselves

The opening words of 2 Timothy 3 are a startling description of what Paul calls "the last days." He strings together nineteen adjectives for these days, the first two with stinging rebuke: People will love themselves, and love money. That has been true of many eras in history. The culture of the west in particular, however, is marked by a self-centeredness that defies previous history to match it. The religion of the average person is to do what will make "number one" happy, no matter what it does to anyone else. The post-modern world operates by a philosophy in which morals are determined by reference only to the feelings of the self. There is no reference to God, and there is little reference to the feelings of others.

Then, there is money. As a culture, we live for it. Capitalism beats communism any day, but the drawback is the cycle of greed that continually feeds itself. In a society where materialism is the main religion, people measure their worth by their money. Many will do few things for which they are not paid at least some money. Even charity is big business. Everywhere you look, people are looking for a way to get more for doing less, to charge more for less quality.

What is the point? We need to see that this is the pattern of things at the end times, and we need to stay out of the pattern and warn others against it. Jesus said our first love should be for God and our second love for others. The love of money is really an expression of love for ourselves. But real joy comes when we get our hearts right with God through a love relationship with Jesus. The little children's song has it right: J-O-Y, J-O-Y, this is what it means: Jesus first, Yourself last, and Others in between.

Father, may true JOY be experienced in our lives today, as we put Jesus first, others next, and self last. Amen.

Exhort servants to be obedient unto their own masters.

The hard challenge of submission

The idea of submission is unpopular, but it is a key teaching of the Bible. The scriptures teach children to be submissive to their parents. Wives are told to be submissive to their husbands. Husbands are to be submissive to the Lord, and members of the church to their elders and pastors. All are instructed to be submissive to Christ. In Titus, Paul teaches Christian slaves to be subject to their masters. He was very clear that they not talk back, but that they try to please them. Some critics charge that Paul approved of slavery. He did not. He faced the fact of the institution and had to say something to those caught in it. Would he say, "Rebel!" Would he tell them to get out, or rise up? No, he taught them to submit, to obey.

This is not to say there would not come a day when the time would be ripe for social change, for that day would indeed arrive. But in order for the gospel to be most attractive, Christians had to show just what humility and willingness to serve could be wrought in the hearts of people who were by nature stubborn, selfish, and proud.

The more general application of this teaching is that whenever we are indebted to someone, especially in the way of obligations we must fulfil—as in the case of employees, people under contracts, or citizens under a government—we should not major on trying to get out of our responsibilities. Neither should we bare our fangs while fulfilling them. We should perform our duties willingly and humbly, and surprise those to whom we owe them. The obligation may be unpleasant, but the important thing is not that we please ourselves but show ourselves to be full of the Spirit of Christ, and thereby make the Christian life attractive.

Do you have to do something for someone today? Do it with a smile, and ask, "May I go the second mile?"

Father, give us grace to have this kind of attitude, by filling us with the nature of Jesus. Amen.

That the communication of thy faith may become effectual by the acknowledging of every good thing which is in you in Christ Jesus.

Witnessing to grow

One of the nicer bits of wisdom we should learn—and one that bears relearning and continual investigation—is the fact that in the matter of faith, you cannot successfully seek deeper spirituality or more extensive witness exclusive of one another: you must do both. Some people want deeper life, a greater experience of the grace of God. Others insist evangelism, pure and simple, is the thing the church and every Christian should be engaged in. One says "experience," the other, "expansion." In fact, there is a fundamental connection between the two: those who really get deep in the faith are going to be irrepressibly evangelistic.

The connection, however, can be expressed from the other side: If you want your faith to deepen, try sharing your faith with someone else. That seems to elude the understanding of many, but Paul makes the connection himself in Philemon 6. He challenges Philemon, the master of Onesimus, to share his faith actively, so that he will come to fully understand the depths of our spiritual possessions in Christ. When you witness, you will grow spiritually. There it is, in plain and simple language.

A pastor nearing his fortieth year in ministry told a younger minister how he handled the stress he faced. He said sometimes things got tough, criticism ran high, depression seemed to be descending. He admitted that at times he felt he had become stagnant. When this happened, he got back to basics and went out to find someone to tell about Christ. In leading people to the Lord, he found he was restored. Witnessing, of course, isn't just a remedy for joylessness, but Paul says it provides an avenue to receiving the riches of Christ.

This must have been the understanding of hymn writer Katherine Hankey when she poured out these words: "I love to tell the story, because I know 'tis true; It satisfies my longing as nothing else can do."

Father, thank you for our Savior, Jesus. Through speaking his name today, may we come to know him better. Amen.

Who being the brightness of his glory, and the express image of his person…

Like Father, like Son

It is interesting to see how many times children turn out looking like the parent of the same sex they are. Little girls occasionally look like their fathers, but to many people's minds they usually look more like their mothers, and boys usually take after their fathers. Like father, like son, is no empty expression, and it is more than physical resemblance. Frequently sons want to emulate their fathers, and daughters their mothers. It may be that this desire appears more strongly in boys. They want to be individuals, but they have a strong urge to be individuals *like* their dads. If Dad is at all worth being like, the son will probably make a conscious attempt to imitate him.

Hebrews says that the Son is the very image of God. The Bible teaches that in Jesus Christ we have seen God. This is what it means for him to be the Son of God. Jesus told Phillip that he who has seen him has seen the Father, and that he, Jesus was "in" the Father, and vice versa. For believers, this means that to know God, we must come to know Jesus Christ. There is no other way. We cannot skip a relationship with Christ and come to know God independently. This is why Jesus said, "No man cometh to the Father but by me."

Not only is this so for the first-time meeting with Christ but also for each day's spiritual experience. If you want to have an active relationship with God, it must be through a walk with Jesus Christ. The reason is that the Father is not fully accessible to us in any other way. We can be his favored children in no way but to be considered as brethren and servants of his one Son, the Word made flesh. This is how he has ordered things.

You have two options today: to walk alone, or with the Lord. Only one brings the experience of the presence of God.

Father, by grace, and through faith, we will walk with your Son. Amen.

Let us therefore fear, lest, a promise being left us of entering into his rest, any of you should seem to come short of it.

Knowing your security

The Bible teaches the security of the believer—if you have had a genuine beginning of faith in Christ, you will be kept secure in him until the full receipt of eternal life. At the same time, the Bible warns us not to get lax in our commitment, lest we prove we never had saving faith in Christ at all. This is the meaning of this verse in Hebrews. Its key words are "should seem to come short." The original Greek words mean, "to be discovered." Some people will be surprised when they discover they were not saved.

This does not mean that every Christian ought to go around worrying whether or not he is saved. It does mean, however, every person should be careful not to fool himself about salvation on the wrong foundation. We are not saved by being members of a church, being baptized, or knowing much about the Bible, God, and spiritual things. We are not saved even by believing Bible statements to be factual. We are saved by the grace of God. It happens when we repent of sin, and receive Christ as saving Lord. That means beginning a lifetime of discipleship.

A man went to a construction site, fell in with the workers, lifted wood, swung a hammer, took breaks with the men, wore the appropriate overalls and hard hat, and did the same thing all week. When paychecks were handed out, he asked where his was. The boss stared at him blankly and said, "Why should I pay you? I don't even know you." The man protested that he had worked all week. The boss concluded, "Maybe you did, but I didn't hire you. You never came to me. You're not one of my men!"

Be sure you don't just belong to a church, but that you belong to Christ.

Father, if there is any doubt, let it be settled today, and thank you for the security of true believers in Christ. Amen.

Through faith also Sara herself received strength to conceive seed, and was delivered of a child when she was past age, because she judged him faithful who had promised.

Faith makes sense

Did you ever hear someone say, "They are as opposite as night and day?" What is interesting is that night and day are not opposites—not really. They do not oppose each other, or conflict; they work together, to form a complete day. They are two parts of a whole.

Sometimes people make faith and reason opposites, as if you either have to live life by blindly accepting propositions without testing them, or live by scientifically or logically provable facts *only,* accepting nothing else. But that is being too hard on both faith and reason. The fact is, reason makes a lot of assumptions it cannot necessarily prove, and real faith is based on many provable facts.

The question is, why does it make sense to believe God? Hebrews describes Sara as having dismissed the usual conclusions about being too old to have children, and having chosen to "consider him faithful" who made the promise that she would. Sara believed she would have a son because the source of the promise was, himself, trustworthy. She chose to believe not because it made sense for her to think herself capable of motherhood; not because *she* felt capable, but because *God* had said it, and God is believable.

Faith still makes sense. It makes sense to believe God. A God who can create the universe certainly can direct its resources and creatures to provide for his children and bless them richly. Did you ever use the expression, "I have reason to believe?" You see, faith and reason are not opposites, but partners. It is reasonable to believe God. The facts will prove him true, even if what he says is difficult to take in. A Christian saying goes, "God said it, I believe it, and that settles it." The Bible really teaches one step better: "God said it, and that settles it."

Father, inspire in us first a real trust in you, and whatever you say we will therefore believe. Amen.

By faith they passed through the Red sea as by dry land: which the Egyptians assaying to do were drowned.

The power of faith

The remarkable feat of the crossing of the Red Sea demonstrated that some things are possible only under the cover of God's power. The Red Sea was normally impassable, but the Israelites walked through on dry ground, because they believed God wanted them to go through, despite the water. In fact, by mapping their route from the land of Goshen to this point by the sea, it is clear that God led them into a place where, if he did not deliver them, they would surely be wiped out.

Sometimes Christians are called on to attempt things that normally would seem foolish. But when God is in it and leads you to it, you can succeed. There are churches that have raised millions of dollars for desperately needed meeting places and mission ventures, when the business world would not have given them hope of gathering together more than a hundred thousand. There are individual Christians who have launched out into some personal ministry, having to give up jobs to do it, and instead of starving, they have prospered, because God was with them. The difference is the purpose and presence of God. Knowing that God is in a thing is a matter of believing what the Spirit says in his still, small voice, and believing what the word of God says you must do. That act of believing, of taking God at his word, is faith. It is not believing in the power of positive thinking; it is believing in the power of God. It is trusting God to do in our circumstances what would not happen by itself or by our own doings.

Someone has said that if God wants a church to do something, there is nothing on earth that can keep them from it if they believe. That goes for you and me as well. We must belong to God, and then we must trust him fully.

Father, you inspire our trust. May we place it squarely in you, and no other. Amen.

By faith the harlot Rahab perished not with them that believed not...

Siding with God

The prostitute Rahab lived in a Canaanite town about to be attacked and wiped out. She cooperated with Israelite spies on a reconnaissance mission. For that, she was given a secret sign which gave her protection in the forthcoming attack. Her life changed when she played this important part in the conquest. Hebrews calls this "faith." She was up against a wall. You might call her desperate; you might call her act self preservation or even treason! But the Bible calls it faith.

The most important observation about Rahab is that whatever it was she feared, she aligned with the people of God and with the God of the people of God. In this last-ditch, skin-saving effort—if one insists on putting it that way—which we might also call finally seeing the light, she sided with the right side and found deliverance. There was a great change of life for her in that newfound loyalty. She was suddenly no longer a harlot, but one of the faithful of God.

You may have felt guilty about reaching out to God in the midst of a tough scrape. In a way, it's good to feel guilty in such circumstances, lest we get in the bad habit of trying to take only occasional advantage of God's forgiveness and deliverance. But God often uses tight spots to drive us to him when blessing and favor haven't kept us there. In such times, run to him unhesitatingly—that's faith. Only let your life come under his scrutiny, because in an "emergency approach" to God, there is the potential for great and wonderful change in your life.

Psalmist David described Israel's folly: "They were at their wits' end. Then they cried out to the Lord in their trouble, and he brought them out of their distress."

Father, it would be best that we walk consistently with you, but when we don't, and we get in trouble for it, help us not to be so proud that we don't seek you for the help only you can give. Amen.

My brethren, count it all joy when ye fall into divers temptations.

Joy amid trials

The Bible often says things to us that run counter to what we may think in our natural minds. Sometimes it advises us to have attitudes that seem totally out of keeping with what most people think or feel in similar settings. For instance, here is a challenge by James to consider our various troubling circumstances to be opportunities to show pure joy. Joy? —When we're in trouble, or when we're under attack? Normally we would be worried or concerned, somber, sober, upset, anxious, nervous, scared, confused. Joy might not seem to make sense at such a time.

But the rest of the verse helps: "Knowing this, that the trying of your faith worketh patience." Ah! Now we realize this joy is a deep attitude of confidence and peace resulting from the knowledge that something good will come out of our trouble. But this deep attitude—if we have it—cannot help but affect our outward, surface attitude. We may not leap in ecstasy when trials come, but the Bible says our response should reflect our ultimate beliefs.

Your trials could be the result of the way life puts you in a bind, and makes doing the right thing hard and costly. They could be physical ailments that work on your spirit. They probably include the direct actions of people around you who test your mettle. The Christian will face these things, and the Bible calls them trials, saying, "Be joyful!" You may think, "Well, all right, if the Bible *says* so, I'll do my best to have joy." But that isn't the attitude the Lord is after. It is celebration, not resignation, God wants. If we cannot feel it, it may be that we are not sufficiently founded on the source of joy, Jesus Christ. Jesus said he lived in his disciples so they could have the full measure of his joy in them (John 15:11). Are you practicing the presence of Jesus, and experiencing his joy?

Father, we need the joy of Jesus, so we need Jesus, in more of his fulfilling Lordship than ever before. Amen.

Be ye therefore ready also: for the Son of man cometh at an hour when ye think not.

When you least expect it

On January 28, 1986, the nation mourned the loss of seven astronauts aboard the space shuttle *Challenger.* Space missions had become almost routine for some people, but somehow, astronauts remained a symbol of courage, adventure, and discovery. In a way, the dream of a nation for pushing back the final frontier was pinned on these men and women who catapulted into space in spite of the danger. With their sudden, shocking deaths, our dreams did not dissipate or die, but they did become more sober, mature dreams. We had always estimated the cost of such missions. On that day, we paid that cost, as we had before, and have since.

President Reagan, in addressing the nation about the fiery explosion that stunned America, called on a line from the poem "High Flight" and said, "they have slipped the surly bonds of earth, reached out, and touched the face of God." Reagan called the attention of the listening nation to the imminence and involvement of God in his universe, and to the silent reminder that this life is not all of life. If among the crew there were those whose trust was in the Christ of God, their speeding chariot of fire delivered them in the twinkling of an eye into the presence of God, from the heavens to the heaven of heavens, in an instant. We could not have known.

Yet all of us can be prepared. At any time, the chariot could swing low to gather any of us, by illness, accident, or age. Few of us have much warning of our impending deaths. By having a personal relationship with the Son of God as Savior, we know that when the chariot comes for us, it will launch us into the presence of our Creator and Redeemer. Jesus said we must be ready, since he may come again—or come for us—when we least expect it.

Father, in somber remembrance of all who have unexpectedly gone to meet you, may we be certain of eternal life, by being certain of our Savior, Jesus Christ. Amen.

All have sinned, and come short of the glory of God.

Sinning for ourselves

Someone wrote, "Nobody knows the age of the human race, but most of us agree it is old enough to know better." Indeed it is. But not really. Perhaps we don't often think of it, but it really doesn't matter how old the human race is: each of us human beings got here only a few years ago, and each must live his own life and learn his own lessons. We do not inherit wisdom or righteousness. Did you ever think of that?

Why should the experience of fifty past generations make you any different morally? It could, if you pay attention to the example of their lives and deeds. Other than that, however, it makes no difference. You have to experience life for yourself. The experiences of generations past are not yours, and their collective maturing does not transfer to you. Those who say the human race is "coming of age" are living on the foundation of a lie, the idea that the race operates as one man, moving toward the goal of improvement.

If anything is true, it is that the race is operating in a unified way toward *dis*-improvement, because of the shared nature of sin in us. It all began in Adam. *The New England Primer,* a book teaching reading, used to say, "In Adam's fall, we sinned all." Some people ridicule that idea, but it is borne out in every person's experience: we all sin. Paul states it as bluntly as it can be said, and 1 John 1:8 says, "If we say that we have no sin, we deceive ourselves, and the truth is not in us. If we confess our sins, he is faithful and just to forgive us." The human race has not arrived, nor has it really learned anything. But you, individually, are old enough to know better. Have you confessed your sin to God and asked his forgiveness through the sacrifice of Christ?

Father, we humbly confess what you say is true, and through the blood of Jesus we ask forgiveness for all our sin. Amen.

If any man offend not in word, the same is a perfect man, and able also to bridle the whole body.

Controlling our mouths

Many of us growing up had mothers or fathers who said to us, "If you can't say something nice, don't say nothin' at all." Exactly where the phrase came from isn't clear. In *Bambi,* the mother of one of the Walt Disney characters said it to him when he was ridiculing another animal. It's a proverb that has been around a while. Its wisdom is simple: it is hard to tame our tongues.

Most of us are somewhat used to saying whatever we feel. Some people have the idea that it is dishonest not to say what they're thinking at the moment. That isn't always so. Sometimes what runs out our mouths is the product of flawed thinking or impulsive emotion. Our first responses are *not* always best, and *not* always accurate, much less kind. The human condition in sin is such that often much revision needs to be done on our thought and feeling before it is fit to be aired before others.

When James says "offend in word," it means "be at fault" or "say the wrong thing." The mouth, then, is a good indicator of the whole body. We say wrong things because we are sinful through and through. God wants us to learn to control our tongues.

Some people have the idea that we Christians are supposed to water down everything we say, even dilute what we believe, until what we say is so bland that no one disagrees with us because what we say is so neutral. They say we should be like the humorous definition of a diplomat: someone who thinks twice before saying nothing. That isn't the idea behind controlling our tongues. Sometimes we must say something that bites because of the truth in it. But most often, our words bite because of meanness—and *that's* what needs changing. If you will surrender your mind to Christ, your tongue will not get out of control.

Father, so often this has been our failing. Forgive, restore, and take fresh command. Amen.

Who, being in the form of God, thought it not robbery to be equal with God: But made himself of no reputation, and took upon him the form of a servant, and was made in the likeness of men.

Equal with us

In America, most people want upward mobility. Many people never attain it, but it is a common dream. In fact, most people in the world want to attain equal standing with somebody who makes more money, has more possessions, more power, better conditions, than they do. This is not only an economic quest, but a humanitarian one as well. People want equality: they do not want to be kept down by an elite. Someone made an interesting observation about equality, however. The defect of equality as a goal is that we desire it only with our superiors. Think about that. Who wants equality with the oppressed, the poor, the troubled, the distressed?

We might say, "Well, why would we?" Unless there were great purpose in it, we would not. Yet the Bible says Jesus considered equality with God something he didn't need to hold on to, but made himself one of us, took on our form and our limitations—equal with us—even to the point that because of his obedience to the Father he was put to death on a cross. Why did he do that? He did it because there was no other way to bring to us what we most need,—forgiveness and salvation—than to be like us and suffer death for us. Ultimately, he sought equality with us so we might gain a kind of equality with him. For in what he did we can be born to new life in him, in which we become co-heirs of his riches in glory.

Upward mobility? The Christian has it as no other!—but only because somebody was willing to be equal with the lowly sinner: me and you. Praise God!

Father, all glory to you for Jesus, who reached down—no, came down, to save us. Amen.

How long will this people provoke me? and how long will it be ere they believe me, for all the signs which I have shewed among them?

Little miracles

"I just don't get it," the man said, "They can send a man to the moon, but can't cure the common cold." Did you ever hear that? "They can send a man to the moon, but can't get rid of roaches." Sending men to the moon has cursed science for years to come! People assume that if the big hurdles can be leaped over, the little ones ought to be a cinch. Well, who said curing the common cold was a little task? If it were, it *would* have been done, long ago.

People issue the same complaint against God. He can make the world, part the sea, multiply loaves and fishes, raise the dead, but why does he not wipe away evil in the world? Why does he allow injustice or natural disasters? Again, these are no little problems. In Numbers 14:11, Moses articulates the thought of God, questioning man as to his unbelief in the face of awesome feats of power. The purpose of many of these feats was to draw attention to God's ability to solve the most difficult problem of all—the sin of man. Actually, however, parting the Red Sea is far easier than removing sin from a human being. The sea is inanimate: man is a living soul, with freedom to choose evil, and he does. The Bible says the problem of evil is a problem of human sin. The evil done by man to man obviously originates in humanity, but what about disease and natural disasters? Romans 8:22 seems to intimate that natural "evils" too are rooted in human sin. In some cosmic way we cannot fully comprehend, our sin set off the disorder of nature, perhaps with retroactive force. That's a deep and challenging thought.

But as for the more immediate issue, God can part the sea—why doesn't he solve the problem of human evil? He does, man by man, woman by woman, when we surrender to him. Soon, perhaps very soon, his promise to eliminate sin and evil totally will come to pass. Christians look forward to that.

Father, may Christ return soon. In the meantime, may we surrender to you to cure our share of the common problem of sin. Amen.

And the merchants of the earth shall weep and mourn over her; for no man buyeth their merchandise any more.

Getting our attention

Much of the challenge of the gospel is to get people to stop being preoccupied with the things of the world and get them to thinking about reality—which is spiritual truth. People are terribly busy making money, pursuing their goals and being self-centered. Once a person pays attention to spiritual things, a good possibility exists that he will believe the gospel and be saved.

After Revelation describes the judgment against Babylon, it says the world's businessmen will complain that there are too few people left to keep them in business. Imagine: the business centers of the world are judged; the men and women who run them are judged by implication; God is speaking through the worsening human predicament about as loudly as he can; and they are crying over their loss of sales! Here is an image of incredibly misplaced focus. Yet how often does God try to turn our thoughts to him and all we can think about is our petty concerns. We don't think them petty, but compared to eternal things, they are.

A man went into his boss's office and asked for a raise. The boss threw a book at him, lectured him about his poor performance on the job, told him how bad business was, kicked over a chair, and finally picked him up and threw him out. Sprawled in the floor, the man raised himself on his elbows, facing the glaring executive, and said, "Does this mean I don't get the raise?"

What will it take to get the attention of most people? What does God have to do? We should realize that God doesn't *have* to do anything, and if we fail to pay attention to the still, small voice, we may not have another opportunity. If you even suspect God is trying to get you to look, pay attention!

Father, now, while we are looking, do something in us that will turn our hearts to you in devotion. May our full attention be on you and your kingdom. Amen.

What doth it profit, my brethren, though a man say he hath faith, and have not works?

Be a doer

There's a story about a river boat steamship whose christening was at hand. Its captain, watching the ceremonies from the pilot house, was busily engaged in pulling the whistle frequently during the whole affair. He had so much fun blowing the whistle, in fact, that when the ceremonies were finally over, and the cue was given to move out, he had no steam left. He spent it all tooting his own horn. How like many of us human beings, tooting our own horns and then not being able to deliver on things we brag we can or will do. Many people tell big stories about things they are going to do for the Lord, or for the church, but they never follow through. Their main talent is talking.

A little Bible verse, Jude 12, describes such conduct. It says simply, "They are clouds without rain." We are sometimes tempted to satisfy our need to do something by making big plans. In the process we spend all our emotional energy making the plans, envisioning in our minds what we could or should do—but never actually doing it. Most of us are far more generous and charitable in our minds than we are in reality. Many of us imagine ourselves doing a lot more good than we actually do. For some of us, we may have honest dreams and desires we simply don't have the courage or knowledge to fulfil. For others, it is a deceptive way of making ourselves think we are being like Christ. But James asks what good it is to claim to have faith but to have no deeds to back it up? Faith without works is dead.

The world needs dreamers and visionaries, planners and motivators who can move us with words, and nothing is wrong with making verbal commitments. But in every person's life there comes a time to stop talking and start doing. Someone said, "Don't brag: it isn't the whistle that pulls the train."

Father, today may we be doers of the word, and not talkers only. Amen.

Neither is this a work of one day or two: for we are many that have transgressed in this thing.

Taking grace seriously

One of the more poignant expressions about God's goodness to us is, "Grace isn't cheap, but it's free." God loves us and offers us salvation which he bought through the death of Jesus Christ, but he charges us nothing to receive it. He doesn't, unless you count the fact that we must give our whole lives in exchange for it. It was not easy or cheap for God to arrange our pardon from sin, and though he offers it to us on the simple basis of repentance and faith, we are not to take it lightly.

Sometimes, however, we do take it lightly and fail to properly turn from our sin or make restitution, figuring God has forgotten all about our sins. The people in Ezra's day were struck with the weightiness of their sin and determined not to make this mistake of treating God's offer of forgiveness lightly. After hearing the accusations against them, they told Ezra they couldn't and wouldn't attempt to make quick work of repentance. They intended to take time to search their hearts, resolve their evil situations, get out of their sin, put away their idols and forsake their sinful connections. They meant business with repentance. Why? Because they realized that their sin was serious to God, and that though he offered them forgiveness, it was based on both his grace and their turning from iniquity. They could not expect him to impart cleansing if they took lightly what he called abomination.

Neither can we. Christ *died* for our sin. Think how serious it must be. Anything bad enough to send Jesus Christ to the cross is serious enough for us to put our whole attention to forsaking. Our whole lives, and every individual component of them—motives, emotions, fantasies, deep desires, habits, goals, careers, hobbies, expenditures, likes and dislikes, need to come under sober scrutiny. God's forgiveness is free, but it was not cheap, and we must not take it lightly.

Father, let us today honor you with true repentance. Amen

Shall he that contendeth with the Almighty instruct him?

Good things, bad things

People often ask why the world has evil in it. A popular non-Christian author wrote a book called, "When Bad Things Happen to Good People," in which he tried to give some answers to that question, but he no more succeeds than many others who have tried to do so. Something comes along to ruin or mar an otherwise rosy life or circumstance and people say, "Why couldn't it have been perfect?"

Perhaps the question is wrong. We don't really have the right to resent the intrusion of evil—the bad things that happen to us. Do you know why? It's because humanity collectively deserves judgment because of sin. The fact that we ourselves are seriously flawed makes it pure hypocrisy to cast a vague but perceptible glance upward and mutter, "Why me, God?" Our problem seems to be that we are willing to welcome the presence of some good things happening in the midst of our badness, but not to accept the inevitability of some bad things happening in the midst of what we think of as our goodness. What kind of arrogance is that?

A boulevard in a southern city was beautified with flowers. Beds of tulips were planted in the median along its length. Each bed had a predominant color. But in each bed, in the middle of scores of tulips of uniform color was planted one of a contrasting color. The contrast defined the true color of the bed.

Van Gogh said, "There is no blue without orange." We should realize that for sinful humanity there is no rosy life without trouble. Into every life some rain must fall, because we ourselves made the clouds. That may not seem to answer all exceptional issues raised. If we can't be satisfied with that answer, however, let the words of God to Job silence us: Do we dare correct God? Let him who accuses God of injustice answer him.

Father, forgive us for arrogance, in resenting what we must admit is far less evil in the world than we actually deserve. Amen.

The ransom of a man's life are his riches: but the poor heareth not rebuke.

The down side of being up

Some years ago a funny TV ad used the slogan, "Success has its rewards." We certainly hope so—otherwise why call it success? Another commercial of the same era said that a particular medicine was for "the stress that can come from success." Apparently success has not only its rewards, but its punishment.

Proverbs 13:8 tells us the rich person has the advantage of being able to ransom his life with his wealth. But it also tells us the poor man doesn't feel any threat (KJV "rebuke") to begin with. The irony in that is that the rich man makes just enough to pay for the demands of the criminal who singled him out in the first place only because he *is* rich. The poor man typically doesn't have to worry about such things. He may have many other worries, but the proverb definitely throws a darker cast on the plight of the rich.

It is often true that the more we have, the more we worry—we stand to lose more if calamity befalls. Relatively recently, insurance companies began to prosper from kidnaping insurance. A client pays x-dollars, and if his little son or daughter gets kidnaped, the insurance pays the ransom, or else pays off if the child is killed. Sends shudders up your spine, doesn't it? Ah, the privileges of being rich.

Yet most people are willing to risk being rich, thinking their chances are slim of experiencing the down side. Perhaps the threat is slim, but the Proverbs imply a host of troubles for the rich, not the least of which is the personal disintegration of spiritual health that more often than not accompanies getting rich. God sometimes delivers wealth and success into one of his servant's hands and makes him or her a good steward of it. But the usual case, when *we* manage to get rich, is that our wealth winds up cursing us in more ways than it blesses us. Success has its punishment.

Father, help us to desire to be righteous, rather than rich. Amen.

Take my yoke upon you, and learn of me.

Learning of Jesus

In the 1960's someone invented a Christian camp staple that eventually found its way into adult use, and today is frequently found as an element of leadership seminars. It's the "trust walk." The basic idea is that one person who is blindfolded, trusts another person, who is not allowed to speak, to lead him around for a time. He also tries in some way to come to know his guide. Participating in the walk, the point comes across almost immediately that the one who cannot see is dependent on the one who can. If left in the same area of a room or even outside, a person could eventually become largely independent, knowing where things are even without sight. But in the trust walk, the guide keeps going different places. The other side of the coin is that the blindfolded person must not think so much about where he is going that he forgets to find out about his guide. One could go through the whole walk, worrying about running into something, and never find out much at all about the one who is leading him.

The walk is a clear illustration of the truth of Matthew 11:29, whose simplest point is that we are to undertake the yoke of following Jesus so we can learn of *him.* We are to learn not just about his teaching, his kingdom or Bible facts, but of Jesus himself. Our prayer lives are not to be reduced to pleas for deliverance from trouble; they are to be opportunities to learn about our Lord. He wants to be a personal guide and friend.

It is altogether possible to be a Christian but have only a minimal, first-introduction kind of knowledge of our Savior. God wants us to know his Son intimately. As you walk with him today as one born again to new life in Christ, draw near and ask him to teach you about *him.*

Father, and Christ Jesus our Lord, thank you for what you are to us. May you be all of it, in a very personal way today. Amen.

So man lieth down, and riseth not: till the heavens be no more, they shall not awake, nor be raised out of their sleep.

A bright tomorrow

The Bible contains many statements that are not true. Before you gasp, read on. Many people quoted in the Bible tell lies. Satan said, "you shall not surely die," but it was not true. The Pharisees said of Jesus, "You use demon power to cast out demons," but that was false. Many people make inaccurate statements in the Bible. This is one way the truth is revealed—by exposing the foolishness of man's many lies. One book in particular contains many statements that reach for truth but do not reflect a full understanding of it. Job is the book. Job 14:12 asserts depressingly that when a human being dies, he "sleeps" until the end of the age. Job—like many other ancients—didn't understand that conscious life continues when the physical body dies.

Job was depressed by his many troubles. He was pouring out his soul about his perceptions of the inevitable. But his negative idea about "soul sleep" until some distant cataclysm is not matched by the rest of the Bible. Jesus said to the thief on the cross, "Today you will be with me in Paradise." Jesus appeared with Moses and Elijah in his transfiguration, and they were very much awake. John's vision of glory in Revelation pictures a heaven with very active inhabitants. Job just did not have the ability at that moment to affirm the vitality of the spirit's life for those who love the Lord God. But later, he did affirm, "I know that in my flesh I shall see God."

Sometimes we go through crises that tempt us to doubt the presence of God or the benevolence of his will. We may not feel much like affirming joyous things, preferring to bathe ourselves in tears and defeatist ideas. In such times it is good for the seed to be planted that for those who belong to Christ as Savior, there is a bright tomorrow.

Father, while the dark clouds dominate, help us to still believe in the Son. Amen.

Every moving thing that liveth shall be meat for you; even as the green herb have I given you all things.

A diet of confession

All of us who aren't vegetarians have a confession to make. Every time we eat anything that once was a living animal, we confess something. Genesis 9:3 tells us God approved a diet including meat for Noah and all his descendants. In Eden, Adam and Eve were allowed plants for food. Then came sin, separation, seedtime and sweat, and there crept into all creation a change of order. Various prophecies in the Bible suggest that when God brings his kingdom in full and eliminates sin from the world, animals will no longer be predatory in nature. Some people believe these scriptures imply that such presently ferocious animals as the tiger and the shark were once plant eaters. Even if that isn't so, it is still true that when God broadened the sanctioned diet of man in his covenant with Noah, it symbolized the violence that was part of the created order. Eating animals meant killing them. The predatory desire extended to man. Eating meat became an implicit confession that man was not what he once had been. Sin had changed things radically for him.

Sin makes your life different from what it would have been had you never departed from the sovereignty of the Lord. It is precisely in admitting this that we become eligible for personal change. To confess the overwhelming influence of sin in our lives, and our personal responsibility for it, is to open the door to forgiveness through Christ and a new experience of overcoming sin.

By the way, that doesn't mean that becoming a vegetarian is part of redemption. Had eating meat itself been wrong, God would never have given it the divine "okay." But the next time you fix a hamburger, remember it is a confession, and let it remind you to be penitent before the Lord always.

Father, even our diet is loaded with meaning. Speak to our hearts through all that we do, and lead us to bow and come humbly to you. Amen.

February 10 **Scripture Reading: Exodus 23:19**

Thou shalt not seethe a kid in his mother's milk.

Respect for life

There are some things that are inappropriate; then there are some things that are downright offensive. Yet in our time, there seems to be the suggestion that human progress means being offended by less and less, eventually to flinch at nothing, no matter how horrible.

God's instruction about not boiling the meat of a young goat in his mother's milk appears intended to address the matter of human sensitivities. Nothing was wrong with eating goat meat—God specifically provided that human beings could kill and eat animals. Nothing was wrong with drinking warm milk. But cooking a goat in its own mother's milk was inappropriate. The mother's milk was supposed to nourish her young. To use it to cook her young was obviously a gross insult to sensibilities.

The broader application suggests many other things that simply are not right, that are out of place, in the most offensive sort of way. It shouldn't need much argument for us to see that calling an abortion clinic a family planning center is an offensive contradiction. What's more, are we aware that the bones of human as well as animal fetuses are used to make the ingredient collagen found in many women's cosmetics? This should be offensive. Where are the sensitivities of human beings who devise such things? Is nothing sacred?

How many of us when we were young found a baby bird dead in the yard? It was explained to us that the bird fell from the nest, was too young to fly, and was killed by a predator or otherwise starved. What did we do? We gently and almost reverently buried it. The bird was nothing—logic would say, 'who cares.' But we were taught to respect life, and to express that profound respect even in death. Is that respect for even human life now defunct in this world? What will we who purport to believe in the Creator and Sustainer of life do to restore that basic respect?

Father, help us to respect what you have made, that we not profane what is sacred in your creation. Amen.

February 11 **Scripture Reading: Matthew 5:37**

Let your communication be, Yea, yea; Nay, nay: for whatsoever is more than these cometh of evil.

Just the facts

Do you lie to yourself? Jesus taught that we should not become extreme with our speech. In the sermon on the mount, he told us we ought not to concoct oaths to convince people we are telling the truth. Rather, he told us to say yes or no, simply and without unnecessary embellishments or expletives. What does that have to do with lying to yourself? Quite simply, most people who swear broadly often do so to convince themselves as much as anybody else. Many times, they need convincing because they know in their hearts that what they claim is not so.

It's funny how we have this tendency to save our strongest speech for our weakest points, our biggest boasts for our greatest insecurities. Jesus said, don't fool yourself—you certainly aren't fooling God.

You and I are known to make claims, if only to God, about what we will do for him or for the church. Why is it we so often fail to come through? Is it that the promise came from only the puny strength of human resolve, and not from the conviction of a heart possessed by the Holy Spirit and mastered by Christ?

Let's not lie to ourselves. Let's not make up a glorious future that reflects our fleshly dreams, impose it upon Christ's plans for us, and vow to fulfil it, only to have our good intentions fall apart and find ourselves thrust into guilt—again. Instead, simply follow Christ every day; say yes to him—yes and nothing more—and when we yield to temptation and say no to him, let our confession be as simple a yes as our yielding was, that we might not boast overly about how we will not sin in the future. God knows our weakness to sin, and the more we boast of our immunity to it, the easier we fall into it. Today, just humbly follow Jesus, and say, "Yes, Lord."

Father, make the path of discipleship extra plain to us today, that we might follow Jesus simply. Amen.

February 12 **Scripture Reading: Ephesians 3:20**

Now unto him that is able to do exceeding abundantly above all that we ask or think, according to the power that worketh in us.

God's indescribable power

Occasionally we hear from missionaries that they have difficulty translating some verses of scripture. For instance, "Though your sins be red like crimson, yet they shall be as white as snow," does not have the impact it should have in tropical islands where it does not snow. Where people have never seen snow, how can they know what "whiter than snow" means? So missionaries in one sunny clime supplied another word: "Though your sins be red like crimson, they shall be as white as chickens." Chickens there are as white a thing as they know in that tropical place.

We do not always know how to communicate with one another. Sometimes it is hard to tell someone just how you feel. It is especially hard for a Christian to communicate fully to a non-Christian what it means to have God strengthen him from within. Unless one knows the fellowship of Christ, what it means to walk with God, it is next to impossible— in fact, it *is* impossible—for him to know what the inward working of God is. How does God bring strength in time of trial, comfort when grief has us in its grips, courage when the world is a frightening place to live? He just does! For those who know him and seek him within that relationship, he is able to move and work from within to meet our needs.

Paul was overwhelmed with this wonderful, inward working, when he said that God does more than we ask or *even imagine,* by his inward power. God's principal work is not rearranging events so that we breeze through life, nor taking away troubles or hardships, but rather it is imbuing us with power to meet life head-on and experience personal victory. When we know Christ, we are plugged into this inward working: God is in us. It is "Christ in you, the hope of glory" (Col.1:27).

Father, may we come to know and experience you in Christ, through a power we cannot explain. Amen.

February 13 **Scripture Reading: Romans 10:20**

I was found of them that sought me not; I was made manifest unto them that asked not after me.

Who found whom?

An age old joke about courtship goes that a man chased after a woman until she caught him. A similar point was made by a cartoon of a bear cub and a man running around a tree, with the tree directly between them. Who is chasing whom? Sometimes we are not sure—with bears, or with people.

In describing how God was amazingly gracious in sending Christ, Paul quotes Isaiah who says that God revealed himself to those who didn't ask to see him. Here is the Lord saying that human beings discovered his truth while they were engaged in suppressing it. Man saw salvation unfolded before him in the middle of his trying to cover it up. Jesus Christ came presenting himself in humility but power as Messiah, and the Jews tried to deny it, and finally tried to stamp him out. In the midst of it all, salvation was accomplished, as Jesus died for human sin. The irony is that the rejection of Christ was the key to his sacrifice for us.

It is like that with each of us. We are not conscious of seeking God sometimes, but we find him anyway. The point is, God is seeking us. We find him because he arranges life so that we run headlong into him and must confront him. Whether we accept or reject, we cannot deny that we have become aware of his demands and claims. This is one difference between Christianity and religion: religions are man's concoctions for reaching God. Christianity is God's reaching down to man. This is also a reason to have confidence: If you are born again through faith in Jesus Christ, it is not because you started the whole thing, but because God did. Consequently, you are not holding onto God. He is holding onto you. Perspective is important. You may have thought you sought after God, but *he* caught *you*.

Father, help us then to take hold of the life for which you took hold of us. Amen.

There be three things which are too wonderful for me, yea, four which I know not: The way of an eagle in the air; the way of a serpent upon a rock; the way of a ship in the midst of the sea; and the way of a man with a maid.

The adventure of love

The proverb writer marveled at four things, unrelated except that all dealt with "the way of" one thing with another. He was fascinated by the flight of the eagle, mesmerized by the slithering of a snake on a rock, intrigued by the navigation of the sea. But his focus was on what rivets the attention of more of us than any of these: being in love. Romantic love, like the fascinating ways of nature, is the design of God for men and women who will be partners in marriage and procreation. It has been called "chemistry," because of biochemical responses of our bodies to scents put off by one another, and chemical changes that actually take place in the brain when we encounter someone who almost perfectly fulfills our fondest dreams and desires. Romantic love has been called many things and has been explained in ways that cheapen it, make it too mechanical, deny it, or conversely elevate it far above its importance. The bottom line is, God created the attraction of the sexes, and ordained romantic love to be part of the mystery and excitement of married partners, not just to guarantee the continuation of the species, but to enhance and enrich the relationship of mates.

The proverb describes love—as it does the other "wonderful things,"—as "the way," or the movement, process, or travel. Romantic love is an adventure, a journey of a woman and a man toward the goal of knowing one another intimately, sharing each other's goals and values, and enjoying the things they accomplish together.

Romance is not everything, but it is one thing God has designed into human life for the joy of the experience. Allowed to take its rightful place without being perverted, romantic love is a great gift. God made a wonderful world. When love reminds us of that, we should praise him.

Father, thank you for the wonder of love, and for your love most of all. Amen.

February 15 **Scripture Reading: 1 Peter 1:16**

It is written, Be ye holy; for I am holy.

Being set apart for God

One of the better known phrases in the Bible is, "be holy." What does it mean? Some suggest it means man ought to imitate God. Others say the thrust is, "I'm watching you, so you had better be holy." Certainly, God holds us accountable for our lives, but the real impact of this verse lies in an understanding of our relationship to God.

We who have repented and trusted in Christ have come through him to the Father, who is holy, and have become his children. For God to be holy means that he is set apart, lifted up, different. If, then, we have come into union with him, we have pledged to belong to him, and we are to be faithful to that pledge. That faithfulness to him sets us apart, and makes us different. Our holiness is found in living for God only in a world of sin and full of itself. In other words, if you have become one of God's people, you have become committed to living in unity with his will and purpose, and you are not to adulterate your life serving other ends.

A newspaper cartoon some years ago showed a man standing before a mirror, dressing, and talking with his wife. She was standing there with arms folded, a very angry look on her face. He was saying, "Be reasonable Phyllis. I made this date with Judy *months* before we were married." You and I would not likely be guilty of such ludicrous reasoning for unfaithfulness or even a date after we married someone else. Why, then, do we plead all sorts of excuses for unfaithfulness to God? The fact is, we are often unwilling to give up our taste for the world, our desire for other thrills, to be holy unto the God who made us and saved us at the price of the life of his incarnate Word. But that's exactly what "being holy" commands us to do.

Father, we are all guilty. Grant not only forgiveness but new surrender, that we may be set apart for you alone. Amen.

I will not drive them out from before you; but they shall be as thorns in your sides, and their gods shall be a snare unto you.

One tiny sin

A young husband described his aversion to yard work: "I'm not much of a gardener, or even lawn man. If I could lay down Astro Turf, I would. I have to cut the grass, but I don't have to put up with thorn bushes. Every time I go by them with the mower, they get me. Those two inch thorns reach out and stab me, on purpose! Finally, I had a friend come over and perform delicate surgery on them, with a chain saw. No more stickers. What a relief!"

Why don't we do that more often with the things that prick and bother us in our everyday lives? Judges 2:3 tells how God responded to the Israelites when they had become slack about driving out the pagan inhabitants of the land to which he had led them. Because they let this influence remain, God said the pagans would be thorns in their sides. The saga of Israel's quest for Canaan has long been a model for the Christian's life. We must subject the sins of our lives and the sinful flesh and desires of our lives, to the routing power of the Holy Spirit. If we do not, the things we tolerate or ignore will become testy, painful encumbrances on the path of progress. Sin will get in your way if you don't get it out of the way.

In an air conditioning system in a car, it is vital to keep moisture out of the coolant line. Even one micro-drop of water will form an ice crystal. It will move freely around the system until it comes to the one small passageway where it will not fit, and then that one, tiny crystal will stop up the entire system. No cool air. Who would have thought one teeny weeny drop… ? Who would think that one teeny weeny little sin… ?

Father, search our hearts, make us conscious of what you find, and move us to repentance and forsaking of it. Amen.

Because this widow troubleth me, I will avenge her, lest by her continual coming she weary me.

Be persistent

Persistence pays off, in almost everything. It must be partly due to the fact that the persistent person will find the way that works eventually. It may have something to do with the erosion of barriers to success through constant pressure and work. Or, the payoff comes when those who are petitioned for help or action finally give in.

Jesus told a story of a woman who plead with a good-for-nothing judge for a decision which would bring relief in her case. Time after time, he did nothing. Finally, Jesus said the judge figured he had better answer the complaint, or she would wear him out. Jesus applied the story saying that God would certainly bring justice to his own people who cry out to him day and night. He taught that though there seems to be a delay sometimes, God is not slack and does not procrastinate, but will act for his people when they are persistent in prayer. When our desired timing is not followed by God, when our urgency is not answered with instantaneous thunderbolts, when our dire conclusions of our condition are not validated by instant healing or liberation, we must understand that God's timing is better, his evaluation of our need not flawed, and his view of the future not a prediction, but certain knowledge. God knows best.

Little Frederick was saying his prayers one night. His mother tiptoed up and heard him say, "And please make Tommy stop throwing things at me. You may remember, I've mentioned this before. He's still doing it." Looked at from a human perspective, the hardest prayers to answer would be those that require the change of somebody else's mind or life. But God's specialty is changing people—especially you. Be persistent in prayer. It will pay off.

Father, we should be glad you did not say yes to our selfish prayers. But help us to be persistent in our selfless prayers, that we may show our faith and then rejoice in your gracious response. Amen.

February 18 **Scripture Reading: Titus 2:2...9**

...The aged men... the aged women likewise... teach the young women... young men likewise... exhort servants...

The everybody book

The Bible is a book for everybody. Not everyone understands it equally, but it has something to say to all people. None of us is exempt. No one is ever too old or too young, too educated or too ignorant, too common or too refined, for the Bible's message. East or west, from one culture to another, the Bible applies to all.

In Titus 2, Paul tells this minister protégée of his to teach old men, old women, young men and women, servants—everybody—the doctrines of the word of God. He covers the spectrum. Why? Verse 11 says it's that the grace of God that brings salvation has appeared to *all*. One application of this passage is that there is no one too down and out, too bad, too lost, to hear the good news that there is forgiveness and eternal life in Jesus Christ. In fact, those who are at the pessimistic extremities of life need that message more, in some ways, than the rest of us. Yet we all need it. For not only can you not be too down and out to hear the gospel, you cannot be too *up and in*, too affluent, to need the gospel. All must repent and believe on Christ.

A few years ago bookstores began selling what was called the "everything" book. It was an attractively bound volume, usually with gold embossing, or an interesting cloth cover. But inside there was *nothing*. Blank pages. The idea was to make it whatever you wanted it to be, a journal, a sketch book, a novel—the everything book. The Bible, on the other hand, is not blank, but filled. It is, however, the *everybody* book. You do not determine the content: God did. But it applies to everyone equally. Yet, in a sense, that makes it just as personal as the everything book, because God speaks directly to you through his book, and writes it new on your heart when you read it. Read the Good Book. It's for everybody, all the time.

Father, thank you for speaking to us. May we hear your Word as never before today as we read it. Amen.

February 19 Scripture Reading: Matthew 22:37

Thou shalt love the Lord thy God with all thy heart, and with all thy soul, and with all thy mind. ...Thou shalt love thy neighbour as thyself. On these two commandments hang all the law and the prophets.

The source of moral law

During a meeting about the problem of pornography in a metropolitan area of the southeastern United States, a Christian man made this concession to what he believed were the mandates of the political system: "I realize that we cannot legislate morality." He believed what he said. Many politicians believe it as well, and certainly pornographers believe it. But it should break the hearts of Christians to hear such a statement, because it simply is not true. It is an example of the rhetoric of immorality being pawned off as truth and the American way, and swallowed by well-meaning Christians. Think a moment: every major law on the books is a legislation of morality. Morality is not just sexual morality. Theft is a moral issue, and so are murder, extortion, graft, drug dealing, and on the list goes. Why stop at sexual morality if we have no problem with legislating our culture's morality in other areas? The question is not *if* we are going to legislate morality, but rather whose morality we are going to legislate.

The two greatest divine laws are the great commandment to love God supremely with everything we are and have, paired with the second commandment to love our neighbors as ourselves. Jesus said all the rest of God's expectations derive from those two. The same moral principles that demand that people not hurt each other by murder and theft also say don't hurt each other with lust and lasciviousness, fornication and adultery, homosexuality and pedophilia. Just because an issue deals with sex doesn't mean it's off limits to law.

Christians have sometimes backed off issues that are hotly contested, and they have rationalized their retreat by saying we shouldn't try to legislate morality. However, no area of life is untouched by God's law, and in your life, no area should be uncontrolled by God's Spirit. No area should be "hands off" to him.

Father, forgive our occasional cowardice in the face of evil. Overcome it with your power flowing through us. Amen.

The sun shall be turned into darkness, and the moon into blood, before the great the terrible day of the Lord come.

Eclipsing the light

Solar eclipses are relatively rare events. A solar eclipse took place in 1984, and for weeks beforehand the media reported that 99.5% totality would be experienced in a three mile wide strip going through various parts of the United States. Ancient people often thought that eclipses were the result of some evil god eating up the sun. Because eclipses were such dramatic events, God actually made use of them as signs. In fact, he will again. Peter broke forth in preaching on the first day of Christian Pentecost, proclaiming the ancient prophecy of Joel had been fulfilled. Joel had predicted a solar and a lunar event associated with the days before the "Day of the Lord." During the crucifixion something like an eclipse had occurred, thrusting the whole land into darkness from noon until around 3 o'clock.

Signs in the sun and moon are also expected before the return of Christ. Consequently, doomsayers sometimes get publicity during these spectacular natural events. But eclipses come and go, and no one knows if God will use one as a sign or not. Perhaps it will not be a natural eclipse at all that signals Christ's return, but a phenomenon that is totally unpredicted and supernaturally caused.

We know what eclipses are. We can tell when they will occur, where, and to what extent. Residents of Lincolnton, North Carolina clustered into a narrow strip of land going through their little town in 1984, at the exact center of the sun's shadow. Modern science is that exact. But with all our smarts about the sun, our ignorance of the Son is overwhelming. The world was made by him and for him, but the world knows him not. Yet soon, heralded perhaps by the eclipsing sun, the Son of God will be unveiled to the world in glory and judgment. Which event should we know more about, and be better prepared for?

Father, may nothing eclipse the Son from our lives today, but may we see him, and worship him. Amen.

For whosoever will save his life shall lose it; but whosoever shall lose his life for my sake and the gospel's, the same shall save it.

Receiving by giving

There must be a law of reality that says that no matter how long or hard you shop for a thing, after you buy it, it will be on sale lower someplace else. Most of us have had that experience. The same sense of lost value is common in this rapidly advancing technological age, when this morning's electronic gadget is depreciated by half by the new model announced this afternoon. Owners of the first home computers paid hundreds or thousands of dollars for them, and then had trouble unloading them for the price of a tank of gas after PC's became successful. That didn't keep some stubborn owners of home computers from trying to sell their machines for something more nearly like what they paid.

The fact is, the more we put into something, the more we stand to lose if it's worthless. This is part of what is involved in Jesus' words about trying to save our lives, but losing them. He is talking about how to get eternal life by surrendering this present life to him. But *eternal* implies something about quality as well as quantity; therefore Jesus' words also teach that the more you invest in life, the more you get out of it. Specifically for the Christian, the deeper your sacrifice of personal will and desire, to the will and desire of God for you, the greater your fulfilment will be.

This is true in personal relationships. The more you put yourself out for another person, the more you will love him or her, and the more you will get from the friendship. It is also true in church. The more you give to its life and fellowship, the dearer it will be to you. The less you give, the more of a troublemaker you are likely to be. Sacrifice is the better route.

Father, salvation is free to us, but for it to be worth much today, we would give our all to you in response to it. Amen.

February 22 **Scripture Reading: Galatians 6:9**

Let us not be weary in well doing: for in due season we shall reap, if we faint not.

Hang in there

It is easy in this troubled world to give up. If we think our efforts will not matter, we may easily choose not to care. This spiral of negativity can affect the Christian. Yet the Bible says we should always give ourselves fully to the work of the Lord. In Galatians we have a promise that if we keep on doing the good God leads us to do, and "hang in there," he will see that we will reap the rewards. We know from Jesus' own words that some of this reaping may be in eternity rather than time, but it will take place.

God does not promise all our problems will be solved here and now. He does guarantee fulfilment and reward for continuing to do his will in the midst of a problem-ridden world. But if we give up, we will be swallowed by those problems and overcome by evil.

The often told story of German pastor Martin Neimoller in World War II bears repeating. He first looked the other way at Hitler's atrocities. Later he opposed Hitler, but not enough to arouse his flock. Neimoller was arrested, and spent time in Dachau concentration camp. Reflecting on his failures he recalled how the Nazis came for the communists. He did not speak out because he wasn't a communist. Then they came for the Jews. He did not speak because he was not a Jew. Then they came to fetch the Catholics; he did not say anything because he was a Protestant. Eventually, he said, "They came for me, and there was no one left to speak."

Hang in there! Speak when you should. Do good in the face of evil. Hold the line. Love God supremely, and love each other, too. Victory is ours in Christ, sooner or later, but always eventually.

Father, give us courage to live for you in all kinds of situations, no matter what the cost, and to believe that you will reward our faithfulness. Amen.

February 23 **Scripture Reading: 1 Peter 5:5**

Yea, all of you be subject one to another, and be clothed with humility: for God resisteth the proud, and giveth grace to the humble.

Keep America together

Riding America's highways you occasionally see signs saying, "Keep America beautiful." They are a positive expression of a campaign to stop littering. The negative expression warns, "$200 fine for littering." The messages are the opposite sides of the same coin. The Bible also uses both negative and positive admonitions about the same moral, ethical, or spiritual issues. It says, "God hates divorce" (Malachi 2:16), but it also gives the positive exhortation to love one another, and to be subject to one another. This is the kind of attitude that will prevent divorce. What would be more beautiful for America, or anyplace in the world, than for homes to be established, and to stay together!

Yet one in three marriages in the U.S. ends in divorce. It's just one example of the broken or strained relationships that characterize our culture. People sue each other over next to nothing. Jobs are lost over problems that should never have existed. All could be prevented by doing things God's way. The chief rule is: Love your neighbor—your friend, workmate, boss, wife, husband—love that person and all those persons as yourself. In applying that rule, Paul said, "Submit," and Peter said, "Be subject." They describe the same thing: willingly serving others, seeking their good, and their joy. We talk about give-and-take relationships. Surely there is such a thing. But we don't need help "taking." We need help "giving," and the New Testament speaks to this great need. To submit is to give respect and give authority. To love is to give self and life. If more couples would do that, there would be less marital discord.

Indeed, if more people, married or not, would practice the idea of submission in all their personal relationships, life would be more joyful, and the world would be a more beautiful place. Help keep America together—love one another!

Father, even Jesus came to serve, and give himself for us. May we do the same today. Amen.

February 24 **Scripture Reading: Genesis 31:49**

Therefore was the name of it called Galeed, and Mizpah; for he said, The Lord watch between me and thee, when we are absent one from another.

God keep us faithful

From his grandfather's home a young man received a little silver tray, engraved with the word "Mizpah." It was a gift from his grandfather to his grandmother long ago, before he took a long, business trip. The word Mizpah is an Old Testament word meaning "to watch." It was often used (in the past, mostly) as a sweet parting word between mates, and is printed on Christian greeting cards and plaques. But the original situation was not so sweet. Laban made the statement to Jacob, and it was an implied threat. He did not trust Jacob, and he expected God to guard his possessions while he could not be there. Jacob likewise invited God to keep them both honest. The place where their agreement of mutual distrust was made was called Mizpah.

Mizpah has even worse connotations than that. It was at Mizpah that eleven tribes of Israel came to wipe out their twelfth, Benjamin, because of the rape of a Levite's wife. In a bloody confrontation, 25,000 Benjamites fell, only after 40,000 from the eleven tribes were also killed. Brother against brother, the blood flowed. Mizpah. Same place.

How our memories edit! Things are often not as good as we remember them. What seems now to have been ideal was probably mingled with disappointment or distastefulness of some sort at the time. But look at it from the other direction. What we are going through now will not be remembered as we might think. We may be defeated now, sorrowful now, blinded to the purpose of events now, doubtful, despairing, worried, but years from now, we will probably see the purpose in the events of this time, a purpose only partly unfolded now. We cannot see it all, because we are not where we can watch the whole event: but God is. So may God keep watch over us, and keep us faithful to him. Mizpah.

Father, who sees all, guard against our resignation to sin. Keep us faithful. Amen.

Although the fig tree shall not blossom, neither shall fruit be in the vines; the labour of the olive shall fail, and the fields shall yield no meat; the flock shall be cut off from the fold, and there shall be no herd in the stalls: Yet I will rejoice in the Lord, I will joy in the God of my salvation.

Praise God anyway

The gospel song that urges us to "praise the Lord, for our God inhabits praise," gets its biblical foundation in Psalm 22:3: "But thou art holy, O thou that inhabitest the praises of Israel." It suggests that in our praise, God is shown to be enthroned over all the earth, and over all opposing forces. Somehow, when we praise God in the midst of troubles, he works through our worship to make us victors—always spiritually, and frequently circumstantially.

Habakkuk's testimony is that he intended to praise the Lord and rejoice in him, despite the failure of crops and cattle. Those things were their economy. Could Habakkuk disregard the disaster all around him and rejoice in the Lord anyway? Why and how?

One reason is that no matter what happens, the Lord is still God and still Savior. If you personally know his Son, the Word made flesh, then not one thing in the universe can shake you from your eternal life and your relationship to God. Another reason one can praise God in the midst of troubled times is that it is the Lord who brings us through those times with sweet spirits and victorious attitudes. In fact, it is just that positive, open, surrendered, confident atititude, centered in the power of God, that allows him to work in our behalf, for he knows his power will be credited to his name when he has blessed us.

Think of it this way: why would God want to bless a sourpuss? Why would he want to invest his blessing in a life that will not magnify him in return? Praise God instead—it makes you so much more pleasant to work and live with!

Father, grant us the grace to praise and thank you. Thank you! Amen.

And we know that all things work together for good to them that love God, to them who are the called according to his purpose.

What can God do with it?

A credit card customer received a letter saying that a charge had been refused because of a computer error. For all practical purposes, there is no such thing as a computer error. Computers do what people program them to do. They respond to the input they are given, and do so with mathematical precision. The error belongs to some human being. "Computer error" is another phrase made up by us when we want to escape the consequences of what we do. Blame it on the computer.

One of Mark Twain's literary characters once said, "People say it was an accident. There's no such thing as an accident. There's nothing in this world that's happened that's not ordered just so by a higher and wiser power, and it's always for a good purpose." Perhaps Twain, as an agnostic, was merely typifying religious thought, but he hit at the truth.

The Bible says nothing escapes God's detection, that he know every thought and action, and that he rules land and sea and all living. We appear to have a need to distinguish the things God intends to do from the things God only allows. We say he "does" some things directly while he "uses" other things when they happen. The effect is essentially the same: nothing is an accident. Romans 8:28 tells us that every event is woven into the tapestry of God's plans, and the final result is the blessing of his people. This isn't a fatalistic statement, or something meant only to quell our questioning why. In fact, it is a positive invitation to God's people to investigate the possibilities of every situation, joy or sorrow, health or pain, life or death. There are no accidents with God. Look for what God can do with even your deepest woe, to bring you good, or to bring good to his kingdom. You'll find *that* approach will *compute!*

Father, run your program for our lives; input our lives with your Spirit; for you make no errors. Amen.

We glory in tribulations also: knowing that tribulation worketh patience; and patience, experience; and experience, hope.

What can God do with you?

Christians frequently look at the news and are tempted to despair. If we had no anchor in our God, we could become extremely depressed and anxious. The sometimes desperate nature of the times creates a temptation for Christians to modify their morality and ethics or abandon their worship and witness. It seems the world is determined to reverse morals everywhere, hopelessly entangle ethics, restrict worship, and outlaw witness. The United States, which many have regarded as a bastion of religious faith in the world, seems to be taking a lead role in this breakdown of principles.

Apparently, it is time for persecution of God's people to come around again. Actually, persecution of Christians seems to be going on somewhere in the world at any given time. In the Bible, Paul among others challenges us to regard present or coming persecution as the road to spiritual maturity. When we endure persecution by turning to the Lord instead of away from him, we develop patience, experience (maturity) and hope—confidence in our victory and reward. If we, being sinful, lived in a vacuum, isolated from resistance, we would not arrive at spiritual maturity. God knows we need the troubles, pains and sorrows, to shape and grow us. It might not have been so in a perfect environment, but this world is far from perfect, and the flesh will enslave us at the least opportunity.

Somehow, God uses the injurious world to make us into something usable to him. A little girl walking with her mother fell on the sidewalk and skinned her knee. She said, "Mom, wouldn't it be nice if the whole world were padded!" I guess we all think so. But we would be the losers. Perspective—that's the key! See it from God's angle. A difficult life in this world is simply God's field of infinite opportunity to do something great with you!

Father, may we let you see what you can do with us, in the midst of our many struggles. Amen.

Ye have not chosen me, but I have chosen you, and ordained you, that ye should go and bring forth fruit, and that your fruit should remain.

Chosen for a purpose

When we were young, most of us at one time were involved in a game where we chose up sides. Those appointed as captains got to choose their players. Many children who are not natural leaders or athletes never seem to have the chance to choose which side they will play for. As well, some kids, bemoaning their lot of being at the mercy of the captains, seem always to be chosen last. In life, however, every person has the opportunity to choose his teammates, to choose which side he wishes to be on. In fact, you cannot avoid choosing sides. Whether you choose intentionally or not, you choose. If you choose to serve God, well and good. If you decide to do nothing, you have chosen to serve self and sin. Either way, you will choose, and have done so already, many times.

Jesus could not have been clearer with his disciples that he had chosen them for an important purpose. They were to represent him. They were to fish for men. They were to choose him over family, jobs, wealth, or anything in the world. They were to be known as his disciples—by their love, by their fruit, by their testimony, by their example—but they were definitely to be known.

A little old man was seen every Sunday morning walking to church. He was deaf. He could not hear a word of the sermon or the choir music or the hymns being sung. He read lips up close, however, and when someone asked him why he went to church when he couldn't hear, he said, "I want my neighbors to know which side I'm on."

We should hope our neighbors know whose side we're on by more than just driving off to church every Sunday, but certainly we should do that, and we should live in every other way so we will make a difference. It is extremely important to take a stand. Whose side are you on?

Father, we remember that Jesus said that he who is not for me is against me. Grant us to be for Jesus today. That's why he called us. Amen.

February 29 Scripture Reading: Hebrews 11:3

Through faith we understand that the worlds were framed by the word of God, so that the things which are seen were not made of things which do appear.

The leap of faith

There will not be another today for four more years. In leap year, perhaps you call today "leap day." People speak of taking a leap of faith. They mean that to accept a certain claim, they have to leap over much of what they think they know, and suspend their questions. Mostly, however, biblical faith is simply a matter of taking God at his word. We cannot figure out many things for ourselves. God has to reveal them. That revelation becomes the object of our faith: we are invited to trust God that it is true.

Hebrews 11:3 teaches that it is through the avenue of faith we come to be certain that the world didn't just "happen," but was put together at the creative command of God. No matter how symbolically some scientists, skeptics, or faithless claimants to Christianity interpret Genesis 1-2, this verse in Hebrews remains clear and unambiguous: what we see—the world around us in its present form—was not produced from itself, but by the purposeful and powerful word of God. The universe came into being in response to God's command. Everything that happened after that emanated from the creative act of God. Unless we simply choose not to believe the written word of God, Hebrews 11:3 confronts us with the blunt truth.

Faith comes into play when you are called on to make a choice. Do you believe, along with most modern, reductionist scientists, that nothing in the universe, including its origin, needs God to explain it, start it or sustain it? Or do you accept the word of God, the revelation of God's truth, to be exactly that—revelation—and do you choose to believe that God created the universe, even if you are ridiculed? The world makes it appear that to believe the Bible is to choose ignorance. The Bible itself, however, says to believe God is to choose wisdom. Whatever the facts may *appear* to be, to some, eventually the facts will manifest the truth of what God has already revealed. You can afford to take a leap, and believe it.

Father, help us believe your Word, in everything. Amen.

If thou shalt confess with thy mouth the Lord Jesus, and shalt believe in thine heart that God hath raised him from the dead, thou shalt be saved.

The resurrection: essential to salvation

There are certain theological beliefs that are essential. The Bible itself defines these beliefs. Opting out of one of them disqualifies a person to be called a Christian in the biblical sense. One of these basics is the physical resurrection of Jesus Christ from the dead. It isn't enough to believe only in some general idea that Jesus lives on in "principle." It isn't enough to believe that his disciples kept the spirit of his work alive, and that he continues with us in that sense alone. The Bible says we must believe in his actual resurrection from the dead. The Bible reports the resurrection as an actual, physical event. Jesus went to some length in his appearances to demonstrate his physical reality. Then the rest of the New Testament repeatedly stresses the resurrection as the event changing death into victory for Christ and for believers. Paul says our response to the gospel must include believing that God the Father raised Jesus from the dead. Only if we believe this can we be born again to everlasting life.

Yet some who wish to be Christians are unwilling to accept this claim. In England a few years ago a bishop stated his belief that the resurrection of Jesus was a conjuring trick with bones. He said he was not convinced that God maneuvers physical things. This high-ranking cleric in the Church of England said Christians do not have to take the resurrection as a literal fact.

Yet any school child can correct this doctor of theology. Disillusioned clerics or agnostic hedonists may take issue with the truth of the Bible, but they cannot change what it says. Romans says plainly: Jesus rose bodily, and believing that fact is essential to our receiving him as living Savior. Since our faith must rest on what Christ has done for us, belief in the resurrection is essential. It's just that simple.

Father, help us not to swallow the lies of those who will not believe your word. Rather, believing, give us power to live, through the risen Christ. Amen.

Be ye doers of the word, and not hearers only, deceiving your own selves.

Do something!

Have you ever been all dressed up with no place to go? Do you ever do something designed to prepare you for some opportunity, but you don't go on to the opportunity itself? Sometimes people go to college, study hard, get a degree, get another degree, then go home and work at a job that didn't require even a high school education.

Christians sometimes do that when they go to Bible studies, training classes, seminars, and sit in worship under preaching, but never make a contribution to the ministry of the church—a contribution not only in money but in themselves and their labors. They receive a lot from their preparation, but they don't give much from their lives. They soak up a lot, but don't apply it in practice. James 1:22 was addressed to just this failure. It not only addresses doing things that are wrong, rejecting warnings of the word from God, but it also speaks to our need to *do* things that are right, when the word of God exhorts and challenges us. Christians are to join in the battle, get involved, become ministers of Christ themselves, not just to be objects of other people's ministry.

Before the days of cell phones and satellite TV links, a metropolitan newspaper once chartered a train to rush a green reporter to a nearby town to scoop all rivals with the first news of a fire that was burning the place down. A couple of hours later the managing editor got a telegram from the bewildered young man reading, "Have arrived at fire. What shall I do?" The exasperated editor replied, "Find the place where the fire is hottest and jump in!"

We have been sent on a mission, not just to stand around, remaining inexperienced. The best cure for feeling ill-equipped just may well be to launch out on faith. God honors trusting obedience with overcoming grace. One who has been a Christian any length of time is equipped to do *something.* So do it!

Father, we have sometimes twiddled our thumbs when there was kingdom work to be done. Forgive us, and give us another opportunity, today. Amen.

For which of you, intending to build a tower, sitteth not down first, and counteth the cost, whether he have sufficient to finish it?

Discipleship Lite?

Common wisdom is that bigger is better. Sometimes that is true. But the new maxim seems to be that smaller is better. Microchips and robotic construction make extreme miniaturization possible. We could name dozens of things that have been reduced in size over and over, because smaller is better. Similarly, many products have not only the original or full-size version, but a "lite" version as well.

But some things suffer by being reduced in size or duration. Some Christians, and sadly some churches, advocate a sort of "discipleship-lite." They reduce the demands of Christian commitment or service to conform to cultural norms or to the amount of time people are willing to give to spiritual things. Many Christians have so thoroughly swallowed the idea of "quality time" that they believe that quantity is irrelevant. So they spend less time praying or reading the Bible, and expect to spend less time at church as well. Such expectations trivialize the life-encompassing dimensions of our faith. The trouble is, our fast-food, quick-stop, drive-in mentality has led us to believe that everything can be abbreviated, produced instantly, compressed, or otherwise made smaller, without loss. It isn't so.

Jesus said we must count the cost of discipleship, and we must be willing to expend everything we are and have in following him. That is a demand that cannot be miniaturized. There is no "lite" version of commitment to Christ.

Father, help us not to minimize the importance of commitment to Christ, and may we never abbreviate what you want done "uncut." Amen.

Behold therefore the goodness and severity of God

Balanced living

Most of us are out of balance at some time in our lives. In other words, we tend to go off on tangents over something. Or we vacillate between extremes. It can be true of our theology, as well. Out-of-balance theology affects negatively the way we live before God.

If, for instance, we think of God as only sweetness and love, forgiving every fault not only graciously but blindly, we will take advantage of such a God by being less attentive to serious moral or ethical issues than we should, or at least by being lax with daily life and witness. If, on the other hand, we see God as a scowling judge with little affection, and we overemphasize the genuinely biblical teaching that the Lord is holy and executes wrath on evildoers, we may become legalistic and hard toward ourselves and others. We may actually scare people away from any gospel we might accidentally communicate.

What is the answer? Balance! Not fence-straddling or compromise, but biblically based balance. As Paul wrote, we should consider both God's goodness *and* his severity, or sternness. They are both essential to his nature. He is a loving judge, and a righteous lover. His mercy is never foolish, and his judgment is never unfair.

This is a wonderful word, because it frees us from both slavery to a driving taskmaster, and from a conception of a god that no one can really respect. Our God, who is holy and merciful, demanding and forgiving, is one who draws us to him, and makes us want to live for him.

Father, thank you for expecting much of us, and for forgiving our failure to rise to it, when we confess our sins before you, claiming the blood of Christ. Amen.

And whatsoever ye do, do it heartily, as to the Lord, and not unto men.

What kind of worker?

Surely an excellent rule for the church is for every believer to work at everything with all his heart, and to direct and devote everything he does to the Lord. In every Christian's private life as well, Paul's general principle in Colossians 3:23 is a wonderful summation of both the right focus and the right attitude for living. Pour yourself into whatever you do, keep the Lord in focus as the goal of your life, and don't worry whether or not self-appointed judges around you approve.

Someone said there are three groups in every church: those who make it happen, those who watch it happen, and those who wonder what is happening. Someone else put it this way—three groups: the plus-plus crowd, which says, "I can do it, and you can do it, and let's get it done;" the plus-minus crowd, which says, "I can do it, but you can't do it, so get out my way and I'll do it;" and finally the minus-minus crowd, saying, "I can't do it, you can't do it, and whoever brought it up was crazy!" Which crowd are you in?

Are you the last to agree with change or innovation? Do you resist anything that isn't what you have been used to? Or perhaps you stay basically uninvolved until you see the way the crowd is going. Or you operate independently, even when cooperation would increase the yield. Or are you one who is always ready to pitch in, always giving input of ideas and energy, and willing to be a part of whatever might work to gain the goals of the Lord's people? Being part of a church means committing yourself to action. Do it, and do it with all your heart, as unto the Lord.

Father, just as you are a God of action, grant us enthusiasm and energy today, to be used in your work and for your glory. Amen.

And as the ark of the LORD came into the city of David, Michal Saul's daughter looked through a window, and saw king David leaping and dancing before the LORD; and she despised him in her heart.

Happy in the Lord

Are you a Christian? If so, are you happy? If not, do you see any conflict in the two answers? Obviously, the list of problems in our lives could go on and on, but are you happy in the Lord in spite of your trials? Can people tell it?

When the ark was brought back to Jerusalem after a long absence, King David was so elated that he led the way dancing in the road. His young wife, however, was a stick in the mud. She was one of those people who are sour and dry-spirited, with no joy of life and no joy in the Lord. Some interpreters say Michal was already disillusioned with David or never wanted to leave her father, King Saul's, home in the first place to marry David. No doubt she had her reasons for bitterness—but don't we all?

Many people choose to let problems make them disagreeable. In addition, Christians can continue in sins or practice ongoing resistance to the lordship of Christ, with the result that they become angry and joyless. A speaker at a Christian conference said, "If you are one of those sour faced believers, *please* don't tell anyone you're a Christian: it will scare them off!"

A happy disposition for the Christian does not require the removal of all his problems. Instead, the best way to have the joy of the Lord in daily life is to do God's will, and the entranceway to God's will is always surrender. God the Son became incarnate in Jesus Christ, and ascended so that through his descending Spirit he could indwell and fill and lead us into abundance and joy. When we are willing to be immersed in his fullness and lordship, our joy will return and grow.

Father, as David wrote, restore unto us the joy of thy salvation, as you fill us with your Spirit. Amen.

March 7 **Scripture Reading: Romans 8:24**

For we are saved by hope

Building on Christ

A morning radio program called "Coffee with the Pastor" was broadcast in the Dallas-Fort Worth Metroplex years ago. It greeted early-risers with the words, "Get up, get out of bed, you sleepyhead! The coffee's on! Get that frown off your face, put a smile in its place, then go out and face the world." Many of us need the reminder.

Some wag's biting versions of first lines of several familiar hymns went like this:

"When morning gilds the skies, my heart awakening cries, "O no, another day!"
"Amazing grace, how sweet the sound that saved a wretch like you!"
"My hope is built on ...nothing."

What is your hope built on? The Bible says we are saved in what Paul calls "this hope." What hope is that? It is written all over the pages of the Bible and expressed well and succinctly in the first verse of the opening chapter of 1 Timothy: "Jesus Christ, our hope." He himself is our salvation. If you have him in your life, you have life eternal. God's kind of hope is not merely wishful thinking; it's, a sure thing, guaranteed in the life, death, and resurrection of Jesus Christ, God the Son. He *is* our hope.

A bumper sticker said, "Don't tell me what kind of day to have!" Okay. But here's a strong suggestion: Have a day built on Christ, and see what kind of day it will produce. No doubt, if you really invest your life today in the things of Christ, frowns will give way to smiles, and as you face the world, you'll be glad to have another day to know and love him.

Father, show me today how to base my hope and expectation in Christ, and to build my every thought and deed on a relationship with him. Amen.

March 8 **Scripture Reading: Mark 12:30**

Thou shalt love the Lord thy God

A relationship of love

We often say things like, "Let's get to the heart of the matter," or "Give me the bottom line," when we want people to "cut to the chase," and simplify something. Often we spend too much time talking about peripheral matters and ignoring or missing the central issue.

What, for instance, is the central issue of the Christian faith? Belief in God? Faith in him? Belief in Jesus Christ? Certainly we could support these answers with scripture. But when Jesus was asked by a scribe about the most important commandment of all—God's chief expectation of man—he said, "The first of all the commandments is this: Hear O Israel, the Lord our God is one. Love the Lord your God with all your heart, soul, mind and strength." Notice that Jesus' answer stressed not just belief in the one God, but more importantly that we must love him. The most important issue of the Christian faith is not a doctrine: it is a relationship. The heart of Christian faith is to love the Lord in whom you believe, the God revealed to us in the Son, Jesus Christ.

Theologian Karl Barth was once asked by some reporters what the core of his theology was. In what is now a well-publicized reply, Barth said, "Jesus loves me, this I know, for the Bible tells me so." There it is again—love—this time, God's love for us. It's that relationship again. God loves us, and wants us to love him back.

How are you doing getting to the heart of the matter? How is your love relationship with the Lord? Does the time you spend communing with him support your claim of loving him? Does your expenditure of time, energy and money say you love him? Does the subject of your conversation evidence that love?

Father, if we get nowhere in any other pursuit today, let us come to the end of the day having learned a little more about loving you back. Amen.

As God hath distributed to every man, as the Lord hath called every one, so let him walk.

God's personal pathway for you

There are different levels of instruction in the Bible. Some things are given as commands, some as strong urgings, some as wise advice. God does not always say, "Thou shalt," but sometimes, "It would be better if you did." For instance, in 1 Corinthians 7, Paul gives many instructions concerning the wisdom of marriage or celibacy. One part he prefaces with, "I give this command—not I, but the Lord." But the next section he introduces with, "I say, (I, not the Lord)." And he caps off the second set of instructions with, "This is my judgment, and I think I have the Spirit of God." Paul attributed some teachings to the direct words of Christ and implied they had the highest imperative. Other teachings were designed to be presented as his urging or wise advice.

Everything God teaches us in his word is to be taken seriously, for all of it is inspired and "useful for instruction in righteousness." But some things are in the word of God to call to those who have an ear to hear them or to resonate with those whose walk of life makes them candidates for just such a message. For instance, in this passage in 1 Corinthians 7, Paul says that his advice to the unmarried not to get married is not a command, but he recommends celibacy as a lifestyle enabling someone to be more thoroughly involved in the Lord's work. He admits plainly, however, that every Christian should follow the path God has laid out for him, since God has given some the ability to be celibate, and some he has not.

So it is with many other of life's circumstances. This is what makes our discipleship so personal: each of us must read the word of God with an open mind and heart, and pray with a teachable spirit, so that the Lord will lead us individually in his customized plan. Some things we must do, along with all others; other things the Spirit leads us to do, out of his will for us alone.

Father, today lead by your Spirit, making your words of wisdom into personal words of divine imperative. Amen.

From whence come wars and fightings among you? come they not hence, even of your lusts that war in your members?

Who started it?

What parent hasn't had to break up a fight? 'Okay, you two, stop it this minute!' 'Well, he started it!' 'No, I didn't—he did, Mom—' 'I did not!' And on it goes. The more things change, the more things remain the same. Few of us are not guilty of blaming the troubles we face on someone else. We especially do not want to be seen as persons who act out of caprice or selfishness. We don't want to be seen as persons who start quarrels or initiate hurtful actions or author injustice. Our line is that we merely reacted to somebody *else's* offense. Our feelings were hurt, or our needs were not met, or something of the like.

James, the Bible writer, has a way of calling us to account for individual responsibility. He asked his readers to be honest about why they get involved in quarrels. He answered the question for them: they start inside each of your hearts, where your own strong desires battle inside you. If James heard us say, "He started it," he would probably interject, "*Who* started it? Wasn't it you? Did someone upset your apple cart because you didn't get your way?" And if somebody else started it, who kept it going? After all, it takes two to argue. Quarrels begin and continue because people are mutually willing to pursue contention in the hope that they can win, thus fulfilling their own strong desires.

Many of the disagreements in which we become embroiled take place because we ourselves are out of step with the God of peace and have abandoned the discipline of being peacemakers, like Jesus Christ.

Father, lead us with a gentle, forgiving hand, and teach us the peace that enables us to let offenses roll off, as we choose love instead. Amen.

Multitudes, multitudes in the valley of decision

Which way do I go?

Joel the prophet gives a striking description of the crisis of people in every age. When he spoke of the "valley of decision," he was describing a place—perhaps a figurative one—where the Lord would bring the history of the world to an end. The term "decision" refers mostly to the verdict of God upon the unrepentant. But even though God's judgment is just around the corner, and even though there are multitudes who will rebel against God to the very end, as long as there is time, there is opportunity to repent, to decide to turn from sin and receive God's appointed Savior, Jesus Christ.

Jesus spoke of this ominous situation when he told Nicodemus that those who don't yet believe in the one and only Son of God are already condemned, but he assured Nicodemus, and us, that he came not to finalize that condemnation but to introduce salvation through him. Yet many linger in that valley of decision, not willing to leave it for the hill of Calvary.

The unsaved often linger in indecision about Christ until the time for deciding passes them by, and judgment sweeps down on them. But the saved also descend into valleys where uncommitted living and indulgence in the condemned things of the world keep their lives from being productive for God, and consequently from being fulfilled and joyful. Just as the only answer for the unsaved is to repent and surrender to Christ, so the solution for the saved is to abandon fruitless and superficial pursuits and to invest themselves wholly in following Jesus daily.

Decision is not just an imperative for life's few great crises, but an essential for everyday living.

Father, teach us today to redeem the time by deciding right now to live for you each moment. Amen.

Let mine eyes run down with tears night and day, and let them not cease: for the virgin daughter of my people is broken with a great breach, with a very grievous blow.

God's grief, God's anger

Few things are as traumatic for a woman as the incidence of rape, and in the case of a young woman or a girl, her parents are nearly as upset as she is. She is terrified, usually, and they are enraged, and all of us can understand why. This is one reason society should be extremely tough on rapists.

We should understand, then, how God feels when he sees the people of his choice deceived by false prophets, violated by corruptive influences, compromised by worldly ways. The word of the Lord through Jeremiah reports that the Lord grieves over the "breach" of his people—a great wound. God is protective of his own, and he hurts for us, and grieves over us, when we are hurt by the evil around us.

It is a liberating discovery when we finally learn that God's chief response to his children is not to get mad at them, but to grieve for them. If we think he is mad, we will hesitate to return, to repent, and to walk with him again. If, however, we realize that God is infinitely more concerned about our condition than we are, we can come back to him without fear of rejection. Sin is not to be blamed on anybody but ourselves, but in a sense we are raped by the world of hedonistic and egotistic philosophies. God hurts for us. His *anger* is directed at the corruptive influences. But his *love* is rich and deep for his children, and out of his grief for us he wants to heal and forgive.

Let us never stay away from God because we fear our sins have turned him against us. No one, not even we, can separate us from his love.

Father, if we are the tempters of others, woe to us, and we repent, but if we are the victims of temptation, may we not fear now to confess and be made whole. Amen.

But go ye and learn what that meaneth, I will have mercy, and not sacrifice.

When you want forgiveness

Despite their best intentions, Christians may come to treat their own sins too lightly. We may find ourselves asking in a brief prayer for blanket forgiveness for things we ought to be confessing individually and in depth. Even more importantly, we may sometimes neglect to set things right with others, while asking forgiveness only from God.

We cannot hurt people and expect to escape the guilt of our actions by going to God in prayer without also going to those people in apology. Praying for forgiveness is easier, but it isn't all that is required. When Jesus told the Pharisees God wanted mercy more than sacrifice, he was quoting Hosea 6:6, where God revealed his desire for his people to have a mutually forgiving and loving spirit toward one another instead of engaging in hypocritical rituals. Jesus was saying that God wants us to express our repentance in the world of relationships with others, not merely in words of prayer.

No matter how much contrition we show in prayer over our flaws, or how many things we say we will give over to God, if we go out and live ungraciously toward others, unbending to their needs, inconsiderate of their feelings or rights, or scorning their imperfections while ignoring our own, then we ourselves have not been forgiven. What if, when we ask God's forgiveness for our wrongs to others, God were to say: "Look, my child, if you want forgiveness, don't ask for it just yet. Go love that one you disdained yesterday. Ask forgiveness of the one you just denied my love, and when you have, my forgiveness will come instantly. Until then, your lips are moving but I do not hear you." Would it change the way we pray?

Father, prod us to forgive and to love others as you do us, so our prayers will be answered. Amen.

The things that thou hast heard of me among many witnesses, the same commit thou to faithful men, who shall be able to teach others also.

Your unique testimony

A fascinating and challenging Christian concept is that in each believer's life there are people to whom that believer is equipped and positioned to witness more effectively than anyone else in the world. Evangelists called and equipped to preach to thousands or millions are not necessarily the most effective tools of God for reaching *your* neighbor or friend at work. Pastors who haven't lived on the wrong side of the tracks may be less effective with those who have, while winos turned to Christ may be fruitless trying to witness to CEOs.

Chief Matamula was a Muslim, but he had attended worship services with missionaries in Salima, Malawi. One Sunday they invited another chieftain and former Muslim, Mphamba, to lead the services. There were several decisions for Christ, but Matamula was not among them. At the next baptismal service, however, when Mphamba came back to the church, Matamula asked him what he must do to be saved. Mphamba said, "If you as a chieftain need Christ, then I know I do, too." What the missionaries had preached urgently, Matamula's unique witness achieved.

Paul wrote Timothy that it was vital for him to train people in the testimony of Christ, and for them to pass on that testimony and train others. The plan of God is not that a few people should tell everyone else, but that each one should reach one, each one win one. Even if it were one and only one person that you could reach, that one might be the key to many others. Sometimes that one person—or that one person just for today—may need to see Christ in your life more than any other, to convince him he needs Christ, too.

Father, help us discover the unique opportunity we may have today to show Christ to someone. Amen.

Is it time for you, O ye, to dwell in your ceiled houses, and this house lie waste?

Cherishing our church

Why are Christians often content to let their churches struggle along with inadequate buildings and budgets when they would not tolerate similar circumstances in their own homes if they could do anything about it? King David once said, "Here I am living in a palace of cedar, while the ark of God remains in a tent." He had suddenly realized that he had provided for himself far better than he had for the house of the Lord. Actually, there wasn't any house of the Lord yet, only the tent, the tabernacle. Now, God pointed out that the tabernacle represented some important things about mobility and the omnipresence of his Spirit; nevertheless, it was important for the people of Israel, who were settling into one place, to take a high view of their place of worship and those who ministered in it.

Haggai echoed David's concern when he pointed out the sin of Israelites in having fine homes indicative of an affluent lifestyle, while the temple was falling down in disrepair. The spirit of his words and David's is the same, and the lesson is obvious: we must place a high value on the house of the Lord. Consequently, we must be responsible stewards of our wealth in order to insure that the total ministry of our church, including its facilities, is not out of keeping with its importance in God's kingdom.

Fixing what doesn't work, painting what is peeling, and cleaning what is dirty is part of this necessity, but so is reviving what is sleeping, populating what has been abandoned, promoting what is neglected, and resurrecting what has been allowed to die. It reflects on us poorly if we treat ourselves well but feed scraps to our church—whether in our offerings or our service.

Father, since Jesus Christ loved the church enough to die for it, may we love it, too, as a way of loving him. Amen.

The LORD our God hath shewed us his glory and his greatness.

God is great

Many children used to learn a simple table prayer, "God is great, God is good, and we thank him for our food..." The first phrase alone is worthy of extended consideration. God is great. How often do we pause, set aside all other issues, and simply think about how infinitely great, how indescribably awesome God is?

Study some of the photographs taken from space of the distant nebulae, vast clouds of interstellar gases from which stars are forming. Consider the almost unfathomable distances across these wonders and the wondrous processes taking place in them. Attempt to take in the concept that there are untold numbers of these clouds and billions of the stars that are suspended in them and in the universe.

Turn the lens around and look at what the scanning electron microscope sees at a nearly atomic level. Look at the mind-boggling complexity of life at a microscopic level and the startling beauty and organization of biological systems, all of which argue demandingly that they were supernaturally designed. One may argue for the formation of things by natural processes that are inherent in the very physics of the stars or in the very structure of DNA. Yet all matter owes its existence to the underlying energy to which it is equivalent, and there can be no source for that energy other than the great designer, God.

God is infinitely greater than the seemingly infinite universe that burst into existence at his creative command. God is incalculably more complex than the most incredibly microscopic building blocks of matter. The God who reveals himself in creation, through a written message, and through Jesus Christ the Word made flesh, is truly great. To muse on this truth alone should lead us to keep ourselves in proper perspective and to worship the God of the universe.

Father, Creator, and Great God, we worship you today, and seek to be awed, as we should be, at your infinite glory. Amen.

And God set them in the firmament of the heaven to give light upon the earth.

The purpose of light

Until the Middle Ages people believed that the earth was the center of the universe. We now know it isn't. The only thing that goes around us is our moon, a mere speck of a sphere. We rotate around our sun, a small star that is but one of billions of stars in a galaxy that is but one of millions or even billions of galaxies in the vastness of the universe. Astronomically speaking, we are insignificant. But when Moses very briefly described God's creation of the sun and moon, he added the creation of stars almost as an afterthought, and he stated unapologetically that *all* the heavenly lights are for the purpose of lighting the world we live in. If this weren't the Bible speaking, we might say Moses was being presumptuous.

But this *is* the Bible, and the message in Genesis 1:17 is plain. It does not tell us the earth is the center of the created universe; earlier human beings inferred that idea where it was not implied. What the Bible does tell us is that regardless of our size and location in the universe, God is uniquely at work right here in our quadrant, our solar system, our planet, and among the creatures he calls Man—a creature who is made in his image. God has placed the lights of the heavens in their place to give light to the earth, whatever other purpose they may serve, and God has created man through the eternal Word, whom the Bible describes as "the light of men." Just as the sun and moon light man's way on earth, the Son of God lights man's way in the world. Just as the stars reveal God's handiwork and speak silently of his majesty, the eternal Word revealed himself as "the light of the world," through whom and only through whom we can see the kingdom of heaven.

Insignificant as we are by some measurements, God sent himself as one of us to show us the light and give us eternal life with him. If God is so interested in you, how focused are you on him?

Father, today may the Son light my way as I seek you above all things. Amen.

And he said unto me, My grace is sufficient for thee: for my strength is made perfect in weakness.

Purpose of prayer

Electronics repairmen have a secret. Every television repairman knows about it; every radio service person knows; every part-time, self-appointed fix-it man knows, too. It's a magic spray. When the volume crackles, when the switch sometimes works and sometimes doesn't, when the computer keys stick, what do you do? Use magic spray! You don't know this, of course, but the repairman does. He sprays a bit of it on your problem, and voila, it's fixed. Then, he charges you big bucks, of course. The spray is a combination of a quickly evaporating hydrocarbon that loosens and floats away filmy, non-conductive dirt, and a light, conductive lubricant that remains on the electronic part. The magic is commonly called tuner cleaner, and it really is amazing how many problems it solves.

Prayer has sometimes been thought of as a magic solution to all problems. In this view of prayer, God should answer immediately upon a single request, and give the petitioner exactly what he asks. However, it doesn't work that way. Paul the apostle once asked for relief from what he called his "thorn in the flesh," and he got this answer instead, clear as a bell: "My grace is sufficient for you." In fact, he tried three times to get God to spray his problem away, and he got the same answer.

There must be some purpose God has in letting some irritating or troublesome things continue in our lives. Indeed, there is. Without them, we would not learn to let him be sufficient. Without them, we would rely on ourselves. Without them, we would assume we were immune to or invulnerable to defeat. God is not a doting granddaddy, and prayer is not a fix-all. It is a means of our putting ourselves at the disposal of God and of being conformed to his will. Increasingly, we should pray not to see if we can get what we need but to see why we need what we get.

Father, since we can't figure everything out, we submit to your will and count on your grace to get us through. Amen.

March 19 **Scripture Reading: John 16:29**

His disciples said unto him, Lo, now speakest thou plainly, and speakest no proverb.

The plain truth

On the last nights of his earthly ministry, Jesus discontinued his practice of teaching in parables and told his disciples plainly that he had come from God and was the only way to God and to eternal life. They were thankful for the plain language. Yet all the time Jesus spoke in parables and used figures of speech and signs, he was not obscuring the truth; he was simply revealing it in more intuitive ways.

Symbols, in both life and speech, communicate at a powerful level. Sometimes we need one image, sometimes another. After a dry spell in our community, the biblical symbol of "showers of blessing" (Ez.24:36) is especially effective, but when flooding has ruined wheat or destroyed homes, the sunshine after the rain (2 Sam.23:4) is a more welcome image. To some, the idea of walking on golden streets in heaven doesn't excite them, but pleasant pastures do. The Bible gives both pictures. The picture of hell as fire probably scares almost anyone, but for those terrified even more by darkness, that image also appears in the Bible.

Likewise, living the Christian life is viewed sometimes as following like sheep, then as building like an architect, then as going to war like a soldier. But it is also pictured as bearing a cross, being in prison, and plowing a field. In fact, whatever kind of image you need in a given situation, you will likely find it in God's word. What does not change is the reality behind all the images: God is love; Jesus is Lord and Savior; salvation is by grace through faith; and Christ is coming soon, and you and I will be either with him where he is, or without him and lost forever. However you picture it, this is the reality. We should be glad that both Father and Son have told us, both with powerful symbols and in plain words, the simple and saving truth.

Father, thank you for telling us plainly all things that pertain to life and godliness. We rejoice in the truth! Amen.

March 20 **Scripture Reading: John 5:6**

Wilt thou be made whole?

The will to change

One of the more penetrating questions ever asked was that of Jesus to the lame man by the pool of Bethesda. This man had lain there every day for years, waiting for some angelic stirring of the waters to provide healing for the first one to jump in. His chance never seemed to come. One day, however, Jesus came by and said to him, "Will you be made whole?" Notice, "*will* you," not "would you like to be," or "are you trying to be." Jesus wanted to know: 'Do you have the driving will, the immediate intention, the determined purpose in this moment to be well, and will you do what I tell you in order to *be* well?' We can speculate about whether defeatism or self pity may have derailed the man in his purpose over the years. But the bottom line is that Jesus by his question challenged him to determine finally to do something about his condition.

In most of our lives there are conditions that hobble us in the full pursuit of Christlikeness, and in most cases we are fully and painfully aware of our lameness. We plan sometime to improve these things, to straighten out some matter, to repent of some continual attitude, to commit ourselves to some gnawing sense of leading. But *will* we? It doesn't really drive us with conviction—the kind that won't and can't wait. Or does it?

While the power to change lies in God, the will to change is our responsibility. It is up to us to allow ourselves to be consumed with God's own passion for what ought to be reality in our lives. We can choose to lie around by the pool of vague hopes, thinking wistfully of what may be, one day. Or we may look into the face of the Master and say, "I *will* be made whole." What will it be?

Father, as we look into the healing eyes of Jesus just now, we say, "I will!" In your power and grace, may it be so. Amen.

Casting all your care upon him, for he careth for you.

Someone to turn to

Everyone needs someone to turn to. Even those who are highly self-reliant occasionally do need a reliable friend. It must be terrible to have no one at all to whom to turn when things get rough. There is a similar need in opposite conditions to have someone to enjoy good times with. Joys often seem hollow when there is no one sharing them, and troubles seem extra difficult when no one helps bear their weight. Human companionship goes a long way toward making life's highs and lows better for us. But sometimes no one seems to care enough, or everyone seems to be taken with his own enjoyments and feels ho-hum about ours. We can't blame people for having their own lives to live. But what about our need of a friend?

Jesus Christ introduces himself to us as the one from heaven who is meant to be our heavenly friend. True, he is presented as Lord, Redeemer, Savior, King of kings, Teacher, Master, Prophet, and Son of God, but he is also Friend. The Bible invites us to cast all our care upon him, because he cares, truly cares about us. When others haven't the time to care or to care enough, Jesus cares for us and is there to be our friend. Is this just imaginary, just a figure of speech, or is it real? Can Jesus really be a friend? Can we know his friendly presence and experience it?

Indeed, we can. To be saved is to have a relationship with God through Jesus Christ, and this relationship has the potential to be more intense and real, because his presence is not just beside us, as another human being can be, but *in* us. We don't need his phone number. We don't need a car to drive to his house. He came to our house, our world, our lives, and he lives in our lives from the day we first say yes to his lordship. Practicing his presence makes it sweeter and sweeter to turn to him, and to find him always there.

Father and Lord Jesus, I turn to you today in the mix of my life's emotions. Thank you for caring for me. Amen.

And the Spirit of the Lord will come upon thee, and thou shalt prophesy with them, and shalt be turned into another man.

A different person

Christian conversion is a phenomenon that cannot be separated from personal experience with Jesus Christ, but conversion was not unknown before the time of Christ. Long before, Samuel the prophet told Saul, who was to be the first king of Judah, that he would experience the entry of God's spirit to his life, followed by an intense awareness of God's truths, and that he would in fact be a different person than before. Moreover, he told him then to do whatever his hand found to do, for God would be with him. In other words, Saul's heart would be prone to do God's will such that Samuel could say, "Go do it, and you're apt to be right."

Christian conversion is similar: God comes to us personally to dwell with us when we open ourselves to Christ as saving Lord. When the Spirit of God enters, we become different. The Word living in us wants to be shared and spoken, and we want to serve God in many ways. This is quite a change for some persons, who could not have cared less about God before meeting Christ personally, or who even may have ridiculed Christian values and evangelism. But now, they are different. This is the heart of conversion.

Those who experience conversion, however, do not become perfect overnight. We receive new hearts, but then we are challenged daily to submit ourselves consciously to the Holy Spirit, God's power for changed living, so that our whole lives continually come into conformity with his character and will.

As a Christian, is there something you wish were different about you? Is there a weakness you wish were not there, an obsession that is improper, an undisciplined way you wish you could master, an area of apathy you wish were filled with zeal? Jesus Christ has already made the difference in your heart. Let him master you, and you can be a different person—even from the one you were just yesterday.

Father, because there is yet change needed in me, may the Spirit of Jesus make even more difference in me today. Amen.

And ye became followers of us, and of the Lord…so that ye were examples to all.

The power of the word

There is a fascinating array of styles in worship. In particular, preaching goes from one extreme to another. There is the soft, mesmeric voice of the one who gets close to the microphone in a studio and half-whispers his appeal. There is the highly energetic type of service where the screaming is so loud that the listener wonders if the preacher counts on being able to speak at all past the age of forty. In between, there are orators, joke tellers, men who use alliteration and allegory and those who don't, people who speak from manuscripts from pulpits high over a crowd of the elite, no-name preachers who just come into the radio studio and simulate a live service, and men who appear entirely normal, whatever that is to you.

The only thing all these persons have in common is the preaching of the word. Isn't it interesting how many opinions there are of what it means to preach with power. Some people don't consider that they have heard preaching unless the pulpit is pounded and the preacher and the congregation both work up a sweat. Others are convinced that in most cases such antics are merely showmanship and emotion, not the power of God. Who can account for taste?

In fact, however, the power of the word is not measured ultimately by any of the styles by which it is preached, or any of the emotions shown in response. Paul wrote to the church at Thessalonica that "our gospel came not unto you in word only, but also in power and in the Holy Spirit." He then told them how he knew: they had become followers of Christ, imitators of the apostolic example, and examples of Christian living themselves unto the church and the world.

The evidence of the power of the word—preached or privately read—is the ultimate response of those who hear it. Changed lives demonstrate that the word has been proclaimed in power. As someone put it, "It's not how high you jump that counts, but how straight you walk when you come down."

Father, most of all, let our living be affected by your word, and we will be truly moved. Amen.

Clouds they are without water…trees without fruit.

False claims

It was only there a short while, that fire hydrant in front of 925 Park Avenue in New York. The address is a ritzy luxury co-op apartment. A fire hydrant appeared in front of it, and had city officials scratching their heads. They didn't order it installed. Where did it come from? It turns out that the residents of 925 had put it there themselves, so that no one would park directly in front of their pretty building. They thought it would spoil the aesthetic value. It was a creative idea, but it was dangerous. If their precious building had caught fire, and firemen had come to hook up to the hydrant, 925 Park Avenue might have been a memory by the time they discovered the hydrant was a phony. It wasn't connected to anything.

People can be phony, too. The book of Jude uses a string of picturesque descriptors for the false teachers who plagued the church, and among them was the image of clouds without water, and trees without fruit—they appeared to be the source of something valuable, but they were not. Sometimes people claim to be prophets of liberating truth when in fact they are carriers of infectious lies. When they come to the end of their way, if they were to be able hold out their phony credentials, their IDs would burn in the fire that will not be put out.

Equally serious is our own responsibility not to be taken in by these dry spigots. Not all that parades as the water of life is really connected to the source. One of the better ways to spot the phony hydrants is to stay in the Bible on your own. Our personal relationship with Christ means that each of us may read and understand the word of God ourselves. While it is wise to be open to the messengers God places in our lives, we must not depend too heavily on any one of them to deliver all the word of God we need. Though he calls many people to equip the saints, the Spirit himself is our true teacher. Genuine spokesmen of the Spirit will always agree with him.

Father, witness in our hearts what is true in what we hear, and make us ever better students of your word. Amen.

Lead me in a plain path...

Reading the leading of the Lord

It can be remarkable how God delivers his word to us just when we need that word the most. A Christian who was rudely admonished by a caustic critic at first reeled and felt hurt. But within the day he encountered in his regular devotional reading the words of David in Psalm 27 asking God for clear leading. The passage went on to say, "False witnesses rise up against me, breathing out cruelty. …Wait on the Lord: be of good courage, and he shall strengthen thy heart!" God spoke to him through that word, and reassured him. When we are listening for God's voice while seeking him and his kingdom in our lives, he will show us the strength, the promises, and the direction we need.

Sometimes our circumstances must be interpreted as God's speaking to us when we need guidance. A lady was with her husband in a grocery store in California. She was reaching for some tomatoes when a tremor in the earth hit the area and shook the building where they were. Cans fell off shelves, fruit and vegetables that had been neatly stacked rolled out into the aisles. Then the tremor stopped. They continued shopping, got home, and while unpacking the sacks the husband said, "Where are the tomatoes? I saw you go over to the tomato display." She replied, "I did—but God said, 'No!'"

Perhaps an earthquake is not sent to make so little a statement. We can get a laugh out of a story like that, but God does work in timely ways to guide us. One of those ways is to make his word come alive in just the right way at just the right time to speak to us. The key is to be reading his word regularly and deeply, to keep a clean heart and mind, and to be listening for God's voice.

Father, let not our hearts be so noisy with other pursuits that we do not hear your word when it comes quietly in a still, small voice. Amen.

Cast thy burden upon the Lord, and he shall sustain thee.

God of our crises

Most of us feel a bit guilty about unburdening ourselves on other people. We say, "Oh, I don't want to unload my troubles on you." Probably each of us knows a few people we wish felt hesitant to share all their problems with us! By contrast, however, God invites us to cast our burdens on him. He is big enough to handle anything and actually wants us to place our weight on him. He really wants to hear us express ourselves to him and consciously entrust him with everything from our deepest sorrow to our hardest problems to our greatest hopes.

A short film once featured a pretty girl out on the highway hitchhiking. Of course, the first car to come along stopped, its male driver seeing this attractive lass in distress. She opened the door, thanked him, then turned and whistled toward the edge of the woods. Out came a dozen or more of her scraggly family members, who filed one after another into the car, making it look like one of those telephone booths college students used to cram for fun.

Sometimes people who invite us to share with them what is bothering us don't know what they would be getting themselves into if we unloaded all our troubles. But God already knows what plagues us: none of it is a surprise to him, and he can handle anything we tell him. One of the underlying messages of the book of Psalms is that God is not upset by our passionate orations and complaints, even if we occasionally exaggerate or bellyache. He doesn't get impatient, embarrassed, irritable, or bored when we're talking to him. He's God. He doesn't act like us.

What grieves God is not when we unburden ourselves, but when we don't. For while we may think we can handle things, down the road we will burst with sorrow, crack from strain, wear out from tension, or burn out from trying to carry it all and deal with it all without God. How much better it is to cast our burdens upon the Lord, and to let him sustain us fully.

Father, thank you for always being there for us to turn to. May we never think we don't need you. Amen.

Be still and know that I am God.

Enjoying God

Some friends who attend different churches got together midweek and conversed about their recent Sunday events. One had thrilled to magnificent seasonal music and pageantry. The other had attended a quiet service with periods of silence, quiet singing, a gentle atmosphere and a short, meditative thought. Both worshiped. While Christians often promote their churches by recounting the size and excitement of their worship events, times of stillness and reflection are just as important to worship.

Church should not always be one exhortation after another, one "thou shalt" after the other "thou shalt not." Sometimes we should just linger in the beauty of God's presence through the Spirit. Worship is communing with God, and that takes place on many levels. Confession and repentance is one level; instruction is another; but simply meditating, praising, remembering, and feeling is another, which we need as well as the first ones.

The Psalmist wrote, "Be still and know that I am God." Other places, he wrote that worshipers should praise God with timbrel and dance and make a joyful noise unto the Lord. But David knew the value of being still before God, of meditating silently, of sitting or standing reverently in God's presence, whether it was in the temple or on a hillside out under God's heaven.

In your daily walk, take time simply to be with God, to love him, to rest in his holiness and love, to revel in knowing the King of heaven. Take a moment now to worship him in silence. Make no promises. Ask no favors. Just be glad to be alive, and in Christ.

Father, how wonderful to be able to call you Father. I worship you, and rest in your peaceful presence. Amen.

March 28 **Scripture Reading: Colossians 1:18**

And he is the head of the body, the church.

Owner and manager

In a story that sounded as if it had been invented for the sake of illustration, a Christian magazine reported on a minister who listened to a group of executives talking about management techniques, and then he introduced them to his own Chairman of the Board, Jesus. The minister showed them how Christ had used all the so-called modern techniques of management with his disciples.

Without suggesting some new paradigm, in some ways Christ is indeed like a Chairman of the Board. Paul wrote that Christ is the head of the church. He appoints many persons to function in the church at many levels, some of whom should have significant leadership authority. But Christ is the head. In many churches, the popular concept is that some group or person is the head, because that group or person makes most of the decisions. In any human organization, somebody winds up making decisions, out of necessity, but ultimately it is not we whose logic, will, and purposes should be behind the decisions: it is Christ who should operate the church. It is, after all, his body.

This is no technicality: it should be a daily reality for the church. The ministerial staff, deacons, all committee or council persons, and all teachers, should consciously deliver control of their church related functions into the hands of Christ.

How about your personal life? Is Christ the Chairman of the Board? Actually, there is no Board—just Jesus. He is the only stockholder if you have given your life to him, so he should make the decisions. Is his direction a daily reality for you? Christ wants to have charge of not only your major life decisions, but each day's adventure and pilgrimage. He may have detailed plans for each movement of your day. Know the joy of being managed by the most successful executive of all time—and eternity.

Christ Jesus, be Lord of all today. You are the owner; you should be the manager as well. Amen.

My God shall supply all your need through his riches in glory by Christ Jesus.

Limitless riches

A woman greeted a guest in her home with the offer of tea or coffee. When the guest chose tea, the woman asked, "What kind? I have Earl Grey, cinnamon, lemon, peppermint, rose hip, mint, Assam, Darjeeling, English breakfast, Irish breakfast, orange Pekoe, spice, and black." Confused by all the choices, the guest replied, "I'll just have coffee."

Christians sometimes are not as aware as they should be of the things God has to offer them. The richness of his promises, the array of his blessings, the dimensions of his power, are only barely touched in their experience. Though God does not exactly present us with a menu, once we begin to enter his will for our lives we do discover the panoramic spread of opportunities for service and growth. As we face both opportunities and hardships, we can experience the depth of his grace and resources to meet challenge.

When Paul penned the familiar promise of Philippians 4:19, he was assuring believers that however desperate their need, however deep their spiritual or material impoverishment, the God of the universe is in control of it all and has the ability to supply any resource for any necessity. The believer will experience God's supply as a blessing imparted to him through—and because of—his relationship to Jesus Christ.

In a real sense, the purpose of our encountering circumstances that place us in need is that we might find in Christ the limitless and glorious supply of God, and thus grow more and more convinced that we should seek and trust him.

Father, may we not doubt your ability and your desire to bring us through every challenge of our lives today. Amen.

Watch and pray, that ye enter not into temptation.

Avoiding sin

How do you resist temptation? How do you go about protecting yourself against falling into serious disobedience, or for that matter any disobedience to God? How do you detect compromising situations so as to avoid them? How do you sense corruptive influences or thoughts so as to reject them? Some people pray, and pray, and pray. Others view everything with the hard, narrow eyes of skepticism and reason. The first people may be counting on miraculous intervention to keep them out of trouble, while the second group may be trusting merely in their own genius at analyzing everything. So the first people fall to temptation because they assume that anything God doesn't keep them away from by divine intervention must be okay. The second ones do wrong because they succumb to subtleties that slip through their self-righteousness defenses. Both were only half right.

Instead, Jesus said that we are to both watch and pray. To avoid falling into temptation's traps, it takes both: watching, which involves our critical analysis, our logic, our observation, our wits; and praying, which involves our openness to the inward voice of God, and which expresses our dependence on him.

To watch without praying is like trying to defend yourself with an unloaded gun. To pray without watching is like taking the ammunition and throwing it by hand at the attacker. Jesus said we need to load the gun.

Father, since the tempter is both subtle and powerful, let us both think and meditate, both watch and pray, today, so we will avoid sin. Amen.

...Jesus Christ of Nazareth, whom ye crucified, whom God raised from the dead

Your picture of Jesus

Through the ages, significant works of art have given us a variety of images by which people have come to picture Jesus in their minds. While we don't know what Jesus really looked like, most of us have chosen—consciously or unconsciously—an image that we regularly associate with Christ. This image may concentrate on his facial features, depicting qualities we most associate with him. Warner Sallman's paintings, for instance, emphasize kindness and compassion in the face of Christ; while the more recent artist Richard Hooks' paintings depict Jesus as both strong and joyful.

The way we picture Jesus may strongly influence our expectation of him, our attitude toward him, even our concept of discipleship. Take for instance Jesus' crucifixion. The Bible says, "We preach Christ, and him crucified" (1 Cor.1:23). Does that mean we should picture Jesus typically as hanging on a cross? In some churches we see an empty cross, and in others, Christ hanging on the cross. Does it matter which image we keep fixed in our minds? A South American, being used to the trinkets of his country's predominant religious tradition, when asked who Jesus is, said, "He is a dead man hanging on a stick." Indeed, Jesus died on a cross, but that event does not define him finally. It was the centerpiece of redemption, but the crucifixion does not go on and on. Jesus himself said, "It is finished."

In fact, even more than it declares Jesus' death on the cross for our sin, the Bible reminds us of his resurrection for our new life. The early preaching of the gospel paired these two events closely so that no one would think the cross was the lasting state of Jesus. Picture Jesus risen, glorious, powerful, and victorious. Picture the cross empty, a symbol of victory won, and a price paid forever. Picture Jesus able to save, not needing salvation himself. Jesus lives!

Father, may your Son not hang dead and useless on jewelry, but instead live in our lives to bring victory through his power. Amen.

April 1 **Scripture Reading: 1 John 4:1**

Beloved, believe not every spirit, but try the spirits whether they are of God: because many false prophets are gone out into the world.

Knowing what to believe

A story circulated a few years ago that the real reason Soviet Premier Nikita Kruschev was deposed was that he had become a Christian. The account appeared in a book called *Like a Dove Descending*, in which author Ian MacPherson quoted Ben Iller, who in turn got the story from Gordon Williamson, a missionary in Pakistan. Williamson was preaching in Durban, South Africa when he was joined for dinner by a Russian ship's captain who was a Christian, and who told of being at a Christian event at a Black Sea resort where Kruschev unexpectedly arrived and gave a testimony about having received Christ. Spies accompanying Kruschev reported his admission, and he was quickly deposed.

The Hollywood Free Paper published this story in the late sixties but later said it was "Christian urban legend." Indeed, the report is *fifth* hand, and the original source is unnamed. Could he who said, "I will display on national Soviet television the last living Christian in our country," really have professed faith in Christ? Some far-fetched conversion tales turn out to be true. The bottom line is that we cannot know about this one.

Christians sometimes swallow incredible stories they want to be true, or they believe in amazing new solutions to chronic struggles. We can be honestly convinced of even blatant lies. How do you know whether or not to believe what any one of myriad Christian teachers write or broadcast? Try every story in the court of common sense, and test every spirit and teaching against the principles of Scripture and the life of Christ. Don't bury yourself in skepticism, but be no fool, either.

Holy Spirit, let me be quick to recognize your voice in all I hear, and just as quick to sense the tactics of the deceiver. Amen.

He was rejected: for he found no place of repentance, though he sought it carefully with tears.

The cost of sin

Esau probably gave no significant thought to the trade he proposed with his brother Jacob. He was famished from hunting, and when trickster Jacob told him he would give him food in exchange for his birthright, Esau foolishly agreed. His sin was his cavalier attitude about precious family heritage and the blessing of his father. He forfeited an important place in his family's future by putting immediate gratification ahead of it. Though he wished to reverse matters later, it was too late. His stew was a more costly menu item than he ever imagined.

A woman went into a grocery store to pick up a few items. She put fewer than ten things in a hand basket and carried them to the checkout. The cashier, as always, rang up all the items and then before totaling asked if that were all. The woman looked on the rack by the register and added a roll of mints to her purchases. The cashier rang up the mints and read out the total mechanically: "$4,594.53." Without missing a beat, the woman asked, "What is it without the mints?"

The cost of our sin is higher than we think. But we are often found bargaining with God about it. We know he wants all of our lives, but we would like to give him limited control, reserving a few areas of our lives where we live as we please. We don't usually admit this is what we are doing, but how else would we describe our declining to let God work on those areas of our personalities that are far from Christlike? What else do we call our insistence on maintaining various habits that present a negative witness? God warns us that the cost of a little sin is more than we really want to pay.

When was the last time you did thorough housecleaning on yourself, and threw out what shouldn't be there?

Lord, to continue to call you Lord means we must let you be Lord of every thought and deed. Amen.

The lot is cast into the lap; but the whole disposing thereof is of the Lord.

Finding God's will

Presented with the biblical truth that God's will encompasses not only every person but every area of a person's life, many of us become increasingly serious about finding God's will. Some suggest that too many people are looking for God's will for their lives when what they should be looking for is their place in God's will—a largely semantic distinction that has value, but still leaves us with the same question: what does God want me to do and to be? And the challenge may not be that we don't have *any* possibilities, but instead that we have too *many* possibilities. How do we know what God's will is? Faced with such a question, we pray, ponder, and seek advice. Not a few of us, frustrated by the search, would have tossed a coin if we thought it would have been the avenue of God's leading.

In essence, the practice of ancient peoples in casting lots was probably something like tossing a coin. When they lacked other means to discover an answer, they left some decisions to God's supernatural control of stones tossed in a lap. Interestingly, God apparently used such methods from time to time (cf. Lev.16:8). But Proverbs says that the Lord is not obligated either to reveal his will through methods we contrive, nor to bless the decisions we make based on arbitrary or circumstantial things. He is sovereign, and his will does not change.

God is not at the mercy of our finding his will in order to arrange that we actually do his will. Our worried search or our protracted prayer may in fact be aimed in the wrong direction, and we may happen on the will of God without even knowing it at first. For God does not wait for us to *find* his will *for* our lives before he starts *doing* his will *in* our lives. Perhaps the best way for us to find what God is going to do with us is to look at what is already underway.

Father, open our eyes to how you have already led us; then may we be easily led onward. Amen.

If these should hold their peace, the stones would immediately cry out.

Praising the Lord

Praising the Lord is appropriate anytime. Some times call for quiet, personal praise. On other occasions, corporate praise in well-rehearsed music and pageantry is fitting. Then there are those events and realizations that should make the hearts of believers burst forth with spontaneous praise, calling attention to the power and grace of God. Even then, some people are inclined to curb expression of praise. But at such times reservation is singularly inappropriate.

The week Jesus was crucified, his ministry had reached an apex of both popularity and opposition. His followers were more than ever convinced he was the Christ. His enemies were more than ever devoted to his demise. The day Jesus entered Jerusalem, friends were ecstatic, believing his appearance signaled glorious things to come. They shouted out phrases from the prophets and Psalms naming Jesus the rightful King and the emissary of God. Jesus' enemies found such praise to be blasphemy, and demanded that he tell his followers to be quiet. But it was no moment for silence. Jesus told the Pharisees that if his followers held in their praise, the stones would start shouting.

Observing the decidedly non-animated worship of his congregation, one church leader quipped there were a few stones in his congregation he wished the Lord would bring to life. The Bible does not dictate one style of worship or the same kind of praise at all times. But Christians should not be difficult to be moved to praise. God is an awesome God who is always doing wonderful and magnificent things. In Jesus Christ he has poured out his love, forgiveness, power, and life, and blessed us with every spiritual blessing in the heavenly realms. We need to praise him for our own good, and through our praise we need to point people to the King who will enter the gates of their lives and save them, when they turn to him.

Lord Jesus Christ—glorious Son, loving Savior, and coming King—we praise you! Amen.

And could not find what they might do: for all the people were very attentive to hear him.

Stemming persecution

Any Christian who has suffered attack from the world around him has wanted to stem the tide of persecution and get on with Christian living. But the Bible teaches that all who are determined to live holy lives for Christ Jesus in this world will suffer persecution (2 Tim.3:12). In cultures that have been profoundly affected by the teachings of Christ, however, persecution slows down for a time. American Christians have often experienced the toleration that gives relief to believers and provides opportunity for less impeded progress of the gospel.

When Jesus cleansed the temple, powerful citizens and religious leaders were furious, but they could not stop him because most of the "common people" supported him. Overwhelming public support put a temporary stop to persecution of Jesus and his disciples. The tension between persecutors and followers teaches an important principle for Christians in every age. Many Christians wish government policy would favor Christianity. While the prospect seems attractive, trying to mold secular government to cooperate with God's people is not God's method of securing his kingdom in this world. Rather, the church's evangelization of the "common people" is the answer. When more of a nation's people love and serve God, governments and the elite realize it is cutting their own throats to move against Christ and his church.

Yogi Berra once said of a popular night spot, "Nobody goes there anymore: it's too crowded." The conflict in his remark makes it funny, but he illustrated the principle that popularity discourages certain actions. A Christian's hope of stemmed persecution is best gained by bringing more people to a saving knowledge of Christ. Here is one more reason for telling the good news that Jesus came to die for our sins and rise to bring us life.

Lord Jesus, help us speak a winning word for you today in the marketplace of competing ideas. Amen.

April 6 **Scripture Reading: Luke 21:19**

In your patience possess ye your souls.

The secret to survival

On Jesus' third day of his last week in Jerusalem he spoke at length about the trouble that lay ahead for his followers in times to come. In one verse he gave them, and us, the secret to survival: endure. The King James word "patience" means endurance—continuing in faithfulness to Christ despite troublesome events that tempt us to compromise or give up. The words "possess your souls" literally mean to "gain" them. Jesus told his disciples that the secret to survival—to gaining their own souls—is to never give up and never give in. While privation and even loss of life in this world is sometimes the price of following Christ, the believer who endures will lose nothing in reality: he will be repaid all, and will inherit glorious eternal life.

The end times of which Jesus spoke, with all their horrible tribulation, are emblematic of the kinds of trouble Christians can expect during all ages leading up to the last days. Blatant hatred of Christianity and its attendant persecution are hard to mistake in their purpose. But even commonplace troubles contain the implicit temptation to back away from devotedly following Christ and to act in an ungodly fashion. Consequently, any trouble is a potential trial of faith. Conflict, failure, obstacles, even multiplied inconveniences, carry the suggestion that God is not supporting or protecting us, or that he has abandoned us to the will of our enemies. But Jesus tells us not to fall prey to the deceitful idea that quitting will bring relief. He says instead, endure!

Winston Churchill gave a speech to the Harrow School in 1941 challenging students to rise to the occasion of the greatest times through which Britain had ever lived. In that speech he said, "Never give in. Never give in. Never, never, never, never—in nothing, great or small, large or petty—never give in." Jesus' exhortation is the same to us.

Father, by your grace enable us to be faithful to your Son and our Lord today. Amen.

Then entered Satan into Judas surnamed Iscariot, being of the number of the twelve.

The danger lies within

Wednesday of Jesus' last week of ministry is often called the quiet day. Scripture records little of his and his disciples' activity on that day—with the exception of one of them. Judas slipped away to temple authorities and made a deal to disclose Jesus' secretive evening whereabouts. That the traitor was one of the twelve was an especially hard blow for Jesus. Yet he had always known that Judas was "a devil." He knew that eventually the devil would come out. It happened on the quiet day, when the other eleven and Jesus were resting.

Times of spiritual retreat can be invaluable to us. But we should never think that the devil respects our need to get away. Nor should we believe when spiritual struggle seems quelled that we are somehow being bypassed by the tempter. Sometimes those very hours of respite are hours during which the adversary is gearing up for major assault. Churches sometimes experience days of comfort followed suddenly by surprising turmoil. All too frequently the trouble was brewing among their own number. Individual Christians can be lulled into lazy discipleship when things go well, and then caught off guard by temptations set up during their spiritual snoozing. The greater threat to the Christian is not so much the opponent who declares himself the enemy, but the false believer among the true, or even the undisciplined believer himself. The danger lies within.

During the 2003 Iraq War, American soldiers camping in Kuwait were sleeping when a grenade rolled into their tent, killing one and wounding more than a dozen. The enemy had evaded guards because the enemy was one of their own, a sergeant who was a Muslim and sympathetic to Iraqis. Never let down your guard. When things are quiet on the front, be alert for attack from unexpected quarters. Always be ready. Our spiritual enemy is always at work.

Holy Spirit, sensitize us today to the smallest move of the enemy, and strengthen us against him. Amen.

Go ye into the city, and there shall meet you a man bearing a pitcher of water: follow him.

The Lord has a plan

From the time Jesus first called disciples they rarely did not accompany him. They knew almost everything he did. But they didn't know that he had made arrangements with someone in Jerusalem to use his upper room for the Passover. They also had not known that, in all likelihood, he had arranged with someone for the use of two donkeys to enter Jerusalem. In both instances people were waiting in place, passwords were given, and certain actions followed. Part of the point of this detail about setting up a secret place for the Passover is to emphasize the truth that Jesus was always ahead of his disciples, planning as well as leading. They did not wander aimlessly from place to place, catching as catch can, making do by hook or crook. While Jesus may have entrusted some of the planning to the disciples themselves, other things he planned alone—things that, for whatever reason, he did not divulge to them until it was time for them to act.

We may occasionally forget that the Lord is more than just a step ahead of us. In fact, to him whose mind and being encompass eternity without respect to our limited concepts of past and future, our lives from beginning to end are an open book and a known quantity. The Lord has a fantastically detailed plan that includes what we call new developments and unforeseen circumstances. Whenever we arrive at a crossroads, the Lord has already set in motion our next steps, and provided for our coming needs. While he guides us in planning some things with him interactively, other events he must prepare providentially. Even our present dilemmas, blind alleys, failures or dangers are part of his preparation for what is coming next. This is why we can trust him. Nothing upsets him. He always has a plan.

Lord, until you're ready to show your plan, give us grace to walk in it step by step. Amen.

And it was the third hour, and they crucified him.

Were you there?

An old spiritual asks the question, "Were you there when they crucified my Lord?" Who is "they"? Matthew, as do all the gospel writers, identifies the Jewish authorities as the ones who arrested Jesus and tried him before their council, determining that he was guilty of blasphemy, punishable by death. However, the Romans did not allow them to carry out executions. Consequently, they delivered Jesus to Pilate. Originally, only the Jewish authorities wanted Jesus dead, but only the Romans could do the deed. In the end, they collaborated, meaning that both Jew and Gentile were responsible for Jesus' death.

Rembrandt was only one of many artists who in depicting the crucifixion have cathartically painted themselves in the shadows at the scene. Countless other people, even many who reject Christianity, have exhibited an obsession with the cross, as if it held a power over them they could not shake. Like it or not, people know the cross was about them.

Jewish groups regularly express concern that Jews are blamed for Jesus' death. The truth is that Jews after Jesus' time are no more to blame for his death than Romans of later years. The truth is also that Jews are just as guilty as Romans, as Greeks, as Ethiopians, and as Indians, Chinese, and Anglo-Saxons. While none of us was around in history when Calvary's drama unfolded, Christ came to die for humanity, whose every individual is wholly encompassed by his eternal love and redeeming purpose. In that sense, we all were there at Calvary. Our sins occasioned the need of God's rescue, and our sins were laid on him as he died on the cross. Our sin crucified Christ. But his very death by our hand paid for our guilt in placing him there. Praise God!

Jesus Christ our Savior, having solemnly confessed our guilt, we quietly celebrate your sacrifice. Amen.

So they went, and made the sepulchre sure, sealing the stone, and setting a watch.

In the grave

Ponder the loss of the Son of God. Imagine briefly realizing the presence of God in human flesh, and then seeing swiftly moving evil nail him to crossed timbers until he was dead. Think of the intense loneliness and the dark emptiness the disciples experienced. The actions of the Jewish authorities must have punctuated their grief. When Jesus died and was placed in a tomb belonging to Joseph of Arimathea, Jewish officials got a contingent of Roman soldiers to guard the tomb. A seal guaranteed any tampering would be known, and the guards themselves made it unlikely that anyone would attempt to steal the body.

Where was Jesus' spirit on this day? Jesus himself told us in what he said to the thief beside him, "This day, you will be with me in Paradise" (Luke 23:43). However, while this verse tells us Jesus' spiritual whereabouts, another fact is equally clear. His body was in the grave.

It is vital to the Christian faith that we be certain that Jesus actually died. If Jesus' body had disappeared immediately after the crucifixion, the situation would have lent modest credibility to the notion that he had not really been dead. But he was dead. After the Roman executioners certified that fact, they released his body for burial. The days spent in the tomb erased any doubt.

If Jesus' life had not come to an end, he would not have paid for our sin. Without his grief, we would have no joy, and without our own grief in conviction for sin, we cannot know the joy of forgiveness. Perhaps for many of us the reason we may not have much joy is that we have not been heartbroken enough over our sin. Let the somber truth of Jesus' death for our sins sink in and bring deep repentance and broken confession. Then the Lord can replace grief with rejoicing when he forgives.

Jesus, Savior, since you died for our sin, may we, brokenhearted, die to our sin, that we may live for you. Amen.

And when they looked, they saw that the stone was rolled away: for it was very great.

Out of the grave

Mark tells us that when the women who were close followers of Jesus came to the tomb, they found that the sealing stone had already been rolled away. Matthew says an angel, accompanied by earthquake, rolled the stone aside, rendering the guards unconscious. Mark's point is that the women saw the first evidence that Jesus had risen.

Many people believe that the angel removed the stone so Jesus could get out. But Jesus demonstrated subsequently that he had the power to appear suddenly in a locked room. He didn't need the angel's help to get out of the grave: the stone had been moved to reveal he was already gone. Clearly what Mark is telling us is that God offered evidence of Jesus' resurrection to those who were open to believing he was alive. The soldiers and the authorities, on the other hand, were predisposed to believing that the disciples were engaged in shenanigans, and they spread that rumor immediately.

All Jesus' appearances after that momentous morning were to persons who had believed in him and followed him. His actions were in accord with his own words a year or so earlier when he told people that those who decided to do God's will would know the truth of his words (Jn.7:17). The lesson of the resurrection appearances is not only that Jesus is alive, but that he reveals himself to those who seek him and desire to know and follow him. Hebrews eloquently gives God's principle: "For he that cometh to God must believe that he is, and that he is the rewarder of them that diligently seek him" (11:6). To experience more of Christ's presence in your life, begin by saying to him, "Lord, I believe. Open my eyes to your living presence in me today."

Jesus, we know you are alive, and in us who believe. Let us experience how real you are. Amen.

Wherefore he is able also to save them to the uttermost that come unto God by him, seeing he ever liveth to make intercession for them.

The day after

The day after Easter, untold thousands of people who got up and out in their finest for Sunday morning services at church are through for another year. Most of them do not return to church after that glorious spring day of remembrance and victory—until perhaps Christmas. Their duty is done. Easter is over—isn't it? Is it?

With little reflection at all, most Christians realize that it isn't. The resurrection of Christ is never over. It is an event that has continued since it began happening. Jesus rose, an event not repeated, but he lives still, and his living presence is continuous. The whole point of Christianity is that Jesus *is risen.* As one who conquered death, he never approaches it again. He "ever liveth."

Consequently, not only is Jesus' ministry toward us a continuing fact, but we must be continuously available to him and our discipleship must be ongoing. Jesus did not do one work in us when we were saved and nothing more. He intended to continue to do a work in us until we switch theaters from earth to heaven to be with him forever. Hardly anything in the Christian experience is merely punctiliar; most of our responsibilities have an ongoing dimension. To be kind once, to love one person for a day, sing one hymn, read the Bible once, and then do none of these things continually, would be an odd way to approach Christian living. Why, then, do some make such infrequent, token trips to church? Why do they shed their acknowledgment of Christ like Easter clothing, hanging it up until another year? Do they not need God the next day? Are they self-sufficient the rest of the year? Does Christ step down from the throne on the Monday after Easter?

If Jesus Christ "ever liveth," then he ever reigneth, ever ruleth, ever calleth, and is ever the deserving Master and Lord of our lives. The only true Christianity is the daily kind, continuous discipleship for an ever living Jesus.

Jesus, Lord and Savior, keep us from the sin of occasional faith, which is really no faith at all. Amen.

Paul hath persuaded and turned away much people, saying that they be no gods , which are made with hands.

What is an idol?

Many modern people find it difficult to understand how anyone ever believed that stone statues were actually supernatural beings. How could people cut stone, chisel and fashion it, place it on a pedestal, and then say it was more than what it was? Actually, most times they didn't really believe the statues *were* gods, but that gods inhabited them. The Greeks believed in the goddess Diana, for instance, and there were thousands of statues of Diana, including many made in silver by Demetrius. But there was only one Diana, who they believed blessed the statues with her presence, and responded when people worshiped them.

We really shouldn't find it surprising that people would imagine that images are mystically imbued with life. How many of us haven't felt just a bit strange being stared at by realistic mannequins? Did you ever find visiting a wax museum a little "spooky?" Even against our good sense sometimes, things can be just a little too lifelike.

Demetrius complained that Paul denied that idols were gods. More telling, however, was his admission that he and the other Ephesians worshiped things "made with hands." The heart of idolatry is the worship of things we have made, rather than worship of the one who made us. Therefore, worshiping anything of human origin, whether images or things or money or other people, is idolatry. Worshiping a thing means to honor and seek it above all other things.

What should really surprise us is how any of us can put anything other than God above everything else in our lives. Is anything in your life occupying a place where only God belongs?

God, help us to see the things that compete for our loyalty, and then to subject everything in our lives to your control. Amen.

April 14 **Scripture Reading: Acts 8:24**

Then answered Simon and said, Pray ye to the Lord for me, that none of these things which ye have spoken come upon me.

Hoping for the best

Whatever happened to Simon Magus, the fellow who offered money to Peter to get spiritual power? Peter called his hand and declared him captive to evil. Simon then begged Peter to pray for him that nothing would happen to him. Considering the way he probably lived subsequently, his request seems out of order. Other early writers say that Simon went on to develop his magic and to make himself out to be an incarnation of God. He apparently had demonic powers enabling him to do wonders. Finally he tried mimicking Christ by having himself buried and promising to reappear in three days. He didn't. Obviously, he really believed he was divine.

Most of us will never become false messiahs, but all of us deceive ourselves occasionally about our capabilities or our nature. It is very common for a person to take charge of his life, and lay out a plan of success all of his own devising, ignore God's lordship, yet then pray that nothing will happen to thwart his plans, or ruin his health, etc. Does it make sense to live for oneself without consulting God and yet expect God to protect against all harm? Simon provides a powerful, negative example from which we all can learn.

Plea bargaining is a process in which a criminal cuts a deal for a lighter charge or sentence in exchange for information helpful to police or prosecutors. Crooks get away with such deals only because they have something the justice system needs. But you and I don't have anything God can't live without. It's the other way around. If we only realized how utterly at his mercy we are every moment, we would not be so bold in living for ourselves while trying to bargain with God to spare us pain and keep the blessings coming.

Father, we pray for humility of spirit and obedience in living today. We are nothing without you. Amen.

For I say, through the grace given unto me, to every man that is among you, not to think of himself more highly than he ought to think.

God confronts our pride

Paul gave us a succinct definition of pride. Thinking of ourselves more highly than we ought says two things: that we ought to think something of ourselves—to have self respect; but that we tend to think of ourselves too often, too much, and too highly. We should have a certain level of self confidence, and it is proper to believe we are worth something. Christ knew us to be worth saving. We get into trouble spiritually, however, when we go beyond self respect and put ourselves at the center of our lives and get our own importance out of perspective. Good indicators of that distorted perspective are selfishness, thoughtlessness, or judgmental attitudes.

Sometimes we aren't aware we're lifting ourselves up or judging people by the standard of our own lives. A young man head over heels about a classmate in college walked with her one evening talking about their plans for the weekend. There were few activities on campus other than fraternity parties. Eager to impress the young woman about his high standards, the boy began to criticize fraternity drinking binges, and then generalized, "Anybody who gets drunk is empty and superficial." A long silence ensued. When he asked her what she was thinking, she said quietly, "My father is an alcoholic." The young man had judged the worth of a human life by an overly harsh standard. Drunkenness is not a good thing, but it hardly renders a human being worthless.

None of us is the center of the universe. Each Christian is part of the body of Christ, and every person in the body is important. When we dismiss the feelings or contribution of others, or constantly compare how we would have done things to the way others do them, we are thinking more highly of ourselves than we ought to think.

Father, before we lift ourselves above anyone else today, remind us that you redeemed us. Amen.

April 16 **Scripture Reading: 1 Corinthians 6:13**

Now the body is not for fornication, but for the Lord; and the Lord for the body.

The Spirit's purpose

Paul taught that the reason to avoid bodily sins, including gluttony and sexual impurity, is that our bodies are meant for the Lord—to serve the Lord, to be consecrated to his purposes. But then Paul turned the phrase around, giving us the ultimate reason for purity: The Lord [is] for the body. This is the original intention of God: that man would be the dwelling place of the Spirit of God. From the perspective of creation, the personal purpose of the Holy Spirit is to live in us. He wants entry and permission to abide and fill.

Romans 8:9 declares emphatically that if the Spirit does not live in you, you are not saved. If he is in you, it is because you have trusted and surrendered to him. But if the Spirit lives in you, how much is he in you? —not 'how much *of* the Spirit is in you,' for he is a person, not parceled out in portions. If he is in you, he is in you. But how fully is he in you? How free is he to control you and change you? Do you confine him or grieve him by restricting his full access? He longs to fill, empower, sanctify, and bring joy and victory to all of your life.

Human beings cannot voluntarily *not* breathe. You may exhale completely and remain motionless a few moments by your will. But when your body runs out of oxygen you will gasp for air. If by phenomenal resistance to common sense you manage to withhold breathing until you black out, your brain's autonomic functions take over and you will again inhale the breath of life. Man has been given a choice, however, about whether or not he will breathe in the Spirit of God as offered. Once breathing the breath of eternal life, we also must continue to choose each day to live in his fullness. Make it your choice today to refresh your heart with a fresh breath of God's joyful power.

Holy Spirit, breathe on us, till we are all your own. Amen.

I went down to the bottoms of the mountains; the earth with her bars was about me for ever: yet hast thou brought up my life from corruption, O LORD my God.

Personalized testimony

Of the many lessons to be learned from Jonah is how his experience of being disciplined invigorated his testimony to the Ninevites. Jonah feared for his life if he went to Nineveh. He did not start out representing well the idea of God's grace. But when he himself was cast into the sea and sank to the root of the mountains, and then was delivered to live another day in the light of the Lord's gracious forgiveness, Jonah's tune changed. He still had difficulty understanding why God would forgive people as sinful as the Assyrians, but he was faithful to preach to them anyway. His trial had become his message.

When we are disciplined by God for our resistance to his will, we often enter times that are soaked in hardship. Even then, however, God has prepared the vessels of our deliverance. His purpose is that our experience should change our perspective, that our trial should become our message. When God's discipline deprives us of life's needs, and then his deliverance shows us his miraculous provision, his purpose is that we should testify to his ability to sustain others in their times of trouble. When we walk through fires of adversity and God provides peace, he means for us to encourage others with the same promise. When we fall prey to temptation and God leads us back to himself in forgiveness and restoration, he wants us to tell others with renewed passion that the Lord is gracious and redemptive.

Often the last effect of our trials we are willing to abandon is our guilt over having failed the Lord. Instead of languishing in self-recrimination, when the Lord restores or delivers us, our trial should become our personalized testimony. Telling others what really happened to us sometimes is a more effective witness than telling them what hypothetically could happen to them.

O God of our crises, turn our trials into living testimony, that our lives may glorify you. Amen.

April 18 **Scripture Reading: Haggai 2:5**

According to the word that I covenanted with you when ye came out of Egypt, so my spirit remaineth among you: fear ye not.

God is with you

One of the more common phrases heard in Christians' prayers is, "Be with me …us …or them." Some foundation exists for the request. Paul closed most of his letters with a benediction that called for God to be with his readers. Peter and John did the same, as had various Old Testament passages. Yet Jesus had told his disciples, "Behold, I *am* with you alway" (Mt.28:20), and the author of Hebrews reminded us, "I will never leave thee, nor forsake thee" (Heb.13:5). Jesus gave us a direct and very specific promise that the Holy Spirit, whom he was sending to be with believers, was going to be a permanent resident in their lives. Not only was God everywhere by his very nature, but his special presence of blessing was going to be granted to all his children by faith.

This personal presence of God indicating his continuing work in our lives is what reassures us when personal failure makes us doubt we can go on—or doubt that God is still leading or using us. Haggai wrote to Israelite returnees to challenge them to rebuild the temple. They were living among the ruins of their former glory, daily reminders of their failure of God and his heavy hand of discipline. Yet Haggai spoke for God: I made a promise to you, and I am keeping it. My spirit is still among you. Don't be afraid to pick up where you left off and follow me.

When wandering produces loneliness, rebellion brings alienation, disobedience generates trouble, and God disciplines us, even when we repent we may fear God has left us—if only in that special way of blessing. When life's paths become confused or dark, when disappointment, failure, and frustration cast us into despair, we may wonder if our plight is due to God's giving up on us. But God has promised us he is faithful, and Jesus has assured us he is always with us by his Spirit. Do not be afraid to pick up your spiritual gifts and serve, and to lift up your downcast face and praise the Lord. God always keeps his promises. He never leaves you.

Spirit of God, as we confess you are always with us, reassure us with the sense of your presence. Amen.

Who are they among all the gods of these lands, that have delivered their land out of my hand, that the LORD should deliver Jerusalem out of my hand?

No other gods

Rabshakeh threatened Hezekiah at the gates of Jerusalem. "Did any of the other gods keep other nations from falling to Assyria?" he boasted. "Well, the LORD won't save you, either." Rabshakeh obviously did not say, "The Lord," with the same meaning that the Jews understood it to have. To him, the Israelite's *Yahweh* was just another of the many gods in the world, a local deity of limited power. Rabshakeh didn't deny the reality of *the LORD;* he simply denied his omnipotence.

The world today sometimes declares war on Christianity by denying the very existence of God, but more often it simply denies the eternal scope of God's being, power, and will. Many people are not able to argue there is no God, but they think he is limited. To them: he is not the creator of all things; he didn't really raise Jesus from the dead; he is not really sovereign or there would be no evil; and he is a pushover who will let anyone and everyone into heaven. People who believe these things will lampoon a Christian's faith.

We who follow Christ must be clear within ourselves that we worship God as the omnipotent, omnipresent, omniscient one and that he has no competition for deity: he is the only God. We must not allow the constant dripping of atheism or agnosticism to wear away our bedrock belief in who God is. But we must also determine to live for God without compromising with the gods of this world, which are not deities, but passions, possessions, and power. God's command, "Thou shalt have no other gods before me," was not a confirmation of other deities; it was a warning against serving and living for anything or anyone else, imagined or real. The way to defeat those who ridicule belief in God, and to get victory over every influence that tempts us to distrust God, is to call on the Lord, keep living for him, and brace ourselves for the way that he will prove our faith well-founded.

God of grace and glory, only God, on your people—on this your servant—pour your power. Amen.

Now where remission of these is, there is no more offering for sin.

Letting God forgive us

Some people who have heard the gospel have not received Christ because they believe they have done things for which God will not forgive them. They may have done things that even they think are unconscionable, and they cannot imagine that forgiveness is available to them. Even Christians occasionally have a problem receiving forgiveness because their guilt over some sin or time of wandering is so great that they imagine that God is withholding his pardon until they pay some premium for their disobedience.

God's earliest plan to demonstrate his offer of forgiveness was the sacrifice. When the Law was instituted, sacrifices made for sin gave people something to offer to God in order to receive forgiveness. They illustrated the deadly price of sin, and they anticipated the once-for-all sacrifice eventually made by Jesus. Hebrews explained that God's plan was to replace a system that was unavoidably imperfect with a timeless event that paid for all sin. Through the cross of Christ, God would write his laws on human hearts, forgive their sins, and remember them no more. In other words, he promised to forgive sin at the profoundest level. Hebrews then declares that where God has forgiven in this saving way, there is no more offering for sin.

He meant two things by saying that: first, that the sacrificial system has been replaced with the once-for-all sacrifice of Christ; and second that when God has dealt with your sins through Jesus, you have no need of any other method of paying for your sins, whether suffering, waiting periods, tortured prayer, acts of penance, or good deeds. No more offering for sin is needed. Can anything we do equal or augment in any way what Christ has already done? Let God forgive you. When you confess your sin and turn from it, calling on Jesus, forgiveness has already come. Accept it, thank God for it, and go your way rejoicing.

Christ our sacrifice, our sins are no small thing, but your payment was sufficient for them all. Thank you again. Amen.

As for Ishmael, I have heard thee: Behold, I have blessed him, and will make him fruitful, and will multiply him exceedingly...but my covenant will I establish with Isaac...

The purpose of earthly blessing

Divine election is often typified by the Bible's statement that God loved Jacob but hated Esau (Mal.1:2-3, Rom.9:13). Even before that choice, God said to Abraham that his covenant would be with Isaac instead of Ishmael. To Isaac's family would come the land of Canaan and the innumerable descendants. Yet God also told Hagar and Abraham that Ishmael would become father of twelve kings and a great nation. But his covenant would be with Isaac alone.

The fact is that God's choice of Israel was not equivalent to automatic salvation of all those who happened to count Jacob and Isaac as their ancestors. Nor was every descendant of Ishmael or Esau destined to be lost spiritually. Ishmael and his family had the choice to live together in peace with Isaac and his family and to worship God with them, but they didn't. Ishmael's resentment toward Isaac, fed by inequities in the family, bore bitter fruit in generations of hostility. The Arab sons of Ishmael now mostly worship another god, modeled on the image of the Lord but claiming that history has it backwards on who was the favored son of Abraham. At the same time, there have always been Arab worshipers of the Lord. Even today, many Arab Christians live in Israel.

Ishmael's blessing demonstrates that having earthly favor from God must not be confused with having a right relationship with him. In fact, sometimes God is good to people in order to lead them to repentance by demonstrating how good he has already been (Rom.2:4). When we look at our lives and think things are going pretty well, it does not mean we are on the right track with God. Conversely, a rough road in life does not necessarily mean we are out of fellowship with God. It is important for us to assess our relationship with God by looking at our faith and our faithfulness rather than our circumstances.

Father, thank you for choosing us in Christ, and bringing us to faith in him. May we walk faithfully in him today. Amen.

Make the heart of this people fat, and make their ears heavy, and shut their eyes; lest they see with their eyes, and hear with their ears, and understand with their heart, and convert, and be healed.

Hardening is interactive

Why does God hardens people's hearts? God hardened the heart of Pharaoh against the Hebrews (Ex.7:13; 10:20,27; 11:10). He stated his purpose in Exodus 10:1: "...that I might show these my signs against him." Yet Pharaoh did his share of hardening his own heart (Ex.8:15,32; 9:34; 10:1). The pattern that emerges is clear. The hardening of Pharaoh's heart against God was not unilateral on God's part; it was interactive. God did not take innocent persons and harden their hearts against him. But then, no totally innocent persons exist. If God hardens hearts, we may be certain they were resistant to him first.

God gave Isaiah the prophet a mission to call Judah to repentance. It may appear at first that God intended for Judah to turn a deaf ear, but Judah's hardening of heart was just as it was for Pharaoh—interactive. Judah, along with Ahaz their king, was already in rebellion against God. If God left them alone, they would not repent on their own. If he sent a prophet to them, their first response would be to reject his message out of pride. Consequently, God had to do what unavoidably would harden their hearts at first, for them eventually to repent.

We cannot blame God for the times in our lives when we have become stubborn or resistant to him. If God has allowed trials to take place and we have responded by leaving his side or becoming angry at his "unjust" treatment of us, we have ourselves and our sin to blame. If God frustrates our attempts to live independently of him, it is only to break us that we might seek him again. The process is interactive. But we may be sure that the moment we are genuinely ready to confess all our sins, repent completely, and return to the Lord, he will do nothing to dissuade us. The way we make the interactive process as short as possible is not to delay humbling ourselves before God.

Father, today may we respond right away to your moving, so we will rub no callouses on our hearts. Amen.

April 23 **Scripture Reading: Jeremiah 18:15**

My people hath forgotten me, they have burned incense to vanity, and they have caused them to stumble in their ways from the ancient paths...

Faithfulness is sensible

When God asks a rhetorical question, there is no answer but the one that brings conviction to our hearts. Through Jeremiah's pen, God asks, "Who has heard of such a thing?" and he gives an example: his people have turned to worshiping idols that they themselves made. They burn incense to vanity. The word *vanity* simply means emptiness—the absence of anything. An idol is nothing. There is no god behind it, no deity represented by it. The god is in the mind of the worshiper only.

Israel seemed to be unable to keep themselves from worshiping idols, which had never done anything for them; yet they were faithless toward the Lord, who had always done everything for them. How does one explain their actions? This was precisely the point of God's question. There is no intelligent explanation.

But the ultimate goal of God in pointing out this weakness that destroyed generations of Israelites in judgment and discipline was to proclaim how wise it is for people to be faithful to God. It just makes sense to love God who loves us perfectly, to serve the Lord who gave his life for us, and to worship the one who has blessed us in countless ways. The "ancient paths" the Lord speaks of in Jeremiah are the ways of close fellowship with God and faithful obedience to him. Christian, do you remember a time when you believed you could almost touch the Lord, he seemed so close? Do you remember sensing the hand of the Lord as he led you? As you look back now, was there a time when you were urgent to obey God in everything, while perhaps today you tolerate much deviation from God's will? If so, what is it you are serving instead of God? What takes precedence over his will? Who or what comes before him in your affections? Remember the ancient paths and return to them. It just makes sense!

Lord, be tender with us as we abandon other attractions and return to the lover of our souls. Amen.

April 24 **Scripture Reading: Psalm 139:5**

Thou has beset me behind and before, and laid thine hand upon me.

Hemmed in by God

David's remarkable 139th Psalm is full of spiritual gems. Among them is a veritable treatise on the eternal nature of God. David realized that God had searched and tried him in his own lifetime, but that God knew him before his life ever came to be, and indeed that God knew David apart from time altogether. David knew also that God was ever conscious of his every thought, even before David considered *having* a thought! These stunning realizations led David to say that God had hemmed him in "behind and before." Our first conclusion is that David had in mind the element of time—time behind him, and time in front of him. But certainly his words could apply to David's circumstances. God surrounded David in his walk, and there was nowhere for David to run, even if he wanted to.

Our concept of God must include an affirmation of the mystery that God is not defined by time in any way. He reveals himself to *us* in history, because we *are* defined by time, but God is timeless—he has no past or future. To him, what we call past and future, is all present. God does not stand in the present, look down into the future and merely predict perfectly what will happen. He is not limited to one perspective on time—which he himself created. He sees all times, in the same moment, all of the time. Therefore all our lives are known by him.

If we reel at such thoughts, we understand why David said, "Such knowledge is too wonderful for me" (v.6). However, such thoughts should have an impact on the way we live each day. God has beset us before and behind, which means that when we disobey him, he hems us in with discipline, but when we walk with him, he surrounds us with his blessing. The omniscience and omnipresence of the eternal God are a solemn reminder to be faithful, but also a standing promise of his perfect guidance and companionship.

O God, we cannot escape you, and we do not want to. Let your surrounding presence bless us today. Amen.

April 25 **Scripture Reading: Mark 10:21**

Then Jesus beholding him loved him, and said unto him, One thing thou lackest: go thy way, sell whatsoever thou hast, and give to the poor, and thou shalt have treasure in heaven: and come, take up the cross, and follow me.

Love is honest

The man we call the rich young ruler ran eagerly into Jesus' presence and asked how he could inherit eternal life. Jesus discerned that the man's real love in life was his wealth. But something was struggling to get free in him and Jesus sensed that as well. So, looking at him, "He loved him." A holy love welled up in Jesus' heart for this man who wanted eternal life but was attached to the material world.

Jesus expressed his love for the man by telling him how to unburden himself of the one thing that held him back from eternal life and always would. He gave him a radical solution for a spiritually deadly problem and then called him to unconditional discipleship. We know what the man did: he went away sad because he was rich. Did Jesus know what the man would do? In the incarnation the Son laid aside much of his glorious power to become a man. Jesus may not have known for certain what the man would do, though he probably sensed it clearly. But even if Jesus knew the young man would decline to sell all and follow him, he would still have told him what he did. Why? Because he loved him, and love tells people what they need to hear—the truth.

God is always honest in his love. He tells us when we are unfaithful that we have gone astray and must return. When his discipline becomes evident in our lives, it is his voice saying, "I love you." Then again, when he opens his hands and gives us blessings out of the blue or provides for us through his infinite ways, he is saying, "I love you," then, as well. Sometimes the Lord leads us through the maze of events that often define our lives and brings us to a point where the only way to be at peace about following him is to give up what we thought was life itself, so as to obey him in something that seems risky. Remember that he is saying, "I love you," by asking us to leave what will not fulfill us for the only thing that will—him.

Jesus, I trust your love today, no matter how high your demand. I know I will be blessed when I obey. Amen.

Whom having not seen, ye love; in whom, though now ye see him not, yet believing, ye rejoice with joy unspeakable and full of glory.

Having joy

Joy is a quality the Christian should exhibit but many of us find in short supply. Bogged down in problems, weighed down with tasks, and embroiled in tensions, we Christians sometimes wonder where the joy is. Did we lose it, never have it, or is it simply buried under emotions evoked by life's concerns? And whatever obscured it, can we get it back?

Jesus told us we will have full joy when we experience his fullness in us, when we are walking in obedience with him, and when our prayer lives are constant and rewarded (Jn.15:7-11, 16:24). In other words, Christian joy is a byproduct of a close relationship with Christ. Peter said believing in a Savior we cannot see but whose salvation is distinctly experienced, brings joy. In fact, the very trials that tempt us to get our eyes off Jesus are designed to pry us away from dependence on worldly well-being, and to tie us tightly by faith to Jesus alone. When that happens, our faith will be more substantial than our sight, and our joy will intensify. Peter described that joy as indescribable.

As often pointed out, joy is not the same as happiness. We can grieve over death and loss, or suffer from troubles or illness, and still have joy. This is possible because joy is not exclusively an emotion. Christian joy is a divine perspective on life resulting from our salvation in Jesus Christ, our knowledge of the Spirit's presence, and the certainty of our future with God in heaven. Weighed against these constants, life's variables are less disturbing, and life's many exigencies can be handled with peace and grace.

When we realize our joy has been submerged in a sea of worries and things, we find David's prayer, "Restore unto me the joy of thy salvation" (Psalm 51:12), especially personal. Most likely our walk with Jesus has become erratic or distant. Focus on him, draw near to him, talk to him, and grasp him again by faith, and joy will return, inexpressible and glorious.

Jesus, forgive us that we ever neglect our walk with you. Restore your joy as we come back to your side. Amen.

After these things the word of the Lord came unto Abram in a vision, saying, Fear not, Abram: I am thy shield, and thy exceeding great reward.

Desiring God

While some material things are vital to life, and having financial security is good, people whose main objective in life is to make money will wake up one day to find they have little that really enriches life. People may try to make themselves happy by buying things, and make themselves secure by amassing bank accounts and insurance. But they often experience misery instead, and they cannot prevent their facing God to answer for their lives and choices.

When Abram settled in Canaan after he and Lot parted ways, he became both powerful and prosperous. He defeated vicious territorial warlords to rescue Lot from Sodom, and as his herds increased, he began to experience what God had promised earlier in his life: "I will bless you." Then God revealed himself in a vision and told him, "I am your shield… I am your reward." God was telling him that while Abram had power and security in his trained servants, God himself was Abram's protection. He was also telling him that far beyond the wealth of material possessions, the Lord himself was Abram's riches.

For most people, the older they grow the more they realize that personal relationships are what count in life, not money and things. Some parents come to regret having tried too hard to give their children things at the expense of giving them themselves. On the other hand, a common testimony of people whose families were not well-off but whose parents were loving and attentive, is, "We didn't know we were poor." Indeed, they weren't. The same principle is true with the Lord. He himself, far more than the things he provides, is your shield and reward. We are to seek God more than any of his gifts. We are to find in him our shield from sin and death, and our reward of righteousness and heaven. As we seek him in prayer, our yearning should be more to know him, and less to get anything from him.

Father God, we confess there is no salvation but in who you are, and no wealth but you yourself. Amen.

Asa cried unto the Lord his God, and said, Lord, it is nothing with thee to help, whether with many, or with them that have no power: help us, O Lord our God; for we rest on thee, and in thy name we go against this multitude. O Lord, thou art our God; let not man prevail against thee.

Getting victory

Christians need to experience victory. From the sins that Hebrews says "so easily beset us" to the tribulations Jesus said "ye *shall* have," life is full of influences and events that seem to conspire to trip us up and test our faith. Satan is against Christians and the church, and desires nothing greater than to spite God by destroying the joy and witness of believers while keeping as many people out of the kingdom of God as he can. This spiritual opposition is the reason the Christian's conscious quest should be to get victory in every area of his life.

King Asa of Judah was one of those few kings whom the Bible says "did right in the eyes of the Lord." He began his rule by cleansing the land of idolatry, and God rewarded the kingdom with rest from war. He also realized the need to fortify against coming hostility, and he built walled cities. The anticipated hostility came in the form of an Ethiopian army a million strong. Asa commanded 580,000 men, but he had something the Ethiopians did not have. He had the Lord. In his prayer Asa did three things: he asked for help from the Lord, who could give victory against a million the same as if it were only one; he invoked the name of the Lord, saying that the Ethiopian attack was really against God and not just Judah; and he gave the battle to the Lord, that the victory and the glory would really be his.

Whether our opponent is merely the nagging force of habit that keeps us tied to petty sins, or the soul-wrenching trial that threatens to break our faith and ruin our lives, God promises us victory when we call on him, claim victory in his name, and surrender ourselves to his working. When we get the victory, it is his, and we must glorify him for all he has done.

Mighty God, may every enemy flee before you as in our hearts we fall before you today. Amen.

Therefore they that were scattered abroad went every where preaching the word.

Wild fire

An early church leader, Tertullian, remarking on persecution of Christians in the days of the apostles, said, "The blood of the martyrs became the seed of the church." The earliest illustration of that truth is found in Acts 8:2. Stephen had just been stoned as Jewish authorities finally lost their collective tempers and began to attack Christian witness in the streets of Jerusalem. They appointed Saul, a fiery young Pharisee, to round up adherents of what was being called "the Way," and to put them in prison. The effect on the infant Christian movement was dramatic. Believers scattered abroad. Unfortunately for the authorities, the Christians' strength was not in their numbers, but in their faith. When they scattered, they simply multiplied.

What effect does resistance to your faith in Christ have on you? When someone attempts to shut down "religious" conversation, does it spell the end of your influence? Or does it spark a new surge of creativity as you try to find ways to communicate your faith to people who are running from God? Is the world's subtle pressure, disapproval, or avoidance of Christian truth slowly killing your commitment to evangelize? Or are you, like the disciples, praying for boldness and open doors in new places?

Whether unbelief or persecution dismantles your witness or intensifies it is determined by whether or not you are on fire to begin with. Campers scatter cooling coals to hasten a campfire's death. But live fires blown about by gusty winds scatter balls of flame that ignite new fires where they land. Wildfire is an awesome force. In the same way, Christian witnesses spiritually on fire spread the word when they are scattered. The winds of adversity only make their zeal hotter.

Jesus my Lord, kindle a flame of love and zeal within this heart of mine. Breathe on me! Amen.

Thou art a great people, and hast great power: thou shalt not have one lot only: But the mountain shall be thine; for it is a wood, and thou shalt cut it down: and the outgoings of it shall be thine: for thou shalt drive out the Canaanites, though they have iron chariots, and though they be strong.

Great things ahead

Joshua gave some memorable challenges to the Israelites during his time leading them in the conquest of Canaan. Among them was a charge to the sons of Joseph, Ephraim and Manasseh, who were worried that their lot in Canaan was not large enough, and that the extra land Joshua offered them was inhabited by enemies too strong to conquer. They didn't have the vision Joshua had. His challenge was meant to impart some of that vision. Perhaps Joshua looked them in the eye until they were silent, and then spoke to them with a soft but powerful intensity. Basically he said, "You can do it!"

We sometimes become discouraged about the prospects of our succeeding at something, or perhaps of ever having more fulfilling days in our lives. Our bleak outlook may result from a record of failure, some catastrophic event, or just the long, tiring process of living from year to year. We may look at the successes or accomplishments of others and think to ourselves that we have been bypassed or set aside. Looking ahead, we may think our lot in life looks confining, or that we don't have the strength to do what it takes to struggle through it. We could use a Joshua to tell us, "You can do it! God is still with you."

No matter how old we are or what path we have walked, great things are ahead of us. When we're young, many of those great things are in the years of life and ministry on earth, if God grants us time. But no matter how old we are, which of us knows the things God has planned for our fulfilment and blessing in this world—to say nothing of the next? And even at life's end the Christian awaits not a defeat, but an everlasting victory. Whether the mountain to be taken is a ministry at life's sunrise or a day's toil at life's sunset, still there are great things ahead—and you *can* do it!

God our Strength, enable us today to possess the lot you assigned us, through your strength and to your glory. Amen.

Thy prophets have seen vain and foolish things for thee: and they have not discovered thine iniquity, to turn away thy captivity; but have seen for thee false burdens and causes of banishment.

Courage to tell the truth

Most of us do not enjoy confrontation: we like to get along with people. In general, this approach to life is beneficial; however, we must not allow our preference for smooth relationships to always take precedence over the need to speak the truth. If we do, our Christian witness will be compromised eventually. We may be able to give a candid witness to friends who permit us to "get personal" about touchy subjects. But people who have antagonism toward Christians and biblical truths to begin with are unlikely to welcome our testimony.

Jeremiah lamented that most of the prophets to Israel after the fall of Jerusalem were not telling them the truth about their circumstances. Instead of identifying the actual causes—their unfaithfulness to God, their idolatry, their sin—these prophets pointed to other things, most likely blaming their enemies. Whether they were consciously aware of their being afraid to pinpoint the sins of Israel as the reason for their predicament, the result is the same. They declined to confront their people with the truth, because the truth was shameful to admit. Prophets who tell people what they want to believe instead of what they need to hear are likely to be popular, but they are also setting themselves up for judgment, and doing a disservice to their listeners.

This message in Lamentations applies to more than just prophets and preachers. It speaks to the need of every Christian to find a way to relate to people in a spirit of grace while sharing a message of gospel truth. We should not regard witness as a bludgeon to be used to offend people intentionally, but neither should we be timid in our encounters with others if truth is on the line. It is common for Christians to have lifelong friends who do not know Christ, and for them to never find a way to tell them the gospel. Let the Holy Spirit guide every thought, word and action. His approach and his timing are perfect.

O Lord, help us to care enough about others to confront them lovingly with gospel truth. Amen.

But in the days of the voice of the seventh angel, when he shall begin to sound, the mystery of God should be finished, as he hath declared to his servants the prophets.

Reveling in the mystery

John wrote that one of the greatly anticipated events of the future would be the completion of the mystery of God. Among the great truths this mystery of God comprises are two things Paul mentioned: the wonder of God's inclusive gospel (Eph. 3:2), and the glory of Christ's internal presence (Col. 1:27). These things are mysteries in the biblical sense: they have been revealed to us, but they are beyond our total comprehension because they are the outworking of the God who is beyond our full understanding.

Think of the inclusive gospel: God has chosen to include us in his eternal family, not because of anything we have done but because of his inexplicable grace. We cannot finally understand the cross. Who can explain how Jesus could die in anyone else's place? The prophets said he would and the gospels say he did, but how he could or why he would we cannot really explain beyond the simple fact that God loves us.

Think of the indwelling Christ. How could the God of creation, who made the vastness of the universe, dwell inside us believers? His presence is not just the intersection of our bodies with his omnipresence, but a personal indwelling of God the Son through the eternal Spirit. Why would a God so immense and all-encompassing pay such personal attention to such small and sinful creatures?

These things are simply mysteries. We know they are true, but they defy explanation by puny minds. We simply revel in them, because they express the inexplicable glory of God's saving plan: to give himself for the redemption of those who sinned against him, that they might live and reign with him forever. Unbelievable? Believe it!

Father, we cannot fathom your salvation. But we revel in the mystery and thank you for our Savior. Amen.

My voice shalt thou hear in the morning, O Lord; in the morning will I direct *my prayer* unto thee, and will look up.

Great expectation

David's morning habit was personal worship and prayer. Psalm 5 demonstrates that his time of prayer reassured him daily that God would bless those who follow him. This confidence in God came from his method of prayer. The Psalm says he first directed his prayer to God. In the Hebrew the words literally say "I will set myself for you." In other words, David aligned himself with God. He realized that it was important for him to be on God's side, knowing that God was already on his side. After he presented himself in surrender to the Lord, then he was able to "look up," a Hebrew word meaning he waited in expectation.

No better recipe exists for successful prayer than to bring ourselves in surrender to God for his will, not ours, to be done, and then to continue life in the confident expectation that he will work out all things according to his purpose. This method does not suggest that we may not ask the Lord for the deep desires that rise up in our hearts. In fact, if we are honest about our submission to God, and faithful in continuing it, eventually the desires of our hearts will be those the Spirit of God has placed there. Praying back to God the requests he inspired us to make is guaranteed to be successful.

It is the waiting we may find challenging. Because of our vastly limited ability to see ahead of the moment, we may think the solutions we ask for our problems are urgent, when God knows otherwise. We may believe what we need is essential, when God knows it isn't. What enables us to wait with great expectation is our being convinced that God is in control, that he is aware of all needs and all dangers, that he is in charge of all forces and influences, and that he loves us infinitely and is always working on his plan to bless us. If we have laid ourselves at his feet and aligned ourselves with his will, we need not worry while we wait. Good things are around the corner.

Father, let the greatest thing our prayer changes be ourselves, that we may have full faith in you. Amen.

If it be a beast, whereof men bring an offering unto the Lord, all that any man giveth of such unto the Lord shall be holy.

Living out our commitments

Jesus once warned the Pharisees about their hypocrisy by citing an example of a man who excused himself from caring for his parents by saying that the money he could have used to do so was *corban*—in other words, already devoted to God. *Corban*, a Hebrew word meaning "gift," was the Old Testament concept of devoting something entirely to God in addition to the offerings he required for sin. In Leviticus, these offerings were typically animals to be sacrificed, but the concept grew to include houses, property, and various tithes. The Jews took these commitments seriously, and God reminded them solemnly to pay the vows they made to him (Deut.23:21).

Modern examples of making vows or commitments to God include pledges to build church buildings or commitments to support a mission offering or endeavor. Christians should be aware that when they respond to calls for commitment to ministries and missions, they are doing far more than obligating themselves to a church: they are committing themselves to God.

Even more than commitments of things or money, however, every Christian has already commitment of an offering of his entire life to God. Some Christians have the idea that they can be saved first and then later commit their lives to Christ. This notion is false. It is impossible to be saved without surrendering one's whole life to God. The simplest New Testament definition of salvation requires that we receive and name Jesus Christ as Lord. While we may not be *paying* our vow and in that sense may not be committed, the commitment was made when we first received Christ. What remains is for us to realize that we have no life or time to waste offering excuses for not obeying God in everything. We ourselves are already *corban,* and we belong entirely to God. Let us get busy serving him devotedly.

Holy God, as you lead us graciously in your sovereign ownership, may we obey you in love. Amen.

It is a righteous thing with God to recompense tribulation to them that trouble you.

The prospect of judgment

Since we are human, there are times when we wish judgment would fall on those who persecute Christians and pervert what is holy. Since we are the children of God, there are times when we respond with broken hearts and prayers for the salvation of these same people. If we are normal, we have a mixture of these two responses, and we should. The Lord taught us to love our enemies and to pray for those who misuse us. He also taught us that many people will hate us because they hate him, and that God will eventually call, "Time's up," and will judge the world.

It is not inappropriate for us to recall, as frequently as needed, the truth that God will "recompense tribulation" to those who persecute God's people. Sometimes the reminder that there is a holy God who will judge the evil that people do, is the only fact that enables us to set aside our own anger, commit our circumstances to God, and act with grace and love. Jesus' approach to the Pharisees was a good example of this tension in balance. He warned them urgently in public, sometimes delivering scathing rebukes of their behavior. But when a Pharisee came to him, Jesus did everything he could to love him and lead him to the truth.

Jude also illustrated the mixture of love and warning. He said we could lead some to Christ through compassion (Jude 22), while others had a chance only if we warned them of the fearful consequences of their deep iniquity (Jude 23). We need not worry that we will be finally heartbroken at the choices some make. In the end, swept up in the glory of our salvation with others who acknowledge the Lord, we will possess the perfect peace of God about the judgment that has befallen the many who to the last refused his grace. Until then, we must go on praying for the lost, whether friend or enemy, and remain on alert to any opportunity to show them the way to heaven.

Loving God, give us both the holiness and the heart of Christ, that we may reach people as he did. Amen.

And the passengers that pass through the land, when any seeth a man's bone, then shall he set up a sign by it, till the buriers have buried it in the valley of Hamongog.

Cleansing the landscape

Some people are neat-niks and some are ...well, some aren't. Sloppiness dogs some of us to our dying day. We call it "disorganization." Not everyone who tends to be disorganized—sloppy— is sloppy to the same degree. Some people appear to be thoroughly neat and tidy until you find that one room, that one desk, or that one drawer that represents their messy gene. For many people it's a home office that seems to collect miscellany and that periodically must be subjected to radical reorganization.

A messy house is only a matter of personality; however, a morally sloppy life is a matter of sin. Do you do things or say things that are beneath the standard of God's righteousness and then just leave them lying around in your life, unconfessed? In most people's lives some moral or ethical garbage accumulates, and they do not collect and jettison it as they should. While messy houses only irritate a few people, sinfully messy lives grieve God.

Ezekiel foretold the day when, after the great conflict of Israel with Gog and Magog, the land will be meticulously cleansed of every desecrating remnant of rotting flesh, until it is free of the debris of invaders. In a similar way, God expects us to go through the landscape of our lives, inspecting ourselves for the remains of the sin nature. We are to bury the flesh, that sinful invader and usurper of what God made for fellowship with him. We are to subject the sinful nature to the mortifying and burying efficacy of the cross of Christ, that our lives might be clean. God wants to inhabit and use a clean life, not one that is cluttered with the rotting debris of sin that we refuse to throw away when we come to him.

Make a plan. Go through everything in your life and get rid of what shouldn't be there. Don't have a messy life for the Holy Spirit to live in.

Holy Spirit, cleanse the landscape of our lives and make us fit vessels for you. Amen.

The sluggard will not plow by reason of the cold; therefore shall he beg in harvest, and have nothing.

No shortcuts

The most obvious application of proverbs about sluggards is to the basic matter of work: lazy people are generally poor. But the lesson of this proverb is clearly broader. Spiritual things, too, require devoted effort if they are to result in fruit. Diligence in spiritual growth and service brings about praiseworthy results. There are no shortcuts to worthwhile goals. We must follow Christ at his pace and partake of his cup if we are to experience his victory and share his joy.

Two brothers were driving to college. On a previous trip, the younger of them had gone with someone else who knew a shortcut along the route. He suggested they find and take the shortcut themselves. At what he thought was the appropriate time, they turned off on a side road. After a while, they made another turn to be back on the main highway. But soon they began to pass places that looked too familiar for comfort. There was a church having dinner on the grounds that looked suspiciously like one they had passed not fifteen minutes before. In fact, it was the same one: they had taken the far end of the shortcut and had gone around in a circle. Anyone who has done something similar knows the truth in the witty turn of Murphy's law #10: "A shortcut is the longest distance between two points."

There are no shortcuts in spiritual maturity. Most Christians have looked at the lives of very spiritually mature persons and wished they might be like them—tomorrow. But each of us must walk the path God has laid out, learn the lessons he teaches, and undergo the trials necessary to the molding of our misshapen lives, so that the end result will be just as God planned it. The spiritual sluggard will not plow because of the difficulty and the seemingly endless task, and he will harvest no maturity, and win no rewards. It will not be so with us—will it?

Father, help us plow only as fast as you lead, and grow as much as you inspire. Amen.

Favour is deceitful, and beauty is vain: but a woman that feareth the LORD, she shall be praised.

Mothers know what's best

One reason children are often partial to their mothers is that most mothers sacrifice greatly. In 1994 a young mother-to-be named Loretta Pullins was diagnosed with Hodgkin's disease, a cancer of the lymphatic system. The disease was curable if treatments were begun immediately. To proceed, she would need to have an abortion, because the chemotherapy would do immense harm to her unborn baby. Loretta said no. She wouldn't kill her baby or take treatments to help her if they would harm the baby. The disease progressed. Loretta developed chest tumors and had difficulty breathing. She accepted radiation treatments as long as they were blocked from affecting her womb. She improved. In May of 1995, Loretta gave birth to little Alana. Of her own health she said, "It doesn't matter."

Infants and young children do not question their mother's importance. But even if adolescents and teenagers lose some appreciation for their mothers' sacrifices, by the time they become young adults they usually realize that their mothers could have done things they did not do, or could have had things they did not have, if they hadn't been so selflessly devoted to them—their children. Men and women's love for their mothers grows as they understand first hand what it takes to rear and provide for children.

Mothers have an uncanny sense of what is truly important, and thus they know their commitment to and sacrifice for their children is justified. A boy announced that he had lost his contact lens in gravel. He had given up on finding it. His mother asked where to look, and in a few minutes she came back with the lens. The boy was astounded, but the mother explained, "You were looking for a piece of plastic. I was looking for $150. Mothers have a way of being able to evaluate the worth of many things, especially their children's lives, talents, feelings, characters, and futures, and they give and give and give more, to bring their children through.

Father, thank you for mothers, and for their love like yours, the half of which we may never know. Amen.

Be ye perfect, as your father in heaven is perfect.

No moderation

Many people have the idea that the saying, "Moderation in all things," comes from the Bible. Philippians 4:5 in the King James Version says, "Let your moderation be known to all men." However, the word *moderation* there means *consideration* or *gentleness*. Actually, it was Aristotle who advised "moderation in all things." People today often adopt this maxim in defense of the idea that it is wise to tame habits such as smoking, drinking or eating, or to go easy on hobbies, sports or sex. By *moderation* they mean to strike a compromise between abstinence and excess, to take the middle ground. But in many things, moderation is not at all the right approach.

In his Sermon on the Mount, Jesus taught people repeatedly that compromised righteousness was not what God desires. His hearers made exceptions to many rules, but Jesus put before them a standard that did not recommend any course but perfection. His startling instruction to "be perfect" still generates controversy—how can we follow it if we know to begin with that we will not, in this life, be sinless? Yet certainly one implication of what Jesus was teaching us is that we must not aim at compromise or moderation, but aim at complete holiness of life and likeness to Christ himself. When we become Christians, we are not given a waver to keep a little adultery, a little stealing, or a little anything else that is ungodly in our lives. Just as important is our adoption of complete commitment to spiritual growth, study of God's word, regular worship, obedient stewardship, and many other things. If we try to moderate the things we used to do, and gradually slip into the things we ought to do, the danger is that we will do neither successfully, but will straddle the fence all our lives. Jesus said we cannot serve two masters.

Mark Twain once said of his habits, "I cannot moderate them. I lack the will power. I can give them up entirely, but I cannot moderate them." Neither should we attempt to moderate either sin or righteousness. Complete obedience is the only godly goal.

Father, we confess we cannot be perfect in our strength, but in your Spirit's fullness we can obey you faithfully. Amen.

The Pharisees and scribes murmured, saying, This man receiveth sinners, and eateth with them.

Complimentary criticism

Two college roommates were very different. John was urbane and cultured, while Steven other was not. John first often acted in a condescending manner toward the Steven. One day, half in humor and half in derision, John told his less sophisticated friend, "You're so easily entertained!" At first Steve did not know what the remark meant, but then he realized John meant to suggest he was a simpleton with no discriminating tastes. But Steve decided it was a compliment after all: he could laugh at little things and enjoy life without its having to be dressed up with complexity, subtlety or pomposity.

People made similar criticisms of Jesus. The Pharisees and scribes murmured that Jesus welcomed "sinners" and sat down at the table with them. How awful! And how wonderful! Here was one, finally, who would come to us on our level and seek to communicate the love of God in the midst of our sinful predicaments. The Pharisees meant to criticize, but they were really recognizing one of Jesus' praiseworthy attributes. If Jesus hadn't done what self-righteous people criticized, the world would not have a Savior. Instead, he did the will of God, and we are the beneficiaries; for he not only ate with, but died for us sinners.

Perhaps today you will face possible criticism for doing the right thing, obeying God, being like Christ, speaking a witness for him, or standing up for truth. Remember that Christ was condemned for perfect living. If people call you a "holy Joe," remember that without holiness shall no man see God (Heb.12:14). If people say you are "narrow minded" because you believe in the one and only Savior, remember that "narrow is the way which leadeth unto life, and few there be that find it" (Mat.7:14).

Father, may we boldly face criticism from the world, taking it as a sure sign that we are following you. Amen.

Beware ye of the leaven of the Pharisees, which is hypocrisy.

Hypocritical criticism

Perhaps no criticism of a church by its community ever troubles Christians more than the charge of hypocrisy. When people say, "There are too many hypocrites there," church members bristle, but they are genuinely concerned that it not be true. Real Christians do not want to be guilty of preaching one way and living another. None of us wants to be a hypocrite or to belong to a group we think is mostly hypocritical.

Jesus frequently warned people interested in following him that they must beware of being like the Pharisees, who taught demanding standards for holiness but did not practice what they preached. But notice that he described hypocrisy as "leaven." Leaven is a stealthy, pervasive thing. It spreads. It contaminates. Obviously, those who recognize hypocrisy in others are not immune to it themselves. In the same sermon in which Jesus made the statement about the leaven, he said, "Woe unto you …for you load men with burdens grievous to be borne, and you yourselves touch not the burdens with one of your fingers!" Some of those who accuse Christians in the church of hypocrisy have done this very thing: they have placed a burden on Christians that they themselves are not willing to bear—the burden of immaculate integrity, of near-perfect example. They expect church people to live perfectly by Christian teachings, but their own lives are not perfect examples even of the principles they believe in, whatever they are.

Are you guilty of expecting from others what you do not do yourself? Probably we have all criticized others for things no worse than those that we do. Seek today to see your own actions in the light of your opinion of others. Be aware of how you live before criticizing anyone in any way.

O God, we are none of us perfect. Forgive our sin through the blood of Jesus, and help us not to have disdain for others for being as imperfect as we are. Amen.

May 12 **Scripture Reading: Psalm 139:8**

If I ascend up into heaven, thou art there: if I make my bed in hell, behold, thou art there.

Cure for loneliness

From time to time, loneliness can be a problem for all or most of us. It is natural for people who have been deprived of human company to feel lonely. Even people who have been known as loners can become very uneasy with having to be alone. Some loneliness is caused by our own attitudes toward people who would otherwise be our friends. Somebody tampered creatively with an old adage and came up with a new one just as true: "An ounce of forgiveness is worth a pound of loneliness." How true! How often have we cut ourselves off from others by our own hardness of spirit.

Other times, of course, loneliness is simply the result of our circumstances. In the middle of these times, there is still a cure. It is found in the truth that God is with us. The Psalmist expressed a glorious wonderment that he couldn't escape the Spirit of God. God's presence was wherever he went. From heaven to hell and everywhere in between, God is wherever you and I are. Sometimes this realization is a warning. But when we are seeking to live for the Lord but find ourselves without much support in the way of close companions, realizing that God is where we are gives us strength. The Psalmist's observation becomes a promise not just of the omnipresence of God but of the personal presence and power of his Spirit with those who belong to him in Jesus Christ. You can count on this kind of heavenly, invisible company to relieve the loneliness and dispel the gloom.

A widow told her pastor, "When my husband died, I decided to invest myself more than ever in the Lord's work, and it paid off. The closer I have come to Christ, the more I feel his presence. I used to be lonely, but I can't really be lonely when my Lord is there the way he is." Here is the cure for loneliness: walk every step of the way with the Lord Jesus Christ, and feel his presence close throughout the days—and the nights.

Father, make the presence of Christ real to me today, and draw me into fellowship with you. Amen.

Even in laughter the heart is sorrowful; and the end of that mirth is heaviness.

More than empty laughter

For many people, Friday as the end of the week's work represents celebration, recreation and escape. The acronym TGIF (Thank God It's Friday) is a workplace watchword, and even the name of a restaurant/bar. Go to the weekend spots and you will find multitudes making merry. Many people will party all weekend late into the evenings, will laugh a lot, drink a lot, sleep it all off Sunday, and go back to work Monday to start all over again. But many of these celebrants will be laughing only with their lips, not with their hearts. The sage of the Proverbs characterized this contradiction by saying that not all who laugh are really happy, and when the laughing stops, the weight of their woes may come back even heavier.

Many people laugh for relief, not joy. For many only celebrate what they have escaped, not what they have found. All of us like to quit work, have a few days off, and change the pace. Getting a break from the daily grind may be reason enough to do something special. But many people's lives and hearts are empty, and they have nothing significant to be deeply joyful about. Their laughter conceals deep pain or anxiety.

It is possible, however, to laugh with the heart as well as the voice. We can have joy, contentment, and release from restlessness. The source of this abiding joy is Christ—not religion, not church, not faith, but Christ himself. He answers questions that trouble lonely souls and removes guilt that plagues wayward hearts. In his forgiveness and love comes true joy that exists independent of happy circumstances. Fridays are still nice, but when you know Christ, Fridays are not all you have to thank God for.

Savior, let us know the joy of finding our purpose for living today in your fullness and lordship. Amen.

Wherefore, my beloved, as ye have always obeyed, not as in my presence only, but now much more in my absence, work out your own salvation with fear and trembling.

Policing ourselves

One of the real tests of obedience is whether or not it continues when authorities are not around. Motorists on a certain city boulevard routinely drive 50 m.p.h. in a 35 m.p.h. residential zone, except for one day a month when policemen set up radar in a church parking lot. Then they glide by at 35 as if they never had a thought of doing anything else. Children often act the perfect gentlemen and ladies their parents brag they are, until the parents are out of sight, and then it's as if someone unstopped a dam or turned on a whirlwind. Christians often put on their Sunday best in more ways than one when they go to church, but how do they live Monday through Saturday when they think they don't have to make a show?

Paul wrote the Philippian Christians with instructions not only to behave when he wasn't among them just as they did the times when he was, but if anything to go further. They were to demonstrate before their world that their lives were lived for the approval of a God who is Lord every day. One of Paul's reasons for challenging the Philippians in this way was that it was not he who was their motivation to do right, but God. In the very next sentence he stated that it was God who gave them both the desire and the ability to live pleasing to him.

If we lack continual motivation to live faithfully for God, we pray to acquire it. The motivation to live consistently holy lives comes from the Holy Spirit. Does he live in you? If he does, are you letting him possess you fully?

Punctuate this sentence: "In the fall a young boy left alone raking leaves" ...Can you do it? Some will object that it is not a complete sentence. It is. Here's how to punctuate it: "In the fall, a young boy left alone, raking, *leaves!*" How true that is! Let it not be true of us that we are show-time Christians who take off their characters when they leave the stage.

Father, forgive us for ever wearing goodness only when convenient or observed. Amen.

Whatsoever hath a blemish, that shall ye not offer; for it shall not be acceptable for you.

Precious gifts

Have you ever cheated God? It would not be surprising—probably all of us have. Leviticus instructed God's people never to offer to him anything that was second-rate, defective, blemished. Moses was writing about sacrifices and offerings in the tabernacle, but the principle reaches down through time to our own lives and speaks to our service toward God. What do you give him? Is it the spare moment, the otherwise useless hour, the neglected talent, the half-developed but squandered ability? Is it the leftover money, the sideways glance, the accidental act of kindness? Many of us are guilty of giving to God not the best of ourselves and what is ours, but only what we are likely to get rid of anyway without feeling much of a loss.

What credit do we think we get for such offerings to the Lord? God wants what costs us much. He wants precious gifts—the time we could use selfishly to great advantage, the money we might otherwise really want to spend on much-desired things, the energy we perhaps used to expend on making money or entertaining ourselves, the ability we could devote to potentially great success in some other way. God wants prime time, full attention, and practiced excellence. Why? It is because he is God, and he deserves it. It's because we owe him even more than that and because we need to honor him with the best. It's because we need to know the cost of our salvation and because we need to be humble. We need to symbolize our submission of life through every gift we make.

Give nothing to God today—unless you can give what is dear to you. The dearest thing to you is your life. Give that. God in Christ gave his life for you that you might live, and he lives for you that you might reign with him. Such love constrains us to live for him fully (2 Cor.5:15).

Lord Jesus, you gave a perfect gift to save us. May we give all we are and have to thank you. Amen.

No man can come to me, except the Father which hath sent me draw him: and I will raise him up at the last day.

Hard fishing

Anyone who fishes a lot, even someone who does it for a living, knows that success is not guaranteed anytime. A productive fishing trip depends on many factors: air temperature, cloud cover, wind velocity, water color, water temperature, proximity of high or low pressure systems, time of day, time of year, how often a lake is fished by others, how much certain baits have been used, how many fish have been taken out of the water, and upstream pollutants, just to name a few. Then there are many factors relating to the fisherman himself or herself: positioning, casting placement, retrieval rate, lure type selection, lure color, lure action, and so on. Some people believe that the position and phase of the moon have an effect on catching fish. But the bottom line, as all true fishermen know, is that you can have almost if not everything on your side, and the fish still might not be biting! Many a fisherman goes home reporting that he "fished hard" and caught little.

Fishing for men is the same way. All your sophisticated spiritual fishing gear, all your guaranteed-to-catch-men gospel tackle, will sometimes leave you empty handed. Sometimes people aren't biting. Jesus said that no one can come to him unless the heavenly Father draws him. The Holy Spirit must be at work in the life of the one you are trying to catch for the Lord. Until he is, that person will not become a Christian. But keep fishing. Fish hard. Keep casting, changing bait, and trying different places. The gospel doesn't change, but our tactics may need to adapt to conditions and needs. Do everything you can, and trust the Holy Spirit to use what he will to touch hearts and reach souls.

Have you been praying about someone, wanting him or her to come to Christ? Be patient. Persistence pays off. Trust God to work in his own time and draw that one to himself. Remember what it took to bring someone else you may know to saving faith in Christ—perhaps even what it took to win you. If you are to lead people to Christ rather than disciple them to yourself, you must let the Spirit do the winning.

Father, teach us to sense where and when to fish for men, and to depend on you for strength and success as we share the gospel. Amen.

May 17 **Scripture Reading: Luke 22:53**

When I was daily with you in the temple, ye stretched forth no hands against me: but this is your hour, and the power of darkness.

Look up!

In one of James Branch Cabell's novels, a character said, "The optimist proclaims that we live in the best of all possible worlds, and the pessimist fears that this is true" (James Branch Cabell, The Silver Stallion, ch.26.). This bit of wisdom makes us realize that the difference between optimism and pessimism may be a fine line. As McLandburgh Wilson put it, "Twixt the optimist and pessimist the difference is droll: the optimist sees the doughnut; the pessimist, the hole" (McLandburgh Wilson, "Optimist and Pessimist," 1915).

Most of us are aware of the benefits of believing the best will happen. Quite often it pays off in a better attitude and more friends, and sometimes it actually affects the outcome of things. Optimism is not synonymous with faith, but biblical faith includes an element of optimism. When we really believe God is good and that he loves us we will be optimistic about things to come. But there are times when Christians have to face the fact that evil dominates and that good things will not come to pass. Jesus was certainly the ultimate man of faith, but in Gethsemane he knew a dark hour was upon him that he would not escape. He faced his arrest, trial and even crucifixion with calm assurance that his ordeal would not ultimately be his defeat, but he knew he must pass through it all just the same.

In each of our lives we face occasional darkness that no amount of optimism will enable us to dispel. We live in a desperately wicked world, and for a time sin will reign. Our optimism is in knowing that sin and wrong will not triumph: God will. We may not live in the best of all possible worlds *now,* but we *will* when God has his day. Look up! God has great plans.

Lord, teach us to weigh present trouble against future triumph, and to believe you for strength to persevere, and finally to win. Amen.

It is better to dwell in a corner of the housetop, than with a brawling woman in a wide house.

Sweet peace

Some scripture verses bring immediate laughter to our hearts because they are so wryly put. This proverb captures such a humorous scene. Imagine a bearded, middle-aged man sitting on his haunches with his chin propped in his hand, leaning into the corner of the low wall that borders the flat roof of his typical Jewish home. Down in the house somewhere, a grating, female voice is cawing, "Jedediah! Where are you? When I get my hands on you …!" Of course, the situation could be reversed, with a domineering husband and a beleaguered wife. But either way you go, the point is clear. The proverb writer says that a mansion isn't a pleasant place to live if the company is disagreeable, but that a hut is tolerable if there is at least some peace.

Not every grand home is cursed with dysfunctional relationships, of course, and just because a home is humble in size doesn't mean it is full of love. But whatever size the house, it's peace that makes it a palace and hostility that creates a true hovel. In a marriage, it's the brawling, the constant squabbling, the arguing over any little thing, the cutting remarks, the sarcasm, the distrust, the griping, and all kindred conversation, that can make life miserable—for mates and for their children. After a while, a husband and wife who live in this pattern become hardened, and they may look elsewhere for their emotional, spiritual and sexual fulfillment.

Some people who continually feud defend themselves by suggesting that at least they are honest: they fight instead of lying about being happy or keeping feelings to themselves. But allowing yourself to become abusive and hostile is never good for a relationship. It hurts both parties. The rule applies to friendships as well. Take a hovel with happiness over a mansion with madness any day.

Lord, let the peace of Christ rule in our hearts so we may love one another in the spirit of him who loved us first. Amen.

Those things, which ye have both learned, and received, and heard, and seen in me, do: and the God of peace shall be with you.

Setting a good example

Have you ever driven up behind, and then passed, a driver education car? Often the driver will be going more slowly than he or she could, and he may exhibit almost excessive caution. Did you become impatient, or did you immediately put on your best driving behavior, give every signal, drive the allowable speed, and make smooth turns, with the thought that maybe the instructor will say to his student, 'Now, there goes a good driver'? If you did, you aren't the only one! Perhaps many people do the same because they want to be good examples.

Whether you realize it or not, people are watching how you maneuver through life. Someone is imitating you if only partly. Are you following the rules of righteousness, driving straight in the plan of God, and giving all the proper signals as you practice what you preach?

Paul reminded the Philippian Christians that he had lived and taught among them, and he exhorted them to follow his example. But in holding up his own life and belief as a model for others, he reminds his readers even two millennia later that it is the duty and joy of mature believers to set a good example for newer and less mature Christians to follow. When people watch your life, do they see a good example of how Christians live out what they say they believe?

A man told a pastor he was going through a difficult time because one of his daughters was struggling with whether or not she really believed Christian faith was true. But he said there was hope because his mother was seriously ill. The pastor was confused and asked him why his sick mother gave hope to his struggling daughter. The man replied that his daughter adored her grandmother and that if she saw her living with joy and victory because of her faith, her example might demonstrate that being a Christian is worth it.

Your walk today may be a test. Watch yourself and see what kind of example you are.

Father, if Christ is in us, let him come out in all we do and say today. Amen.

For every one that asketh receiveth; and he that seeketh findeth; and to him that knocketh it shall be opened.

God listens

Answering machines have made it a familiar sound: "Hi, I'm not here right now, but if you'll leave your name and number, I'll call you back." It's convenient to be able to contact people through messages since they aren't always at home. But what if you heard, "Hi, I'm not home right now. If you need me, forget it—I'm fishing. If it can wait, why didn't you call later in the first place? If you have a computer, email me—I'll check my email in a week or so. If you don't have email, write it down and mail it; what do you think the post office is for? Come to think of it, what good did it do you to call me at all? At the tone, hang up." How would you like to have that answer in a recording? Some business answering services are nearly as aggravating. You get a recording that gives you options, each of which gives you another set of options and so on, until you have no more options but to listen to the list again or simply hang up.

Aren't you glad that when you pray, you don't get an answering service? Some people don't feel they get much response at all, but if you *practice* prayer, you will begin to realize that every time you go to God, he is waiting, as if you were the only one talking with him, the only one who needed him that moment. In fact, God has no difficulty spending one-on-one time with every person in the world. His loving heart goes out to you and listens, and when you listen for him, he speaks to the waiting heart and the spiritually attuned ear.

Jesus' instructions were to ask and keep on asking—that's the meaning of the verb he used. He said to seek and keep on seeking, and to knock and keep on knocking. He promised that when we pray, God listens and meets our needs out of his gracious and merciful heart.

Father, thank you that we may find you in the quiet place of prayer and that you never turn a deaf ear if we come honestly and humbly, not hiding our sin or our need. Amen.

For the preaching of the cross is to them that perish foolishness; but unto us which are saved it is the power of God.

Foolishness?

Government from the national to the state level has involved itself in campaigns to encourage the wearing of seat belts in cars. In many states, seat belts are mandatory for persons under a certain age, and in some places laws may be enacted soon to require belts on all passengers regardless of age. There are serious arguments against fining people who don't wear seat belts, but no one can argue successfully that seat belts don't save lives—they do. Similarly, life jackets and other flotation devices save lives of boaters. Yet many people go boating and fishing without jackets, and every year we hear the statistics on how many people die because they were not wearing safety devices.

Why is it that we have just enough of a streak of pride or foolhardiness in us that we say to ourselves, "It won't happen to me—I don't need sissy things like seat belts or life preservers"? The foolishness is not limited to earthly dangers, however. The Bible says that through the crucifixion and resurrection of a man named Jesus, people can be forgiven of sin and have the gift of eternal life. To many people that idea seems unlikely at best. In fact, it seems foolish to them to talk about the cross and the blood of Jesus as having anything to do with living life in the twenty-first century. They laugh it off or scoff at it, believing that their own method of dealing with the prospect of eternity without God will be good enough. But it won't. God is in charge of heaven's gates and is the sole arbiter of who enters them. His plan is to receive those who receive the message of the cross.

We who have believed on the Jesus who died on the cross for our sins know that it is the only power of God unto salvation. Men may call it foolish and promptly turn it down, but that old cross of Jesus contains our heavenly crown.

Father, help us not to take lightly the cross of Christ. Let it be both a reality to us and our message to others today. Amen.

Your fathers did eat manna in the wilderness and are dead. This is the bread which cometh down from heaven, that a man may eat thereof, and not die.

How often do you eat?

Imagine a poll being taken on a sidewalk in your town:

"Hello, sir. We're taking a poll: would you tell us what you had for lunch?"

"I'd be glad to, but I didn't have lunch."

"Well, then please describe the last meal you had."

"Oh, let me see, turkey and dressing, cranberry sauce, sweet potatoes…all the usual Christmas fixings."

"In February?"

"Oh, no, it was on December 25."

"You must have eaten since then."

"No, I really don't see the need. Christmas dinner is such a special event. I never miss holidays like that—or Easter."

"I thought you looked a bit thin. But what about daily food?"

"I never saw the need. *(Looks at his watch)* Sorry I have to run, but I have a doctor's appointment. He thinks I have some serious condition. Malnutrition or anemia or something."

Long ago, the Jews celebrated the ancient miracle of manna, recalling how people were fed by God in the wilderness. It was a wonderful, miraculous provision. Yet Jesus reminded the Jews of his day that their forefathers, who had eaten this miracle bread, all died. His point was that amazing experiences did not change biological realities: we all die. However, Jesus went on to teach that he is the bread from heaven who changes spiritual realities. Christ, the Bread of Life, brings eternal life when we partake of him. Jesus said we are to live daily by every word that proceeds out of the mouth of God. We need this spiritual sustenance from the word of God every day.

Don't make the mistake of depending on some special spiritual experience of your past to get you through life. Spiritual bread needs to be eaten every day. Jesus is that bread.

Jesus, feed us with your own living Spirit and presence as we turn to you through Scripture. Amen.

I was glad when they said unto me, Let us go into the house of the Lord.

Mondays

Mondays have gotten a bad name. Probably it's because of the use of Sunday just to play—maybe a bit too hard. Or perhaps it's due to staying up late trying to eke out the last fragment of recreation before going back to work on Monday. Of course, some people are in jobs they hate. Monday is a bad day if you see it primarily as the weekly end of your real life.

Many Christians, however, find Mondays pleasant or even exciting. The difference, said one believer, is church. He explained: "Have you ever read in the Psalms, 'I was glad when they said unto me, let us go into the house of the Lord'? After church on Sunday night, we say, 'It was good to be in the house of the Lord.' I believe that makes the difference in Monday. Church refreshes me. It starts me out new, with spiritual energy, with a sense of cleansing and power, with fresh hope and a revived outlook."

The Psalmist was glad to see the weekend come, not because of the prospect of recreation, but because of the promise of worship. Christians who worship genuinely with the body of Christ on Sunday will, like David, be glad, not only for the experience of a few hours, but for the positive effect that church tends to have on life during the week.

A couple seriously in love went to schools two hundred miles apart from each other. But every weekend each drove a hundred miles to the little town in between where they had grown up. They spent every waking hour with each other for a day, and then drove back late Sunday night. People asked if it was difficult to maintain a relationship when they were so far apart. They admitted it could be challenging, but as one of them said, "The day we spend together gets us through the whole week. I literally float through Monday."

If Monday is a down day, perhaps Sunday needs to be more "up." Look to see if the time you spend with the bride of Christ is feeding your soul. Perhaps more preparation is in order.

Father, let us not only attend worship but also meet you there and be recharged regularly for all of life. Amen.

My mouth shall show forth thy righteousness and thy salvation all the day; for I know not the numbers thereof.

Because time is short

It is curious what people choose to do sometimes when they muse on the fact that they don't know how long their lives will be. Some people, in the spirit of the old maxim, "Eat, drink, and be merry, for tomorrow you may die," become desperate to engage in every pleasure the world has to offer—the permissible and the forbidden alike. To those for whom death is the end of all life, it appears reasonable to throw caution to the wind and pack as much entertainment as is possible into this brief existence.

Some people are not so hedonistic, yet they procrastinate about "getting right with God," because they aren't yet ready to settle down. They, too, believe that they may miss out on something fun if they walk the strait and narrow too soon. Often, time runs out before people finish sowing their wild oats, and they don't get right with God at all.

The child of God, however, should be convinced that this life is only a minuscule prelude to the wondrous eternity that follows. Sin introduced death into the world, along with every human and natural evil, and death is an enemy because it threatens to make permanent the alienation from God every human being experiences. But receiving the gift of God, which is forgiveness and eternal life in Christ, changes our eternal destiny. Death becomes a moment that, while often unpleasant, is no longer to be feared. Instead, it transfers the believer from earth to heaven, from mortal to immortal, from the sinful world to sinless glory.

Consequently, the Christian must not consider his time on earth the only opportunity to enjoy life. In glory he will have all the time in the world. However, since most people do not have this eternal certainty, the Christian has an important priority for his earthly years. He should join the Psalmist in filling his days with praise and witness because the time *is* short, and multitudes of people need to hear there is a Savior. If you knew there were no tomorrow on this side of life, how many people would you try to tell about eternal life in Jesus Christ today?

Savior, with thanksgiving for your salvation, I renew my commitment to share it with others. Amen.

For if, when we were enemies, we were reconciled to God by the death of his Son, much more, being reconciled, we shall be saved by his life.

What a friend we have

A bitingly funny description of acquaintances who slight us suggests that "with friends like that, who needs enemies?" People do not always treat their friends right. But God always does. Yet many people apparently think that God isn't very kind to his friends. On the one hand, we talk about God's love. But the idea is very common that God is waiting to pounce on us for the least infraction, or that he withholds his blessing until we really deserve it. Until then we may imagine that he looks at us with one lifted eyebrow all the time, monitoring us with a stern dispassion.

With friends like that, who needs enemies! If that is your image of God, you have the wrong God. The God of the Bible is not that way. If you are a Christian, you need to learn the immense implications of Romans 5:10 for your life. Christ *died* for our sins: much *more* will he deliver us by means of his life. If God loved and saved you even when you were ignoring him, fighting him, or even mocking him, what attitude must he have toward you now that you are his friend? God has not replaced one system of law with another. The Old Covenant is based on law. The New Covenant is based on grace, since we could never deserve God's love by obedience to laws. Grace says, "I know you are miserable in your sins. What you need to know is that you can never deserve my love. But I love you anyway. Come to me for fresh forgiveness and a new gift of life and strength."

You cannot imagine God's love and desire to bless you. Be confident in the love of God. He is grieved when you sin, but he is eager to receive you when you confess. Your forgiveness is already finished in the work of Christ. Today, let no negative image of God keep you from coming close to him as your heavenly Father. Stay in good fellowship all day, knowing he loves you dearly, and is your best friend of all.

Father, thank you for your undying love, expressed through your dying Son. May we never doubt your heavenly welcome to our repentant spirits. Amen.

All scripture is given by inspiration of God, and is profitable for doctrine, for reproof, for correction, for instruction in righteousness.

Being corrected

The Bible says of itself that it is God-breathed. A major function of the inspired word of God is the correction of our errors, both of belief and of action, and the instruction of us in ways that are right. The Bible finds us living one way and teaches us to live another. Yet, how often the word of God finds unwilling subjects, resistant to being told anything different than what we have always believed or done.

In his nationally syndicated column, Sydney Harris once commented on human stubbornness: "Our emotional reflexes are so strong that the moment an adversary challenges our views, we become more dogmatic about them; thus, all opposition tends to make us more extreme." How true! However, in spiritual things, when it is the word of God instructing us, it is not merely emotional reflexes but sin within us that balks at being told what is right. Sin makes us hate being told we are in sin. Sin even begrudges us the need of forgiveness. Sin doesn't want a Savior. Yet salvation for the unsaved person, or renewal for the saved one, is all about this very thing: humbling ourselves to receive the instructing word of God, and obeying it, first repenting of our sinful ways. At some point, we will tire of sin's enslavement of us, and we will be attracted to Jesus Christ, who can free us.

No doubt today God will move upon you by some word of his, prompting you to leave some way, habit, belief or pursuit, and to come into conformity to his word and will. He may bring to your mind a verse or phrase from the Bible, a proverb, a lesson from an Old Testament story, a prophet's exhortation, or a teaching of Jesus, and through that word whispered in your heart he will correct and instruct you. Your question right now, even before that encounter with the Holy Spirit takes place, is, "Will I obey?"

Father, as by the one Teacher, your Spirit, you speak to me today, may I above all be teachable. Amen.

And all things whatsoever ye shall ask in prayer, believing, ye shall receive.

Optimism in God

Pessimism simply does not pay. Nevertheless, some pessimists insist that it does. Their humorously-put wisdom goes this way: the optimist is typically disappointed because things are almost never as rosy as he expects them to be, while the pessimist is happy most of the time because he is delighted by the number of things that go nicely, in spite of his dire predictions.

That "wisdom" works on paper, perhaps, but not in real life. Optimism and pessimism, it turns out, are not just attitudes; they are factors in what happens. This was the essential message of Jesus when he taught the disciples how to pray. He told them that what made prayer effective was a certain attitude accompanying their requests. Jesus recommended optimism, but not *just* optimism, but optimism *in God.* Christians call it *faith.*

Faith is believing: that God is good; that he has good plans for you; that he is in the process of working out those plans; and that in whatever situation you find yourself, God is going to work for your good, keep you spiritually safe, and stand with you through it all. Other people may doubt what you believe. Even close friends or relatives sometimes will not share your trust in God, or may not have grasped by faith the thing you seek and believe God will give. But the very essence of faith is that you go on believing that God will act and will bless you as you live confidently in him. Your continuation in believing is the difference between the believer and anyone else.

A humorous rule of life says, "The one who says it cannot be done should never interrupt the one who is doing it." God wants us to be the ones surprising everybody by doing the doubted thing, through his strength.

Father, our trust in you is completely founded. Help us to display that trust today, grasping by faith some blessing our hearts have longed for in your will. Amen.

Whom have I in heaven but thee? and there is none upon earth that I desire beside thee. My flesh and my heart faileth: but God is the strength of my heart, and my portion for ever.

Who can you trust?

Do you go through times when you come to realize that everything in this world is ultimately untrustworthy? Our friends are faithful, but there is so much they can do for us, and no more. Promises may be made in all sincerity, but things happen that none of us can predict, and promises may become null and void. Ultimately, the only unfailing foundation we have is the promises and proven faithfulness of God. The Psalmist expressed his reliance on God because of this very fact that human beings, as well intentioned as they may be, do not have the power and reliability of the King of Heaven. Therefore, as dear as people may become to us, our supreme desire should be toward the God who made and sustains us and who alone is sovereign over life.

To many people, to speak of the peace of the soul resting in God sounds simplistic, as if it amounted to nothing. To dismiss the concept reveals the absence of a relationship with God. Those who know the Lord know the calm that can come over a person from the very depths of who he is, a peace in knowing that God is in charge, and that whatever is unknown does not need to be known.

The basic confidence of most people is in themselves. But ultimately, we fail even ourselves, and we cannot help ourselves through passages we have not traveled. God wants to be our unfailing guide, our companion, our strength. But we must rest in him and commit our ways totally to him. When trouble comes, sickness comes, or death draws near, our trust in God makes the difference between standing firm and falling to pieces. It makes the difference between loneliness and not being alone, the difference between despair and confidence. Is your life in the care and keeping of the Almighty?

Father, let every sunbeam of this day light our way to you, and finding you, we will find life at peace. Amen.

And saviours shall come up on mount Zion to judge the mount of Esau; and the kingdom shall be the Lord's.

The final victory

Many places in the Old Testament prophets as well as the New Testament writings tell us of God's final victory over the enemies of righteousness. Obadiah prophesied against the Edomites, perennial thorns in the side of Israel and in particular of Judah. No doubt what Obadiah received from the Lord agreed with his own spirit as he looked at the way the Edomites had skirmished with Israel, had condemned them in their misfortune, and had taken advantage of them in their losses. Obadiah knew one day the Edomites would be repaid in full. His prophecy included a national defeat and rebuke.

The Edomites as a people have long been gone from history's scene. But Obadiah's message speaks to all those who pester, pelt and persecute the people of God. God's hands are held out in invitation to anyone to turn to him for forgiveness and a right relationship with him. But in the end, God will champion his people, oppose their enemies and his, and give the kingdom to his children. In the age of grace, the people of God are those who follow Jesus Christ by faith. The Christian should avoid a smug attitude about the world's being judged. However, God gives us the promise that the kingdom shall be his so that we may have the quiet confidence that our trials and the world's enmity will not last forever. The last page is known from the first to him before whom history is a book all in present tense.

God's promise of saviors to judge Esau ultimately finds its fulfillment in the Savior who came to judge sin, die for it, and deliver from it those who turn to him. He has become our assurance of final victory, and therefore our peace. We can both rejoice and rest in the risen one. He is in charge of history and of that part of history that concerns us most: our lives.

Father, your kingdom come. May it come in our lives today with peace and power. Amen.

Woe unto them that call evil good, and good evil; that put darkness for light, and light for darkness; that put bitter for sweet, and sweet for bitter!

Ancient evil

Someone coined a phrase called Voltaire's Law, that says, "Nothing is more respectable than an ancient evil." The wry remark is regrettably true. Adultery is becoming a respectable pastime for many people. Fornication is now innocently called "living together" by the generation that first promoted it. Homosexuality is championed by a public movement to recognize it as a perfectly valid lifestyle. Abortion and prostitution are other ancient evils with significant public support.

Isaiah pronounced fearsome woes upon those who declare wrong right and lambaste right as wrong, and the Psalmist said, "He that justifies the wicked and he that condemns the just, both of them are abomination to the Lord." The culture that celebrates perversion and castigates those who disapprove has crossed a line that should cause everyone to shudder with fearful anticipation.

One wonders how a culture so infused with Christian values could so quickly devolve into one so infested with immorality. The answer is twofold. Godly values must be held in the converted heart to be preserved, and they cannot be instilled by laws. Christians have failed to be the salt and light Jesus told us to be. Our complaints have often been private or restricted to the safe environments of church buildings. We have shrunk back from bold, costly and prophetic witness in public. Some of us, through the practice of silence, have pronounced virtual consent. Insufficiently opposed, evil has ascended.

The worst part of our culture's degradation is the prospect that an infant generation will grow up in a world where disapproval of immorality and perversion is so slight that it will be thought without merit. Our children and theirs may wonder why they should reject pleasures and lifestyles that virtually everyone else accepts. Such a prospect should shake us sober and motivate us to preach the word and change the world.

Father, help us to be clear on what is right and what is wrong, and to share with others the word of God, with love and urgency. Amen.

But what things were gain to me, those I counted loss for Christ.

The principle of conversion

Total changes in attitude may occur in our lives sometimes, when forces at work in us either overwhelm us suddenly or overtake us gradually over a period of time. The principle of conversion is that Christ brings about changes in our mentality, spirituality and activity that are often like night and day. For those whose lives may be mired in the deepest and worst kinds of sin, this conversion often is dramatic and fast-paced. For those who grow up in Christian settings and never really know a time when their lives are not deeply affected and controlled by moral influences, conversion may seem slower and less dramatic. But over time, the differences show up.

The apostle Paul experienced dramatic conversion, yet to a new covenant in the same family of faith. So his conversion shared aspects of the dramatic and undramatic. Yet he came to be able to distinguish things in his very religious past that were at odds with what God wanted of him. He told the Philippian church that he saw his previous advantages as interfering with his life in Christ. Before Christ, Paul valued most his ability to keep laws and to show himself righteous. After Christ, Paul realized he was not righteous at all without Christ, and he valued not his own abilities and worthiness, but that of Jesus Christ alone. The difference in his perspective was spiritual maturity.

It is troubling that we sometimes reverse values gained by conversion and again take a carnal view. Charles Adams, the 19th century diplomat, kept a diary. One day he entered: "Went fishing with my son—day wasted." His son, Brook Adams, also kept a diary. On the same day Brook's entry said, "Went fishing with my father—the most wonderful day of my life." How perspective changes our valuation of things. What is most important to you in life? Does your attitude need to "grow up?"

Father, you know where our hearts have values backwards of yours. Help us discover our need of a daily dose of conversion, until finally we are like Jesus. Amen.

Whatsoever thy hand findeth to do, do it with thy might...

Enthusiasm!

Children often learn verses such as Ecclesiastes 9:10 in Sunday School. The rest of the verse is usually not quoted with it: "for there is no work, nor device, nor knowledge, nor wisdom, in the grave, whither thou goest." The down-side of the verse suggests that our limited time in the world should prompt us to be energetic in everything. Better reasons exist. 1 Samuel 12:24 encourages us to serve the Lord with all our hearts, "for consider how great things he hath done for you." With or without Ecclesiastes' more depressing reasons, the first part of the verse is excellent advice: Be enthusiastic! What a difference enthusiasm would make in our everyday lives.

A therapist told his patient to overcome the doldrums by injecting enthusiasm into everything he did, even if he had to put on an act. He advised the man to get out of bed with enthusiasm, eat with enthusiasm, and work with enthusiasm. The patient went home but came back the next week more depressed than ever. The therapist wanted to know if he had even tried to follow the instructions. The man said, "That's why I'm depressed. The first day, I got up with enthusiasm, ate with enthusiasm, and then I kissed my wife goodbye with enthusiasm—and I was two hours late to work, and got fired."

We have to use good sense in everything, of course. But almost anything we do would be made better by an enthusiastic approach. Depression tends to bleed off on everyone. Blessedly, so does enthusiasm, and the Christian need not worry about having to keep up a pretense of passion or zealousness when he really doesn't feel it. Every believer in Christ has the power to be truly enthusiastic in serving and living for the Lord. It's called "the Holy Spirit." In fact, the word *enthusiasm* comes from the Greek meaning *"God inside."*

Even if at first a Christian must simply discipline himself to respond to difficult circumstances with an optimistic attitude, something about enthusiasm brings faith alive, and faith moves mountains. Go ahead—make your day. Do everything with enthusiasm!

Father, we grumble too much. You knew that. Turn our mouths up, and our hearts up, today. Amen.

June 2 **Scripture Reading: 1 Peter 4:8**

And above all things have fervent charity among yourselves: for charity shall cover the multitude of sins.

A covering of love

The Bible tells Christians to use love as our secret weapon to destroy the barriers erected by our many faults that otherwise would keep us from getting along. This timeless wisdom will facilitate not only Christian fellowship, but Christian witness as well.

A minister described a sloping path in his backyard leading to a little basement room where his shop was. As often traveled as it was, it got a lot of wear. At first, there was some grass there, but as the path was used more and more and hot weather and too little sunshine to grow the grass took their toll, the grass disappeared and the pathway became bare. Over several years, heavy rains caused the path to erode. Soil washed down into the lower parts of the yard, and as it did, the roots of the trees and all sorts of rocks appeared, making the path rough and even treacherous to tread at night. What once was a smooth path to a daily destination was now a rocky way of stumbling. The grass had been its savior, but now it was gone.

Love is like that grass, covering over many of the things that trip us up in life. Love smooths over things embedded in our personalities which when left open and raw can cause rocky relationships. Love is a blanket or a buffer between us and others. Neither Peter nor any apostle nor Jesus suggested in any way that a Christian who sins should think that repenting and asking forgiveness of those he offends is unnecessary. Peter's instruction is simply that those offended should not use the sins of others as ammunition to hurt them in return. Rather, they should let their love of those who hurt them outweigh any offense. In response to this love, others will seek forgiveness, and friendship will deepen and grow stronger.

We all have many deep-seated flaws, prejudices and lusts. Love is the humble recognition of our common failures. Let love bind us together where sin would tear us apart.

Father, the world doesn't operate as you do. But help us understand your wisdom instead, and use the secret weapon of love to overcome the disruption of our mutual sins. Amen.

He that speaketh truth sheweth forth righteousness: but a false witness deceit.

Honesty on display

Somebody said that nobody knows we are honest until we pass our samples. Proverbs 12:17 taught this truth some three millennia ago. It declared that someone who is righteous—a heart-and-soul characteristic—would speak truth—a live demonstration. While a person may believe he is honest at heart, it is what he does in his life that demonstrates it, both to others and to himself.

Stories abound of persons who were honest in a crisis and their honesty counted heavily in their witness. During the days when bus drivers actually took money and dispensed change, a man got on a bus and made a transaction, then took a seat. He found he had too much money returned, and he went back up front to tell the driver. The driver said he knew he had given the passenger too much change, and in fact that he had done so intentionally. "Why?" the man asked. The driver said he wanted to know if the man would call his attention to it. For the passenger was a Christian speaker the driver had heard the night before. Because the man was honest, the driver listened to his witness, and he was saved.

Honesty does count. Sometimes we are tempted to choose honesty when it will not hurt us, but fudge when it seems profitable or more comfortable. Some humorist wrote, "Isn't it interesting how we all want the butcher's scales to be scrupulously honest, but don't mind if the bathroom scales fudge a bit." Setting the bathroom scales to weigh a pound or two light does little harm to anybody. But perhaps such superficial actions underwrite a general tendency to be approximate about honesty. The Christian certainly doesn't need to go in that direction. Instead, believers need to scrupulously avoid the "white lie," "the spin," or even "the dodge" if it is designed to misrepresent the truth. Since our witness is all about what is true, we want to assure people they can trust what we say.

Father, since, as Jesus said, your word is truth, let ours be no less. Amen.

June 4 **Scripture Reading: 2 Corinthians 6:17**

Wherefore, come out from among them and be ye separate, saith the Lord.

Being above average

Did you know that on average there are some 950 million phone calls made every day in the U.S. alone? Or did you know that the average married couple converses twenty minutes in an entire week? The average person laughs fifteen times a day. An average American is exposed to 2,400 commercial messages every twenty-four hours. The average person in this country will move from one home to another twelve times in his life.

Are you average? In many ways, most of us are. There are things in which we don't mind being average. But there are things in which we all should want to far outstrip the average. We should want to be better than average Christians. Such a desire is not pride: it's holy aspiration. The average Christian spends about fifteen minutes per week praying. He or she averages talking specifically about the gospel about once per year. The average believer attends church only about one out of every five services, and gives only about three dollars out of a hundred to the Lord's work. By God's grace, we should hope to rise above the average Christian's performance.

The scriptures characterize the Israelites as a people set apart, or separate, from the other nations. The New Testament commands the same of Christians, not to be stand-offish, but to be markedly different from the world in the way they live morally, ethically, and spiritually.

Interestingly, most of us don't want to be lost in the crowd—to be considered completely average. But quite a few of us neglect to do anything above the norm. In fact, sometimes we avoid sticking out or being different. Consequently, we turn out average. The secret of being different is to be constantly enlivened and energized by Christ, so that we think his thoughts and do his works. God has a plan for us that is unique. When we follow his daily leading, our lives will be anything but average.

Father, thank you for being extraordinary. May we enter into your surpassing nature and rise above the world through Christ. Amen.

But the men marvelled, saying, What manner of man is this, that even the winds and the sea obey him!

The Lord our mighty friend

Some people expect too much from God, while others expect too little. The first sort may grow up outside the influence of Christian teaching, and may have a concept of God that he is for emergency use only. They are like people on a commercial airliner ignoring the flight attendant or the video demonstrating the use of flotation devices and pointing out exits. But let the plane get into trouble, and suddenly there is frantic interest in the escape routes and life preservers. Such people expect too much from God not because God couldn't step in and save them from all harm, or perhaps from themselves, but because his purpose is not typically to do so. Yet if he doesn't, they think they have further reason to ignore him in the future.

Other people are the opposite. They have been raised in church and have adopted a mild, moderate pursuit of God. Their concept of him is that he is with them but doesn't wish to make himself obvious. When these people get into trouble, they may indeed pray for help, but mostly they expect solace and gentle companionship. They may not imagine that God will do anything unusual to help them—certainly nothing miraculous.

Jesus' disciples were out on the sea one day when a storm arose, while Jesus slept in the bow. They came to him frantic and woke him, really just wanting him to make their worry unanimous. When Jesus stilled the storm with a word, they were flabbergasted. They had never expected such intervention.

Jesus is not just for emergencies, but neither is he simply a silent presence who will cry with you when trouble comes. He is the Lord of heaven. He is God. If you are his, and you daily walk with him, you will find sometimes he will display his power to forge the way for your safe passage. What you face today need not defeat you. The Lord is equal to it all, and he can make you the victor through his power.

Lord, show us both your compassion during things we must endure, and your mighty power to deliver us according to your will. Amen.

In the world ye shall have tribulation: but be of good cheer; I have overcome the world.

Accepting the unchangeable

Most of us are familiar with the famous prayer penned by Reinhold Niebuhr. The first four lines are the most remembered. They say, "God grant me the serenity to accept the things I cannot change, the courage to change the things I can, and the wisdom to know the difference." The first thought in Niebuhr's prayer expresses a deeply biblical idea. God's people need to stop worrying about things they have no ability to affect. Many believers waste much of their emotional and spiritual energy being frustrated over factors in their lives, circumstances and relationships that are not going to change.

What are some things you cannot change? Your identity is one. Many of your personality traits or talents cannot be either augmented or erased. You cannot change the inevitability of war, hatred, or violence, and perhaps you cannot stop the onslaught of unjust government. You cannot change your heritage. You cannot change the past. You cannot change other people's pasts, and unless other people allow you to, you cannot change them. Some of our most tiresome battles are fought with things we cannot budge. God, grant me the serenity to accept the things I cannot change.

In John 16:33, Jesus assured his disciples that they would have trouble in this world. The key to having peace in this life is first, of course, to know God through Jesus Christ. In addition, however, we need to accept the fact that knowing God does not give us immunity from trouble or miracle power to change everything around us. Some things will not be changed, as long as this age continues. We need the unruffled, tranquil composure to accept that. When we've learned what business God didn't put us here to do, maybe we can get on with what he did.

Father, we need to trust you to take care of things beyond our power, knowing that nothing is beyond yours. Amen.

But ye shall receive power, after that the Holy Ghost is come upon you…

Changing your world

The second part of Reinhold Niebuhr's famous "Serenity Prayer" is a petition for the kind of fortitude many of us desperately need: "Grant me…the courage to change the things I can." Often we are tempted to give up on our convictions too easily and say, I won't make any difference; my one little part will never change anything." With that excuse, we often let our convictions slide into meaningless statements of intellectual belief, unmatched by decisive action on our part.

The difference between believing and acting is often a thing called courage. It takes courage to act out our beliefs because some of the things a Christian believes demand a change in the world around him, or invite rejection, criticism or attack. The believer says, "This is unjust," and it takes courage to attempt to set that thing right. The believer says, "God wants this to happen," and it takes courage to make it happen for the glory of God. Our greater virtue lies not in the rightness of our beliefs but in the boldness of our actions. Winston Churchill said, "Courage is the greatest virtue. It makes all others possible."

Many things *can* be changed: people can be won to Christ; laws can be changed to reflect godly values; relationships can be mended; hundreds of other things that admittedly take some work on our part can be changed. For most of us, what we lack is not the ability to change things, but the courage of our convictions to get up and do it.

Jesus said we would receive power when the Holy Spirit came upon us. Then he told his disciples to go out and be his witnesses. We have no idea what the upper limit of our ability in the Spirit is, if there even is one. Jesus said we would do greater things than he. Whatever else that may mean, it certainly means we can make a difference in our world for Christ. God give us the courage to do it.

Father, like the disciples when first persecuted, let us not ask for relief, but for boldness to do even more for your glory and the name of Jesus Christ. Amen.

There was given to me a thorn in the flesh, the messenger of Satan to buffet me, lest I should be exalted above measure. For this thing I besought the Lord thrice, that it might depart from me.

Focusing your energies

If it is important to know what unchangeable things to accept, and what changeable things to change, it is extremely important to know the difference between the two. Much of our failure in life results from butting our heads into that which is immovable, or dodging the obstacles that need to be moved. Reinhold Niebuhr's "Serenity Prayer" expresses the desire for God to lead us to focus our energies on things we can affect or influence.

In the Bible, sometimes the difference between an illness being healed by miracle and another being treated with human remedies was merely that one *could* be treated and the other could not. For instance, Paul healed the father of Publius by the power of Christ, but he merely prescribed treatment for Timothy's stomach. Paul's own thorn in the flesh was not healed as he had prayed for, but rather endured. Yet, it took him a while to know just what attitude he would have to have toward this thing that plagued him.

We need wisdom when facing similar circumstances. We need to know when to do battle and when to wait calmly with grace and acceptance. The wisdom to know the difference is a heaven-sent thing, a sort of seeing with soul's eyes what course of action is of God. This wisdom is developed through practice, and perfected through exercise. It begins with little things like knowing when a friend is ready to hear our witness, and it grows until we begin to know the profitability of a pursuit before we get into it. At times, however, we cannot make a judgment confidently and we must pray to know God's direction, and he may lead us to focus on something that seems to yield little fruit. But our perceptions are frequently cloudy and limited. The key is to discover God's leading by whatever means, and then to pour ourselves into the task without reservation. The results we must leave up to him.

Father, let us not waste one moment today, but spend them all willingly on your perfect will. Amen.

Now do ye Pharisees make clean the outside of the cup and the platter; but your inward part is full of ravening and wickedness.

Deceiving appearances

In conversation, a Christian man told how he had a businessman friend who was one of the sharpest dressers he knew. His hair was always conservatively and immaculately kept. His clothes were always crisp, fresh and stylish. He never looked as if he needed a shave. His image was perfect. But this friend, said the Christian, was one of the worldliest, most casually immoral agnostics he knew. By contrast, another friend lived on a secondary road on the edge of a farm. She owned next to nothing. She tried to look presentable, but she was not always clean, and was generally unkempt looking. Her image was anything but perfect, but she was one of the sweetest, finest Christians imaginable.

Looks can be deceiving. Yet many people are more concerned with their looks than with their character. But are we what we make ourselves appear to be? For instance, are our religious habits and rituals indicative of the kind of people we really are, or are they misleading? Jesus indicted the Pharisees for polishing the exterior of their lives while leaving the interior full of filth. What he said strongly suggests that some people may make the errant assumption that God cannot see the inside of us, or that he ignores it.

Not only *can* God see what is inside us, he is always looking at it. If he ignored anything (which he doesn't), it would be the show we put on for public consumption. We ought not to be sloppy in appearance if we can help it, but far more important is that we not appear ragged morally and spiritually to God's eyes. Most of us need to spend more time bathing our hearts in prayer and the word, combing our conduct to remove sin's kinks, and dressing our lives in the righteousness of Christ, and less time in front of mirrors tending to appearances.

Father, lest we be decorated shells with death inside, help us tend to our hearts first and foremost. Amen.

Behold, now is the accepted time; behold, now is the day of salvation.

The only guaranteed time

Most of us don't have enough time to do everything we want to do. At least, that's what we say. We work, play or study at a furious pace. But in other matters we tend to think we have all the time in the world. Sometimes Christians put off being faithful in church until another stage of life when they expect to have fewer competing things to do. We may defer witnessing until some more suitable circumstances. Or we may procrastinate about our devotional lives or make excuses about getting involved in missions, because we just can't find the time. Some of us Christians who make such excuses are aware that non-Christians often do the same thing—they say they won't become Christians today because they aren't ready yet, and they believe they will have time later. In fact, they believe they have lots of life ahead of them to make the one decision the Bible says ought to be made *now.*

The reality of limited time applies to both non-Christians and Christians. The believer's mandate is to grow, to serve, to become. None of that mandate happens automatically: it is achieved by conscious decision and continuing obedience to God's will. What if we don't have as much time to obey later as we might think?

During a parachute jump, a sergeant instructed his men, "When you jump, from this altitude you have fifteen seconds to pull the main ripcord. If for some reason it does not function, pull the backup chute cord." A recruit raised his hand: "If the first chute fails, how long do we have to pull the second one?" The sergeant dead-panned his reply: "Son, you have the rest of your life."

You *do* have the rest of your life to do God's will, but that may be no longer than today. Why not adopt the bright and optimistic side of the same coin: I have today to serve the one who gave his life for me. Now is the day to fulfill his plan. Now is the time to make a difference for Christ. Whatever it is you may have put off until tomorrow, do it today. Right now is all the time you are guaranteed.

Father, not taking anything for granted, may we take the time you do grant us, and joyfully obey you. Amen.

Then said Thomas, which is called Didymus, unto his fellow disciples, Let us also go, that we may die with him.

Willing to die

Upon hearing of Lazarus' life-threatening illness, Jesus waited until death occurred and then announced he was going to Bethany where Lazarus lived—which was near Jerusalem. The disciples were alarmed because recently Jerusalem officials had threatened Jesus' life. Jesus' insistence on going despite the danger prompted Thomas to say what he did about going to "die with him." Many commentators believe that Thomas was being fatalistic, inviting martyrdom. It is just as possible to read his statement as a vow of brave commitment. We do not have enough context to say for sure. All we have are the simple words inviting people to go with Christ even though it meant death.

Most of us do not fear for our lives at any hour. Soldiers in the battlefield do; race car drivers and high rise steelworkers may; but the common person doesn't. In this context of relative safety, the words of Thomas are especially chilling. He was determined to go with Jesus even though he had good reason to believe it would be his last act. Most of us would find it challenging to have that kind of attitude. There are many things we want to do in this world. There are relationships we want to continue, things we would like to see, loved ones who need us. But we are aware that there really have been martyrs for Christ—many of them, and we know that the initial decision we make to receive Christ as Lord contains the pledge of ultimate commitment. We give our lives to Christ, even if living for his glory means dying for his name.

Two things help us to live with utter abandon for Christ. One is the experience of life's uncertainties and trials, which tend to make our eternal future more attractive. The other is the nature of spiritual growth, when we undertake it. When we come to Christ we not only resolve to be prepared to die, we *do* die—to sin and to self. With that death should go our selfish reasons for wanting to live. If we are called on to die for the name of Christ, God will certainly take care of whomever and whatever we leave behind.

Lord, as human beings we want to live. Help us to want more to glorify you, live or die. Amen.

Neither shall they say, Lo here! or, lo there! for, behold, the kingdom of God is within you.

Where can I encounter God?

Most pastors visiting the homes of infrequent attenders have heard someone say, "I love that church up there." Some of these folks are hypochondriacs who think they cannot go—or want you to think so. But they *love* the church *up there.* Aside from the lesson in phony love, something else lies in their words. Why is the church "up there" or "over there"? It is as if the person thought the church were somewhere else, and that he himself was not part of it.

If you have had an experience of new birth from the Holy Spirit as you placed faith in Christ, you *are* part of the church. What's more, the church isn't anywhere else so much as it is in you, shared with all others who know Jesus in a saving way. Jesus told his disciples that when people tried to divert their loyalties to this or that charismatic leader or movement, they were to remember that the kingdom of God was right where they were, because it was in them.

The church is the focus of God's kingdom work in this age, and Jesus' words about where his kingdom was to be found have a vital practical application. If we Christians want to encounter God, we should look in our hearts, where Christ was invited to live when we said "yes" to him. The implications for this truth are important for an age in which people are looking for a worship "experience," and churches are hiring worship designers, or even producers. Aside from the fact that worship can be truly inspiring in a church building with other believers, it is also a fact that many Christians are under the impression that *real* experiences with God are the result of a unique combination of place, music, leaders, and style. Where they *go* to church seems to be more important than whether or not church is *going on* in them.

Let us orient our lives less toward *experiences* and *places* and more toward our relationship with the Savior inside us, and our walk with him in his Spirit.

Father, remind us that while you are in heaven, you are also in Jesus, and that Jesus said he was with us, till the end of the age. Amen.

Ye shall know them by their fruits. Do men gather grapes of thorns, or figs of thistles?

What did you plant?

Some foods we don't think twice about eating nowadays were once thought to be poisonous—tomatoes, for instance. But in other cases some varieties of the same basic plant are indeed poisonous—take mushrooms, for example. Many of us enjoy mushrooms, fresh in salads, or sauteed in lots of butter! But our enthusiasm for them may be diminished when we first learn that most varieties of mushrooms are not edible, and some of them are deadly. But we have no reason to fear. We don't hear of people buying poisonous mushrooms in stores, for the simple reason that the people who grow them know what they are planting. Mushroom spores of good varieties were introduced to their growing areas and all other kinds were kept out. When harvest time comes they don't have to pick through the crop to weed out the toxic varieties.

It only makes sense that what you plant is what you will reap. That's true not only with vegetables but with character, morality and spiritual values. Grapes do not grow on thorn bushes, and responsible adult behavior is not the result of sowing wild oats while young. Figs do not grow on trees with thistles, and compassionate service is not learned by a regimen of self-centeredness. Jesus said to his disciples, "You shall know them by their fruits," but the reverse is just as true: They shall know you by your fruits." What do we wish people to know or think about us? What, then, have we planted—because that's what fruit will appear in time.

Do you long to be influential in others lives for good and for God? Then are you planting the seeds of character and solid relationships now? Do you want to have an honorable and godly family? Then are you planting the seeds of discipline and devotion now? Do you hope to hear God say, "Well done, good and faithful servant"? Then are you planting the seeds of sacrificial service and faithful following now?

Father, we want to enjoy our lives' fruits, and we want them to redound to your glory. Help us to recognize continually what seeds we are planting. Amen.

June 14 **Scripture Reading: Luke 22:32**

But I have prayed for thee, that thy faith fail not.

The intercession of Jesus

If you are like many people, at times the greatest obstacle you have is a feeling of defeat. You made promises to yourself you haven't kept and set goals for yourself you haven't reached and believe you never will. You are certain God is disappointed in you and perhaps will not forgive you for your miserable failure. If this doesn't describe the way you have felt at some time in your life, you are wonderfully blessed. Many of us have run headlong into this debilitating emotional mire.

Besides putting a depressive damper on your attitude, lingering disappointment in yourself contributes to a cycle of failure—feeling you are a failure nearly ensures that whatever you attempt will fall through. Perhaps the disappointment is not entirely justified. Miles Stanford said, "To be disappointed in oneself is to have trusted in oneself." We may have been trusting in our own strength to accomplish God's will or Christian living, when we should have been trusting in God. Trying to draw supernatural strength from ourselves to accomplish a supernatural goal, it isn't surprising that we would fail.

The apostle Peter faced severe self-condemnation just after the rooster crowed. He realized he had done just what Jesus said he would and just what he vowed he wouldn't. He had made a "do-or-die" promise to Jesus believing he had the wherewithal to keep it. He didn't. Yet Jesus reassured him: "I have prayed for you." While Jesus was on the earth, he carried out a ministry of intercession for his disciples and others. It must have been the greatest encouragement of all to Peter to know that Jesus himself had prayed for him. However, John 17:20 says that Jesus prayed for all of us who would believe the gospel and follow him. Another scripture, Hebrews 7:25, may imply that Jesus' eternal role in the presence of the Father may include a permanent state of intercession for his followers in all their trials and challenges.

Since the Lord is pulling for you, trust him today to work in and through you what you have been unable to do while depending on yourself.

Lord, failure has reminded me not to count on myself for everything, but on you instead. Amen.

The foxes have holes, and the birds of the air have nests; but the Son of Man hath not where to lay his head.

An appeal to faith

A television program on mail fraud provided an eye-opening look at one of the more deceptive enterprises of modern criminals. All of us have had experiences with fraudulent offers. It's just that some of us are taken in by them. For the most part, there is no shame in that; however, there are some clues that an advertisement may be promising more than it can deliver. One of the surest signs is the promise of quick money, and lots of it. A want ads publication ran a notice stating, "Make money fast! Grow fish worms." Another said, "Little known secrets! How to buy a new car at $125 above dealer cost." A chance exists that these ads were not fraudulent, but the odds are two to one or better that they were not all they seemed to be.

The appeal to great gain is attractive to most of us—so much so that the promise of gain is cause for suspicion, and the conspicuous absence of any such promise is a fair sign of trustworthiness. Jesus knew this, and his own invitations to men were straightforward, not promising all kinds of things that people's greed would respond to. In fact, he told one man who followed on his heels that he didn't even have the certainty of a bed to go to that night. He never promised worldly goods as an incentive for following him.

We may be tempted to think that if we live for Christ this morning he will proportionately bless us with a bank deposit this afternoon. But the blessings Christ offers are real, and more lasting than money. In fact, the Lord does not even promise the shimmering lure of miracles, celestial visions, or earth-shaking experiences—at least not now. What he does is to offer us spiritual riches, wisdom, love, peace of heart, and fellowship with God. His appeal is not to greed, or even to the powerful desire for "experience," but to the challenge of faith. He calls us to believe him, to want him for himself, and to follow him at any cost.

Lord, help us to seek the Giver rather than the gift today, and to trust you to grant us what we really need. Amen.

He that is not with me is against me: and he that gathereth not with me scattereth.

No neutral ground

Some people who have traveled to Europe note that in many cases their cities are litter-free while many American cities are strewn with trash. Perhaps the observation is not so accurate, as quite a few European spots are not so clean. The same contrast exists in the United States, where some cities are remarkably attractive and others bear witness to the slovenly habits of their residents. Back in the sixties when the modern anti-pollution movement began, a phrase made the rounds of T-shirts and bumper stickers: "If you're not part of the solution, you're part of the pollution." While some people might resent the implication that they are less than good citizens, the point is clear: most people pollute mildly. If you're not helping keep things clean, you're helping keep them dirty.

In many areas of life there is no truly neutral ground. Either you are involved in solving a problem or you are by implication part of it. Jesus laid out this truth when talking of himself. He frankly told his disciples that they were either with him or against him. Quite simply, we are either Christians or not; we belong to him or we do not. We either serve him or we serve ourselves; we love him or we do not, we obey him or we defy him. There is no in-between. We may wish we could straddle the fence and still say we are Christians dedicated to God. But the call of Christ is to confess him openly, to take sides with him, to choose him and no one else. This is what it means to make him Lord.

Perhaps because it so clearly announces whose side we are on, witnessing to our faith is a key area where our true loyalties become known. We either "gather" with Christ by sharing him with others, or we help the world to obscure the gospel by our remaining silent. Do others know we know Christ? Have we left the myth of neutrality for the open confession of discipleship?

Lord, may we choose to be on your side in our principles, our actions, and our words today. Amen.

If he trespass against thee seven times in a day, and seven times in a day turn again to thee, saying, I repent; thou shalt forgive him.

Neutralizing acid

At one time, doctors researching stomach ulcers noticed that people with more than the usual anger, worry or stress seemed to develop ulcers more frequently than others. For a while the common treatment was a bland diet and relaxation. Then, continuing research discovered a physical cause: the bacterium *Helicobacter pylori*. Twenty percent of people under forty have it in their stomachs already. The bacteria bore into the lining of the stomach or duodenum and weaken it. Then, some people develop ulcers, but not all—why?

Scientists are having to come back to the first, common-sense answer. Bacteria make the ulcer more likely. But often the trigger is still the production of excess acid resulting from unresolved, negative emotions that "eat" at us. One of these is an unforgiving attitude. Close kin to bitterness, an unforgiving spirit is a lingering anger. We may repress it or wear it on our faces, but the effect is the same. Since people are whole beings, body and soul, the one affects the other—sometimes brutally. The required treatment is obvious: we have to neutralize this acid of the soul.

Some people say, "I don't *feel* I can ever forgive." There is the problem. Forgiveness is not something you must feel in order to do. You must do it by choice. Jesus told his followers to forgive, repeatedly, habitually, lavishly. We often ration forgiveness and mentally put people on probation. But every implication of Jesus' words, "seven times in a day," is that forgiveness is first a disciplined decision. He didn't suggest that we should live a lie; he simply taught us to obey first, trusting him, and expect feelings to follow faith. When you choose to forgive, release your feelings of anger and resentment to God, and do not go back on your choice. Soon you will feel the forgiveness, and you may stop a lot of ulcers from ever beginning.

Father, forgive us for not forgiving. Heal the wounds our attitudes have caused, especially those between us and others. Amen.

For the Son of man is not come to destroy men's lives, but to save them.

New lives for old

Sometimes the worst part about getting something new is anxiety about getting rid of the old. For example, we tend to get attached to our cars and hate to give them up. We know a new one will look better, drive better, and be more reliable, but we've gotten attached to the old heap. Or consider the church that learned from a building inspector that its sanctuary had been found unsafe and had been condemned. Fixing it was not an option. They had to tear it down and build a new one. For longtime members, it was a painful event. But the new one was even better.

Jesus taught his disciples that his ministry was not about destruction but construction. He didn't come to make people miserable, but joyful. The gospel is not the bad news of what God hates about you, but the good news of how much God loves you. Many people are reluctant to become Christians because they fear the destruction of their current lives. They don't want to give up this or that. They see Christianity as a negative state: denying things, forbidding things, losing things. They do not understand that Christian faith is positive, too: receiving a new and eternal life, acquiring profitable character, knowing the God of love and power.

When a person becomes a Christian, his new birth results in his not wanting to live in the gutter—so there isn't much to miss. The other side of the coin is that some things in our lives *do* need to be forsaken in order to have eternal life. But what would a man give in exchange for his own soul? Non-Christians may forfeit eternal life itself by being unwilling to trade their old lives for new. But as a Christian, have you been held back in spiritual growth because of resistance to God's purifying work? Is Christ unable to continue his saving work in you because you are holding on to things that need to go? Count the cost and surrender fully. You will discover what God actually gives will outweigh what you thought you would lose.

Father, help us defeat the temptation to think of your will as restriction instead of freedom. Amen.

Children's children are the crown of old men; and the glory of children are their fathers.

Cherish them now

Father's Day was conceived in 1909 by Mrs. John Dodds, whose father had been both father and mother to her. Mrs. Dodds felt that a day honoring fathers was as important as one honoring mothers, and a campaign to establish Mother's Day was being carried on at that very time. Woodrow Wilson proclaimed Mother's Day in 1914. Father's Day also caught on generally, but curiously enough it wasn't until 1972 that Richard Nixon signed a congressional resolution making it official.

Plenty of bits of wisdom inform us that children are the pride of their parents. All you have to do is ask most parents—not to mention grandparents!— what they love most. But the Proverb writer said also that fathers are the pride of their children. The Bible salutes the pride children take in their fathers. Wonderful fruit can be produced in the lives of children who have and admire a dad who is a worthy model to emulate. Yet the father who is the best model does not pretend he is perfect. Frank A. Clark said, "A father is a man who expects his son to be as good a man as he meant to be."

Most of us need to be reminded to cherish our fathers, and more generally our parents and grandparents, while we still have them, for the years quickly slip by. At four years old a child says, "My daddy can do anything." At eight he says, "My dad knows everything." At twelve he thinks, "My dad doesn't know what's going on." At eighteen he says, "Dad is out of touch." At twenty-five he thinks, "Dad may have been right." At thirty-five he says, "Daddy, what do you think?" At fifty, he says, "My dad was so wise." And at sixty-five he pines, "I wish I could talk it over with Dad once more."

Whether you have the privilege of celebrating a living father's love or honoring your father's memory, take time to cherish those whom God places in your life to love and guide you.

Father, thank you for your plan for the family. Deepen my love for my own family, and my godliness as a model for all. Amen.

For through him we both have access by one Spirit unto the Father.

No lines

Everybody waits in lines. While you wait, you begin to notice things, such as how often the shortest line is also the slowest, or how you always seem to pick the line where someone has an item with no tag, and the cashier is waiting uncertainly on a clerk to call back with a price. In the spirit of Murphy's Law, someone has compiled the laws of lines: 1. If you're running for a short line, it suddenly become a long line; 2. When you are waiting in a long line, the people behind you are shunted to a newly-opened, short line; 3. If you step out of a short line for a second, it becomes a long line; 4. If you are in a short line, the people in front let their friends in and make it a long line; and finally, 5. A short line outside a building becomes a long line inside.

Waiting is a part of life. But aren't you glad you don't have to wait in line to get to God? Hebrews teaches us that Christ opened the way to God through his own blood and that we should take advantage of it by coming boldly to the Lord, and Paul taught that we have access to the Father by the Holy Spirit. That simple statement in the present tense means there is no waiting, no line, and no barrier. This intimate access means that there is no reason for our ever feeling profoundly alone. Full access means we are not denied anything we truly need to live for the Lord—any provision, any strength, any counsel, any wisdom. Instant access means we need never fear God's help will come too late, so long as we ourselves do not procrastinate in prayer.

Occasionally we may have the feeling that other people have had encounters and blessings in the Lord that we have missed out on. We may conclude that God has placed us on hold, or that we're waiting in line for something we have so far been denied. God's plans for people differ, but his plan for you is perfect, and his supply for you is complete. He is ready to provide when you are willing to leave whatever else has been occupying your mind, heart, and time, and there's no line in prayer.

Lord, grant that today I will not cheat myself of your rich provision by failing to take advantage of the access I have through the Spirit. Amen.

I am poured out like water, and all my bones are out of joint: my heart is like wax; it is melted in the midst of my bowels.

Needing a refill

If you have lived very long, you have felt something like the Psalmist when he described himself as being poured out—you feel you don't have strength to go on or the heart to care. The Psalmist's words painted a picture of despondency and weakness of the very soul. You may experience this same dissolution when everything in general comes crashing down around you, or when some specific adversary, spiritual or physical, assaults you with particular ferocity. A death, the loss of work, personal illness, trouble at home, or a multitude of other things can leave you feeling empty and impotent. What do you do about it?

The Psalmist responded to the need he described in Psalm 22 with the supply he described in Psalm 23: "The Lord is my shepherd: I shall not want." Throughout that psalm, David told how God met his every need through his inward working and providential leading. When life left David needing a refill, he got it from his spiritual pastor—the Lord himself.

Many people have found that repeating the 23rd Psalm or the Lord's Prayer has a soothing effect when they are troubled. But if we are to have a refilling of strength, a rebuilding of boldness and commitment, a renewal of faith and vision, we must do more than repeat words by rote, even divinely inspired words. We must dig deeply into devotional life, studying and internalizing the Bible, praying honestly and passionately, meditating and listening for the still, small voice of the Spirit of God. The Bible says it is when we keep our minds stayed on the Lord that he keeps us in perfect peace.

Lord, life is very hard sometimes—as you said it would be. Keep our cup filled with your joy, our hearts filled with your praise, and our minds filled with your purpose. Amen.

As he went out of the temple, one of his disciples saith unto him, Master, see what manner of stones and what buildings are here! And Jesus answering said unto him, Seest thou these great buildings?

What do you see?

Everyone ought to have his eyesight tested now and then. Vision problems have a way of sneaking up on us gradually. The same is true with spiritual vision. Remarking on the grandeur and the sheer immensity of the temple building in Jerusalem, Jesus' disciples said he should "see the size of those things!" Jesus' response was a question that aimed the same idea back at them: "Do *you* see?" They saw impressive structures, monuments to man's ability to create, feats of engineering—in short, they saw monuments to the glory of man. Jesus saw another thing: the temporal developments of human vanity, the misplaced hopes of a people blinded in unbelief, buildings signifying the trust of man in man, not in God. He saw them as symbols of religion not matched by hearts of worship, and thus delivered by the hand of God into the hands of coming armies. Jesus was not so much as impressed as he was sorrowful.

When we see, do we really see? When you see the world of amazing technological development, are you so awed by the inventiveness of man that you forget that it will soon be wiped away in the destruction of this present world? When you see evil, are you completely depressed, as if it will always prevail—forgetting that it will be overthrown when Christ returns? Or when you look at normal, everyday life, do you just see what everyone else sees, or do you see in it the unique opportunity to serve God through the minutes and hours of every precious day God gives you to live?

How we see determines how we live. If we see only what the world sees, we will live as the world lives. If, with the eyes of faith, illuminated by the indwelling Spirit of God, we see what God sees, we will mind the things of God. That's what God is always trying to get us to do.

God who sees all, let us see through what is false and past what is temporary. Let us instead set our sights on what is godly and for what is eternal. Amen.

Ye must be born again.

New beginnings

Fast food restaurants follow each other's leads with every new twist in menu items. When all chains were offering hamburgers, a new chain introduced biscuits. The biscuit wars were on as each of the other chains came out with its own biscuit offering, and each in turn boasted that its biscuits were the biggest and best. Actually, that title probably still belongs to a farm wife in a little country church.

During his 1975-76 campaign for the U.S. presidency, Jimmy Carter characterized himself as a born-again Christian. The subject of being born again rapidly swept the country and continued to energize conversation among non-Christians, some of whom exhibited breathless excitement in their quest to find out what this "new" development was. Others knew already, and showed prejudicial disdain. As we know, the new birth is an old subject. Jesus told Nicodemus he had to be born again. In fact, he said being born again was essential to seeing the kingdom of heaven—another way of saying *going* to heaven. Being born again is not a higher level of Christianity, as if there were more than one level. It is not a deeper experience or a fine classification. Being born again is the way anyone who really is a Christian became one. Some people who call themselves Christians don't think of themselves as having been born again, but the Bible is clear that we must be born to new spiritual life because our spirits are dead from sin until we are.

There is a time in your life when you are ready for what God wants to do. If you have not been born again by God's power, you may be ready to seek the new beginning only God can work in your heart. If you are already a Christian, perhaps it is a fresh work of God that you need. God may be calling you to a new step of faith or a deeper surrender to Christ, so that he may inaugurate a new time of growth, holiness, or excitement in your pilgrimage with him. For every soul who turns to him in hunger for his best, God prepares new blessings and eternal life.

God, let us discover the newness and excitement of blessings that have been waiting for us since the beginning of time. Amen.

A fool's wrath is presently known: but a prudent man covereth shame.

Opting out of anger

Do you have trouble keeping your temper? We all know people who fly off the handle at the least little thing—hopefully we are not those people, ourselves! On the other hand, most of us marvel at a few people we know who either never or almost never get angry. Most of us are in between: our thresholds of anger are not exceeded by the littlest provocation, but we don't hold off forever—we let off steam under pressure. The Proverb writer spoke of the wrath of the fool as being "presently known." That's King James English for, "He blows his top right away." Instead, we should be like the prudent man, who "covereth shame," meaning to overlook an insult.

Some experts tell us that it is good for us to let anger out, and that if we don't, it will bury deep inside us and cause high blood pressure, or come out later in a destructive way. But if what the Proverb writer is saying is to be followed, we must not bury anger but either re-channel it or just not have it to begin with. Some people express anger through sports, exercise, or even art or writing. But what Solomon had in mind was probably that the wise man simply doesn't let himself get mad over things that don't truly warrant it.

Some will object that psychologists say we shouldn't repress anger. True enough, but we don't have to *be* angry at all, outwardly or inwardly. It is possible to grow in spirit to become a person who is not angered by unworthy things. Anger is a choice. Our response to people and situations is up to us. People don't make us angry: we choose to become angry, even if only automatically. The best defense against the automatic choice to be angry is to draw close to Christ until we are so satisfied with his life and purpose that we become joyful within and are not always on edge. As his life is recreated in us, we learn his peace and power, and we begin to deliver up to God the things we cannot handle alone. In this way, any Christian can have the proverbial "patience of a saint," and never have to be plagued with a quick temper.

Father, help us to make Jesus our all in all, so that his peace and patience will rule our lives. Amen.

June 25 **Scripture Reading: Colossians 3:1**

If ye then, be risen with Christ, seek those things which are above, where Christ sitteth on the right hand of God.

In our element

Paul's explanation of the way we are to live the new life we have in Christ focused on the fact that we are dead to the world and alive in Christ. We are dead to sin through the cross, alive in Christ through his resurrection. But Paul's concern was not simply to explain how redemption works, but to urge us who have been raised with Christ to become habituated to our element: to live in the resurrected life instead of wallowing in the old ways of death.

An old myth has it that a mermaid desired to become human. Finally her desire was granted. One day she swam onto the beach and walked out on new, beautiful legs. For a while she enjoyed dry land immensely. But finding things difficult and not being disciplined to adapt, she began to pine for the old life. She went down to the water's edge and gazed at her old home. Finally she became so nostalgic that she ran into the surf and dove deep into the sea. Not a mermaid anymore, however, she could no longer breathe under water, and she drowned.

Christians who slide back into old ways instead of fully embracing life in Christ are trying to live in the wrong element. Once risen with Christ, our element is no longer the world but the Spirit. While we may be tempted to believe that doing something God's way is too hard and that acting the old way is easy, in fact living in the sinful element will bring only intensified emptiness and a magnified sense of futility. It will be worse than before we became Christians, because now we know life can be much more than before we came to know Christ. The most miserable people on earth are not lost people, but saved people who are living outside God's will. For our own sakes as well as God's glory, we who have been born into the world of the Spirit must breathe in its freedom, live in its power and move in its glory. We don't belong to the world anymore, but to the Lord.

Father, help us to see through the adversary's tempting us to dive back into the world, lest we drown in its emptiness. Amen.

As a jewel of gold in a swine's snout, so is a fair woman which is without discretion.

Gold or sterling?

Everyone has his or her own idea of what makes someone beautiful. Beauty is said to be in the eye of the beholder. If you are talking only of a person's appearance, the observation is true. But what about what we call true beauty—the inward kind? Is that a relative matter, subject to the standards of the beholder? Or is inward beauty judged by a never-changing standard, set by the Lord God?

Body jewelry has been around for millennia, especially in middle eastern culture. But the interest of western culture in body piercing—for men as well as women—renews the poignancy of the Bible's imagery here in Proverbs. Solomon said a pig with a nose ring is a fitting illustration of a beautiful woman with bad character. The simile pulls no punches. The pig was a detestable animal to the Jews: unclean, both ceremonially and in point of fact, and certainly not a pretty animal. A gold ring in the nose was an ancient ornament for a woman to enhance beauty. But what would one do for a pig? Nothing. The pig is not changed. The ring would be a contradiction. So is the woman who is stunning to look at but who throws all restraint to the wind and adopts the motto that "anything goes."

Living out the principle in this proverb requires that we apply it just as much to men as to women. What your life *appears* to be like to others is not nearly as important as your actual conduct. As you live through this day, you will likely be tempted to present an image of yourself that casts you in good light but doesn't match who you are on the inside. Beautify the inside first. Let your conduct be honest, moral, humble, thoughtful, loving, godly. If you character is sterling, you won't need gold—in your nose or anywhere else—to attract others.

Father, with all our hearts may we long to be, and seek to be like Christ, the most beautiful one of all. Amen.

Only by pride cometh contention: but with the well advised is wisdom.

The trouble with pride

Did your parents ever tell you things you didn't understand? A minister related several things his father said that dumbfounded him as a lad. One of them he heard when he and his brother got into—let us call them—arguments. His father would say,"It takes two to argue, son." He realized the obvious: an argument was a heated debate involving at a minimum two persons. But he didn't catch on to what his parents were trying to imply. It didn't occurred to him that his father was suggesting that he might choose not to be involved in a disagreement, ending the argument. It didn't occur to him, he says, precisely because it never crossed his mind *not* to pursue his side of an disagreement. If anyone should back down, it should have been his brother!

The proverb says that the only thing pride breeds is quarrels, but that people who listen to the opinions of others develop wisdom. When people constantly bicker, you will find in one and probably both of them a deep vein of pride running through their personalities. Pride is the unwillingness to commit hurt feelings to God, to turn over injustice to the Lord. Pride is the drive in us to win, when the Bible says we are not in competition. Pride is the fear of being thought wrong or weak, or as fallible as everybody else. Pride is insisting that we are a cut above.

Wisdom, on the other hand, is about being willing to hear the truth in anybody's point, and being ready to learn from anyone God chooses to use. Wisdom does not demand that we bow to every opinion or let our convictions be swayed. But knock-down, drag-out arguments are not usually over these things, but over the little issues of getting along with one another. It is the wise person who is quick to acknowledge the value of other people's views.

Try exercising your humility today. Agree with people. You will shock some and silence others. But at least you won't argue. Because it takes two to do that.

Father, make us more like Christ, who submitted himself to you fully, in part that we might learn what it is like not to be proud. Amen.

June 28 **Scripture Reading: Romans 13:8**

Owe no man any thing, but to love one another: for he that loveth another hath fulfilled the law.

Debt ceiling

All of us would like to be debt free, though it is difficult not to be in hock to someone in this world. But money is not the only way we may be indebted. We are familiar with the expression, "I owe you one," or, "I'll return the favor." If someone does something for us, we want to stay even. Maybe, however, that's not so good.

Paul taught us not to owe each other any debt but to love each other. He wasn't mainly talking about money. He was talking about personal debt, the feeling we have that good deeds are commodities that must be bought or traded for even value. He was talking about our tendency to feel that we are placed under moral obligation to people, bound by gratitude or custom.

We may think it is only fair to be bound by gratitude. But imagine how it could get us into trouble. Suppose we feel we "owe one" to someone who then asks us to get him out of a jam by doing something dishonest. Would we be obliged? Paul's point was that love is meant to be the debt ceiling of all obligations. In godly relationships people owe each other only one thing: love. This love is not principally a feeling but a set of actions. Love does only good to our neighbors.

Does it matter if a person has opportunity to do much more for you than you can do for him? You are still not in debt to him or her but for one thing: love. When you are the one who does the greater amount of giving, you must not feel that your friend owes you anything either, except one thing: love. That way, we never work under the burden of pettiness and record-keeping. We simply act in love as God gives opportunity. Give your good deeds away with no expectation of return. Receive the love of others with simple gratitude, pledging them only one thing: love.

Father, may we see Jesus as he loved—simply, spiritually and sacrificially— and may we do the same. Amen.

And he walked in the way of Asa his father, and departed not from it, doing that which was right in the sight of the LORD. Howbeit the high places were not taken away.

Exporting values?

U.S. foreign policy has variously favored either self-defense only, or the exportation of democracy—which is right? If we believe in liberty, how far should we go in trying to establish liberty elsewhere? This enormous question almost certainly cannot be answered the same way for every circumstance. But it prompts us to think in personal terms: if we believe something, how far do we take our belief?

2 Chronicles summarized the reign of Jehoshaphat, king of Judah, by saying that he was a principled man, but that he didn't remove the high places. The high places were local worship sites on hilltops, most of them probably devoted to Baal sacrifice. Some of them may have been used to carry out sacrifice to the Lord, but God had commanded Israelites to sacrifice only at the temple. In either case, then, the high places were demonstrations of rebellion. The Chronicler praised the king for his personal morality, but indicted him because he could have cleansed the land of a scourge, and did not.

Many Christians keep their beliefs to themselves, attempting neither to witness nor to influence their culture or government for righteousness. Some people honestly think that either one constitutes imposing beliefs on others. But if what we believe is truth, we are responsible to try to persuade others of it. If we have the means to right wrongs, we must consider our role in doing so. It takes character to be righteous for yourself; it takes courage to establish righteousness around you. When critics say we shouldn't legislate morality, remember that *all* law is a legislation of someone's morality: the only question is whose.

Lord, help us remember that to him that knoweth to do good and doeth it not, to him it is sin. Amen.

Cast thy burden upon the LORD, and he shall sustain thee.

Who is in charge?

Some years ago a commercial for a cologne product advised in a commanding tone, "Take charge of your life!" It then suggested that a certain after-bath splash was the way to do it. Not hardly. But the advice by itself is not bad. There is a sense in which we should take charge of our own lives. Galatians tells us that each man must carry his own load, and Peter, Paul and others praise self-control (KJV "temperance"). Every person should assume responsibility for his own life and problems, not push them off on others. Some people never shoulder their own load, but run to others for decisions only they should make, or answers that only they can give. They live in misery all their lives because they have no peace with their own approach to living.

On the other hand, there is a deeper sense in which we should not take charge of our own lives. The word of God challenges both those who do and those who do not carry their own weight to give charge of their lives to Jesus Christ. He alone can give the direction and relief from life's burdens that really satisfies us. The Psalmist's insistence that we cast our burden on the Lord means that we ask him to do for us what no one else, not even we ourselves, can do: give us peace with God, forgiveness of sins and eternal life, and direction of our lives into true fulfillment and godly success. While we learn to accept responsibility for our own lives and actions, we also recognize that human wisdom or strength cannot do some things, but only God through Jesus Christ.

When interbank charge cards such as Visa and MasterCharge (now MasterCard) first came out, someone made a cute but meaningful variation. It looked very much like the MasterCharge card until close inspection revealed that it actually said, "Give the Master Charge of your life." Good advice.

Lord, We know no one is responsible for our lives but us, but no one can make them what they ought to be but you. So take charge! Amen.

So likewise, whosoever he be of you that forsaketh not all that he hath, he cannot be my disciple.

The price of life

Some people claim that everyone has a price, but that is cynical and untrue. Nevertheless it is a practical truth that every*thing* costs something, and every goal worth attaining costs something. The popular proverb for this truism is, "You don't get something for nothing." This is true even of the most gracious gift of all, God's salvation. For though the Bible describes it as a "free gift," it cost the blood of Jesus Christ, and it costs us our lives in surrender to him to receive it. It is a gift, but it requires our return of our very lives. It is a paradox, perhaps, but that's the way things work.

What do you want out of life? Every dream of success has its price. Someone said that successful people dislike doing the same things that unsuccessful people do, but they do them anyway. All of us would like to have something, but are we willing to pay the price for it?

Two ladies were talking about the children of one. The other said, "I would give my life to have children like that." The reply was, "That's exactly what it costs." So many of us are not willing, however, to give up other pursuits in order to do what is necessary to gain worthwhile goals.

Jesus said that if we are unwilling to give up everything, we cannot follow him. What this means in terms of specific sacrifices varies from person to person, according to the will of God. But it means one thing for all who would be Christians: from the time of that first step of faith, all we are and have must be regarded as belonging to him, not to us anymore. Whatever he chooses to put in our hands to use is up to him. But he owns it, and must control it. That is the price. Are you paying the price of life?

Father, help us realize that we don't manage the store, so we don't set the price and don't have the privilege of bargaining with you. Amen.

...Neither cast ye your pearls before swine, lest they trample them under their feet, and turn again and rend you.

Don't waste your witness

One of Jesus' most interesting metaphors was "casting pearls before swine." The idea of scattering pearls on the ground inside a pig pen is ludicrous. It helps make Jesus' point: in sharing the message of Christ with people, the Christian is not to make the mistake of believing that just anybody is a ready subject. Some persons are willingly hostile to the gospel, and engaging such a person in an in-depth attempt to convert him will result only in patent rejection and even retribution. Why subject yourself to this when there are persons who would readily receive the good news?

We must be careful to understand that all need the gospel, including those who hate it. Sometimes the time to witness to the enemies of Christ is laid before us and we must not shy away from it. But Jesus' warns against trying to win the hard case just to prove we can do it, rather than preaching the good news to those who are open to it now. In fact, by dogging the resistant, we may be robbing the receptive.

A strong Christian woman described how, in a way, she had been on the other end of this teaching. A cult church's members tried to sell her their faith. Later, they sent her free videotapes, in a further attempt. She could have told them it was a waste of time, and certainly of money. She said she had the odd thought that they probably thought she was the swine that refused their pearls—when she was really more like a saint refusing their pig slop. At any rate, they should have saved their "witness" for someone more likely to respond. She concluded her tale by saying, "I wish no one would respond at all."

It's interesting to see it from the other side. It makes the point that we must make the best use of our witness, seeking the receptive wherever they may be found.

Father, we don't always know who is ready for Jesus. Help us to be discerning. Amen.

And he spake a parable unto them, Can the blind lead the blind? shall they not both fall into the ditch?

Our great influence

Parents should be amazed by their tremendous influence—not just good, but bad influence. A father notices that when his children are with him, they mimic not only his actions, but his words, even his attitudes. If he gripes at another driver on the road, they parrot his sentiments—even if they don't know what he was complaining about. If he gets excited, so do they. If he acts afraid, it makes them scared. If he tries something, they try it, too. That's real power!

This influence exists not only in the parent-child relationship, but in others as well. New Christians watch older Christians. Some become warped or ruined as a result. Fortunately, some also are led into genuine discipleship by the ones they choose to watch. Neighbors watch you, to see what you do. Although adults will not mimic you as children would, what your neighbor does about Christ and his church may have more to do with what *you* do than you would like to think.

Jesus asked us if it is possible to follow someone who doesn't know where he is going, and still wind up getting to the right place ourselves. Someone who does not know God cannot lead others to know God. But even if you're a Christian, you are not automatically a good example or leader. A Christian who lives poorly may in fact do more damage to someone watching him than the rankest hedonist. The bitterness someone develops because of the hypocrisy of a Christian acquaintance is often harder to overcome than the influence of an immoral, but honest pagan. If your neighbor is watching you, will he come to know Christ and follow him devotedly, or will he take a pass, thinking from your example that Christianity isn't worth the effort?

Father, we have been put here as salt and light. May we function faithfully as both. Amen.

Honour all men. Love the brotherhood. Fear God. Honour the king.

Christian patriotism

The Bible doesn't say much about what we call patriotism. It stresses our loyalty to the King of kings, not lesser powers. Yet the Bible contains good examples of the loyalty of people to their country, even when that country was not really their own. Peter gives us the bottom line: we should respect legitimate authorities and be good citizens.

John Witherspoon was not the only Christian but was the only minister to sign the Declaration of Independence. A Scot, he had been a devoted pastor and a servant of the King. But he became president of the College of New Jersey in 1768, and quickly embraced his new country. He was elected to the Continental Congress in 1776, and joined the body three days before the adoption of the Declaration. Though there were many who begged the delegates to remain loyal to England, Witherspoon's challenge was followed instead:

> "There is a tide in the affairs of men, a nick of time. We perceive it now before us. To hesitate is to consent to our own slavery. That noble instrument upon your table, which ensures immortality to its author, should be subscribed this very morning by every pen in this house. He that will not respond to its accents and strain every nerve to carry into effect its provisions is unworthy the name of freeman. For my own part, of property I have some, of reputation more. That reputation is staked, that property is pledged, on the issue of this contest. And although these gray hairs must soon descend into the sepulchre, I would infinitely rather that they descend thither by the hand of the executioner than desert at this crisis the sacred cause of my country."

There are things bigger than our personal dreams of wealth and success. We should be thankful that many have chosen sacrifice, so that many more could be blessed.

Father, Jesus Christ, most of all, sacrificed that we might live forever. Grant us courage to live for you, and serve others, even to the point of sacrifice. Amen.

For other foundation can no man lay than that is laid, which is Jesus Christ.

Building on the perfect foundation.

The secretary-treasurer of a Baptist association watched as crews tore down a building near his office. It was only a little hut of a building that had been there a long time. He noticed in passing by regularly that there was evidence of more than one structure having been there. But it looked as if two or three buildings had been constructed on the same footings. It reminded him of Jerusalem, as well as many ancient Israelite cities. One can plainly see the walls and foundations of many former constructions in excavated sites. The ancients did not bother to remove all the former stones. They simply built on top of them. Once a good foundation, always a good foundation.

A life may be built on solid foundations, too. Jesus said, "Therefore whosoever heareth these sayings of mine, and doeth them, I will liken him unto a wise man, which built his house upon a rock." It turns out that rock is none other than Jesus Christ himself. The thing about a rock is that it is good not only once, but continually.

All of us fail to keep promises made to ourselves and to the Lord about what we are going to do with our lives. Perhaps the better thing to do is simply to surrender to what God wants to do with our lives. But we fall away from that commitment, too. What shall we do? Find another foundation? Start all over from scratch? No, the foundation is still faith in Jesus Christ. It is still the gospel. It is still the doing of his will that is important. When we need a fresh start, we do not need to find new foundations. Simply dig back down to what is firm and valid in life, and start from there.

Why not ask God to renew you in your commitments today, and refresh you in your *foundational* love for your Savior?

Father, let me build on faith in Jesus Christ, with the gold, silver and precious stones. Amen.

Not forsaking the assembling of ourselves together, as the manner of some is; but exhorting one another: and so much the more, as ye see the day approaching.

The fellowship we need

Most of us who grew up with television think, at least in some fashion, of the old favorite characters as being some of our best friends. But of course, when you really need a friend, you could not call one of them. The characters were only make-believe, in the first place, and if you could get hold of the actors who played them, they would not want to come be the friend you need—they couldn't. It's not that they aren't nice people: it's just that TV was never meant to be a personal thing.

Take that to heart! It is convenient to be able to switch on the television and get your gospel there, to turn on the shouting, crying, orating, gyrating, criticizing, dramatic, healing, charismatic figures who mount TV pulpits day in and day out and appeal for your eyes, ears, and money. Some of them have a good word to say, and among them there are some genuine ministries to the truly confined or occasionally sick. But what about personal attention? Try calling one of them when you are sick or troubled. They won't come. They can't, and it's understandable.

This implies that your attention for worship and teaching should be focused on your local church—the fellowship of real people—not the television. If you are essentially unknown to the church, when trouble comes, the church you call "yours" may not know you, either. Hebrews says we mustn't stay out of the church, like some people do. In fact, considering the nature of the times, the needs we have, the command to worship, the price of alienation, the value of friendship, and the strength of sharing, we ought to seek out the real, live church all the more. It's the fellowship we need.

Father, help us today to be examples of loyalty to the church, which Jesus loved enough to die for. Amen.

Let every man abide in the same calling wherein he was called.

Sitting tight

We've all heard the frequent urging, "Don't just sit there: do something!" But at other times, it may be that the word of advice we need the most is, "Just sit tight." It is often the appropriate word, because it is a firm, biblical principle. In discussing why a wife shouldn't decide to leave her husband just because she had become a Christian, and he hadn't, Paul expanded the matter to give this more general teaching: whatever you are when you find Christ, 'sit tight.' Stay where you are long enough to find out why God called you while you were that particular setting. Have you considered the probability that God wants to use you right where you are?

This was a hard thing for slaves to hear, but Paul said it, anyway. It was wrong for people to make slaves of others, but there was no sin in someone's being, himself, a slave. It was unjust, but only for the one perpetrating the act. The one receiving it did nothing wrong. Paul was trying to say that it might have been precisely God's will for them to bear this injustice, so that they could be witnesses to the freedom that comes in Christ, a freedom that transcends and therefore supercedes the bondage of social situations.

This is a challenging teaching. It calls for submission, patience, grace, and discipline. What is it that you want to get out of? Is it a problem, a lifelong hardship, or a sickness? No one can say with finality for you and your life, but could it be that your situation is just what God wants you in, so you can do something, say something for him, or simply so you can grow? There is no sin in being subjected to poverty or moderate means, or in being sick or beset with unearned problems. It's how you *act* that brings in the question of sin, and it may be that God is trying to tell you, "sit tight!"

Father, it is a hard word, but it is your word. Apply it where needed in our lives today. Amen.

They are new every morning: great is thy faithfullness.

Fresh blessing

There is something exciting about new things. New clothes give a lift to the attitude. New toys—children's or adults'!—engage and delight us, and new cars—it's hard to describe their effect. But once a few moments or days have passed, the new wears off, and things can never be new again. They wear out, get used up, or disappear. Refurbishing can go only so far.

But some things in life can be new or like new again, although we do not always let them be. Lamentations 3:23 describes the mercies and compassion of the Lord. Every day, his mercy is new. Every morning, his compassion is fresh. The blessings of God are not old and worn out. The salvation he gives has the potential to be experienced by us as new and fresh every time we contemplate it, each time we review it and probe it in worship or devotion. This is principally because the new life God gives is too deep for us to ever fully comprehend, too wide in possibilities for us to ever totally exhaust. If your new life in Christ is not so exciting anymore, it isn't because it couldn't be: it's because you won't let it be.

A student attending graduate school halfway across the country drove the thousand mile trip for the summer every year, and then back in the fall, in a single stretch. He would usually arrive at school late at night, when the lights of the beautiful city suddenly became visible over a rise. It was like a new place every time he returned, and he said, "It gave me the feeling again and again that I had a new chance to live better, and accomplish more."

The experience of life in Christ we should be having is regular renewal—re-*new*-al. "Be ye transformed by the re-*new*-ing of your mind" (Rom.12:2). In Christ "all things are become *new*" (2 Cor.5:17). An old hymn says, "Every day is a *new* day, when you live it for the Lord!"

Father, this day is not the same as yesterday. May we not be, either. Amen.

Some trust in chariots, and some in horses: but we will remember the name of the Lord our God.

Whom do you trust?

From the beginning of the nation Israel, God charged his people to trust him, and he would fight for them, and save them. The deliverance from Egypt was the symbol of this pattern of divine intervention. Occasionally thereafter, the Israelites won a battle victory by miracle—Joshua at Jericho, Jehoshaphat against Moab and Ammon, are just two examples where, with no weapons, the Israelites conquered their enemies. God confused or terrified the enemy by some other means. At other times, however, they fought battles under the same divine instruction, but used swords, chariots and horses. So what does it mean that Psalm 2:7 exhorts God's people to trust in him, instead?

David was simply saying our ultimate trust should be in the Lord. We may use physical means as tools to solve problems, but we should not trust them as if they were the answer itself. Often we trust in money, or might, or our own wits to get us through. These things might be *used* to help us. But God should be trusted to be our deliverer. The distinction may seem fine, but in reality it is immense. The Christian who will not tithe because he says his bills are too great, is not trusting God. Trust demands obedience and reliance on God to honor that obedience by providing our needs. The person who forces his will on others because he isn't sure what he thinks is right will take place otherwise, is probably not trusting God, who says through Paul in Philippians 3:15, "Let us be thus minded, and if in anything you are otherwise, God will reveal this to you." We should trust God to move others, and not attempt to take his place.

Subtle differences often make all the difference in the world. Whom do you *really* trust—you, or God? Is it evident from the way you are living your life right now?

Father, there is no reason not to trust you, and there is every reason we should. May we, today. Amen.

The effectual fervent prayer of a righteous man availeth much.

It all comes down to prayer

The Bible challenges us to pray often, pray believing, pray persistently, pray thankfully—pray! But if there were no scripture telling us to pray, even logic would tell us that if God can do anything, we ought to ask him to take action in our lives where there is a need. So much for logic. In practice, we usually ignore the ability of God, and count on our own abilities. This is why Jesus so often reminded us, as did his apostles in their writings, to pray—to ask God for the answers to our needs.

John Wesley once said, "God does nothing but by prayer, and everything with it." This is one of those amazing statements about prayer that startle the average Christian, who doesn't realize prayer is so important in God's design for the Christian life. The statement is firmly based in Bible truth. We simply underestimate the role of prayer in God's work.

A report came from a Southern Baptist missionary in Bolivia a few years ago that a theater had been built right next to his church. The noise from the theater was severely impeding the progress of any meetings. No amount of complaint was effective, either through courteous requests of the owner or reports to the authorities. Finally the members decided they could only resort to prayer. So they prayed, and they prayed. It was a short time later that the roof of the theater caved in. The owner picked another site to rebuild.

When no one else hears you, the Bible says, "The Lord hears my complaint." A seminary professor regularly said to each of his incoming classes, "When all your other resources run out and all you can do is pray, well, then, praise the Lord! For then you have been brought to rely on the most powerful source in the universe." It makes sense to ask God.

Father, we're asking. For everything we need this day in order to walk with Christ and do your will, we ask now. Amen.

And Peter answered him and said, Lord, if it be thou, bid me come unto thee on the water. And he said, Come. And when Peter was come down out of the ship, he walked on the water, to go to Jesus.

Surrendering our un-gifted-ness

Many Christians have paid special attention to identifying their spiritual gifts—areas of spiritual strength. We are assured that God will give us the gifts necessary for doing the things he calls us to attempt. But what about when we find ourselves facing something we don't think we're at all fitted to handle? Some say we should avoid these situations and just focus on our strengths. What we may need to do, however, is learn not only to use our gifted-ness for the Lord, but also to surrender our un-gifted-ness to him.

Peter saw Jesus walking on the water, and asked for an invitation to do the same. He got it. Although walking on water was something Peter had not previously been gifted to do, he stepped out in faith.

God may call us to places in life where our gifts mostly fit our challenges. Often, however, there is some duty or need that frustrates or scares us, and too often that's the area we neglect. We need to trust that if the Lord says, "Come, do this," it implies he will give whatever ability is needed to accomplish it. What God does not give by birth or by spiritual rebirth, he will supply through grace.

Every major Bible character had an identifiable area of weakness. Jonah lacked love and mercy. Elijah tended toward self-pity. David tended toward sexual lust. Even Moses was occasionally impressed with his own position. As God grew the men he had called to his work, in many cases these areas of weakness were refined and changed. God will work on you, and less painfully if you let him. He wants not only to polish your gifts, but also to fill your voids. Surrender your *un-gifted-ness,* and see if you can walk on water.

Father, when I am tempted to avoid what could be your will simply because I feel inadequate, remind me that where I can't, you can. Amen.

And thou shalt make holy garments for Aaron thy brother for glory and for beauty.

What do you wear to church?

In a previous generation, families often called a certain set of clothes "church clothes." That meant suits, ties and dress shoes, and dresses, hats and heels. Times change, and people in many places don't feel they must dress up for church. They often reason that those who don't have nice clothes would feel out of place and would be discouraged from attending.

Maybe it's an issue people make too much of, and maybe not. But regardless, there is another sense in which we must certainly pay very careful attention to what we wear to church.

When God met Moses in the mountain to instruct him in the building of the tabernacle, he described the priest's garments, which were to be very special, and were to lend **"dignity and honor"** to him as priest. The clothes were constructed to symbolize important religious things like holiness and purity. He was not to go just "any old way" into the worship of God. According to the New Testament, now we have one high priest, Jesus Christ, and we don't have to wear robes and tassels and bells like priests of old. But that doesn't mean God isn't particular about how we come "dressed" for worship.

God expects us to come with hearts bathed by prayer and repentance. He expects us to be clothed with the righteousness of Christ. He does not want us to come in the sloppy garments of unchaste lives, unbending wills, unconsecrated hearts. Such spiritual apparel is undignified and dishonorable.

What do you wear to church? Even the best clothes cannot cover lives draped in unholiness. Before you go to church, dress yourself in the dignity and honor of a cleansed life, and a consecrated heart.

Father, as I worship you alone today, I ask for the clothing of holiness, that I may be properly dressed for worship. Amen.

But if ye will not do so, behold, ye have sinned against the LORD: and be sure your sin will find you out.

Sin detectors

Are you ever afraid on leaving a store with a security device by the door, that it will go off and you will be stopped and searched? Of course, they won't find anything (would they?). But the imagination can play out the paranoia: the store insists you have stolen something, you are taken to jail, wind up in court, and have to plead for your acquittal on the basis of the lack of evidence. Did you ever have such wild imaginings?

A minister exiting a department store heard the detector beep as he went through the door. No one called out or tried to stop him, and since he had neither stolen nor even bought anything, he walked on and tried to look nonchalant, and never knew what set off the alarm. In our times, we are so used to scanners and surveillance that it shouldn't be a surprise that some of us have wild daydreams about what would happen if …

It isn't good to be too paranoid about such things. But it is good to remind yourself that breaking the law is dangerous. You are likely to get caught. It is also good to remember that God does not miss anything, and he often allows the strangest of circumstances to act like "sin detectors" to find us out. Things we thought well hidden wind up in the spotlight.

If men can build machines to detect shoplifters, why should we marvel that God who knows all will detect and reveal sin in us? His purpose is not primarily that we be afraid, but that we turn and trust him and live for him. Sin grieves him. He calls us to holiness out of his love for us.

But if we sin with impunity, we have good reason to imagine all sorts of scenarios about the day when we are caught. Today, prefer to please the Lord in everything—then you will have to be afraid of the Lord in nothing.

Lord, help us to shun the evil, and do the good, through the power of the Spirit. Amen.

And as he reasoned of righteousness, temperance, and judgment to come, Felix trembled, and answered, Go thy way for this time; when I have a convenient season, I will call for thee.

I'll call when I need you

Many people do door-to-door selling honorably. But it makes most people nervous. Perhaps it's our isolation, or the dangers in our culture. But probably most people find themselves thinking they would like to say to door-to-door salesmen, "Just give me your card, and don't call me—I'll call you." Many of us hate to put people off indecisively, so we would like to leave things ever so slightly open, though it would be clear to the salesman that we didn't intend to look him up again.

That's what Felix, governor in Caesarea during the days of the apostle Paul, was trying to do when he answered the gospel salesmanship of Paul. Acts 24:25 records Felix's response, which was essentially, "I'll call when I need you."

Many people reach that point very quickly when they hear preaching or Bible teaching, or are confronted by a Christian message on television or radio. The moment the message makes a demand on them or touches a sensitive spot, they put it off, turn it off, turn themselves away, so as not to be moved to any kind of conviction—lest they be sold on the truth and have to do something about it.

Jesus remarked on the irony of people's rejection of divine salvation, and quoted Isaiah who said, "their eyes they have closed; lest at any time they should see …and I should heal them" (Matthew 13:15).

All day long, God tries by his Spirit to speak to us, lead us, teach us. How do you respond? Do you listen, take notes, learn, correct your actions, obey? Or is it, "Okay, God, that's a good thought, and I'll take it up sometime when I feel like improving my life—but not now?" How often do you tell God, in one way or another, "I'll call when I need you?"

Father, help us to leave the door open to your patient salesmanship, buy everything you offer, and then put it to use in our lives. Amen.

Study to shew thyself approved unto God, a workman that needeth not to be ashamed, rightly dividing the word of truth.

Putting our minds to it

It's an old complaint that when people go to church the preacher talks over their heads, or the Sunday School teacher confuses them with doctrines they don't understand. So, some people don't go to church very often, for that excuse. Yes, excuse, not reason—because that's what it is. The same excuse is used privately, to explain why the Bible is not read and personal study is not done. Some say, "I don't get much out of it," or "I don't understand it."

But if these same people had jobs where things were unclear, they would ask for explanation and help, so as not to lose the job. If they took up a sport where the rules were unclear or the techniques confusing, they would do their best to learn the game, even if they had to take private lessons. It all depends on what you want to do.

A little girl who had just finished her first week at school said to her mother, "I'm wasting time. I can't read, I can't write, and they won't let me talk!" Some casual church attenders feel that way. But the whole point of listening to teaching and preaching is to learn. Unfortunately, some people don't want to learn. They turn off their learning switches when they come to church. Paul the Apostle challenged young Timothy to "study." That word means to "do your best," or "try hard." We need to study the word of God, learn the doctrines it teaches, learn the faith of Christ, in order to live by it.

"The preacher is too deep," or "the Bible is too hard to understand," is no excuse. In the final tabulation, it is you and your commitment to learning and growth that make the difference.

Father, sometimes we get lazy, and neglect to be mentally and spiritually serious about learning the Christian faith and way. Help us to see how important it is to be conscientious about it. Amen.

A bekah for every man, that is, half a shekel, after the shekel of the sanctuary, for every one that went to be numbered.

Equal responsibility

Old Testament passages about the building of the tabernacle, or later the temple, or the wall of Jerusalem, provide wonderful illustrations for our study. A reading of Exodus 38 reveals that an enormous amount of gold and silver was used in the making of the tabernacle, the wilderness tent-dwelling of the Lord. In today's values, the gold was worth many multiple millions of dollars, and the silver was proportionately valuable. One of the curious things about it was that nobody was particularly rich. They were all fugitives and had been a slave nation. But God had made it clear that "the rich shall not give more and the poor shall not give less" (Exodus 30:15). When the tabernacle was first built, there was a numbering of Israel done, and each man was assessed a half shekel to go toward the service of worship. Each had equal responsibility to build the "church," we might say, because each had been redeemed in the same way, at the same price.

Since our abilities differ, we cannot all be expected to produce the same fruit for God. But in a more fundamental way, our responsibility to build the church is the same. The house of the Lord is his church, the people of Christ. Each Christian was purchased with the blood of Christ, and came into eternal life the same way—through faith in Jesus as Lord and Savior. Occasionally, a church has a sweeping sense of what it owes to Christ, and gives and sacrifices to build the church up. When a church building is constructed, money and participation increases. In between these times, however, a church sometimes languishes, suffering from the indifference and sleepy commitment of the people. Building up the church itself—the people—falls way down on the list of priorities.

Where is "building the church" on your list of priorities? Are you doing your share?

Father, accept our new pledge of loyalty, and prick our consciences about our duties to Christ's church. Amen.

The hour is coming, and now is, when the dead shall hear the voice of the Son of God: and they that hear shall live.

Get up from the dead

The phone awakens you from deep sleep. You groggily say, "Hello?" And an amazing voice on the other end replies, "Rise up from the dead!" That would be a surprising message to hear, wouldn't it?

There are many people who have reported what we call "NDEs"—near death experiences. People say they have separated from their bodies and have been in some realm of the spirit, and some have heard a voice saying, "Go back. It is not time yet." Some of these claims are laced with contradictions to the Bible. Other stories seem believable and less problematic. We must keep in mind the scripture that says, "it is appointed unto man once to die, but after this the judgment" (Hebrews 9:27).

What about Lazarus or the other persons raised from the dead by Jesus or the apostles—were they actually in heaven and then had to return? We may not be able to say with certainty. But this we can believe without hesitation: Jesus calls people out of death into life. John 5:25 teaches us that ever since the day of Jesus' appearing, he has been calling out to the dead in sins, "Repent, turn to me, and live." Countless persons have responded to that call, and have received new life in Christ. This life is true, real, joyous, abundant, and never ending. Nothing else can truly be called life. That's why John calls the state of being here but not knowing Christ, "dead." It is "the dead" who hear the voice of the Son of God." As Paul says, "You who were once dead in sins and trespasses has God made alive in Christ." If you can say that of yourself today, that you are alive in Christ, then praise him! And share that peace, joy, and victory with others. Perhaps it will be through your own testimony that Jesus speaks, and "the dead" you know will hear his voice.

Father, thank you for making me alive in Christ. Let Jesus call to others through me today. Amen.

For if any be a hearer of the word, and not a doer, he is like unto a man beholding his natural face in a glass. For he beholdeth himself, and goeth his way, and straightway forgetteth what manner of man he was.

The mirror of the Word

Memorize the verse above, then repeat it to yourself with your eyes closed. What do you see? You say, nothing. But in a real way, whenever you read or hear scripture, hear the word of God preached or taught, you are looking at something—a mirror. God's mirror, what James calls "a glass," shows you what you are like, points up things that need attention. Do you pay attention to what it reflects? Or do you interpret what you see mostly as an indication of what *others* need?

A backwoods mountaineer found a mirror that a tourist had lost. As he looked in the mirror, he said, "Well, if it ain't my old pappy. I never knowed he had his 'pitcher' took." He took the mirror home, sneaked into his house, and hid it. But his action didn't escape his suspicious wife. That night while he slept she slipped out of bed and found the mirror. "Uh-huh!" she said, looking into it, "So that's the old hag he's been chasin'!"

Are you unaware of the reflection of your own life you have been seeing in the words of the Bible? Could it be that you have applied the lessons taught to others, to the world, to poor sinners down on the other side of town, or to your enemies, but not to yourself? What trouble we make for ourselves when we refuse to see that our lives, our actions, our beliefs, need changing, rearranging! Today, as God speaks, ask yourself: Is this something I need to do? Is this something I have been wrong about? Have I been ignoring God's voice? Do I need to alter my life to line up with God's will?

Father, our subjective vision often will not let us be objective about ourselves. Open our spiritual eyes to see as you see us, so we may do something about the way we look to you. Amen.

Choosing rather to suffer affliction with the people of God, than to enjoy the pleasures of sin for a season.

The price of selling out

The case of Moses was just one of many the writer of Hebrews used to illustrate how faith—believing God and counting on his promises in spite of the cost in this world—is the kind of life God rewards.

On a busy city street in a major metropolitan area a few years ago there was a lone house standing back from the road, surrounded by groves, and flanked by stable houses and barns. It stood in stark contrast to the thriving business district all around it. An elderly couple refused to sell out to enterprises that wanted to transform the stately old place into another shopping center. The commercial value of the land was tremendous, but the owners went on sticking out like a sore thumb, standing in the way of progress.

Bravo! There was something hopeful, honorable, and courageous about their stand. Here are two people who lived in the house and on that bit of ground for their whole lives. Suddenly, their familiar turf was altered overnight, and they were expected to give up what they had and go elsewhere—and for what? A few dollars and the vague and questionable concept of progress?

Make this application to Christians: the world around us is busy, even frantic, in pursuing its ends at a breakneck pace, and it expects us to go along with it, giving up our values in the process. It offers us pleasure, money, success, in exchange for our heritage. What kind of trade is that? Every Christian must have the courage to stand alone for Christ, a stalwart witness in the midst of a frivolous world, a testimony to the enduring values of our faith and the unchanging principles of our God. Like Moses, we must choose the enduring joys of God's people rather than the temporary thrills of worldly pleasure. Sell out to the world? Never! People have given their very lives for the faith of our fathers. Will we?

Father, grant us grace to choose today to stand out noticeably as followers of Christ. Amen.

But let judgment run down as waters, and righteousness as a mighty stream.

A swelling tide of righteousness

Living in one of the southeastern states, one often experiences the expansive effects of Atlantic hurricanes. Rains of several days saturate the mountains, swell the streams of the foothills, and bring many a river far downstream to flood stage. Travelers in upstate cities are hampered by the abundance of water overflowing creek beds and saturating the parks, woodlands and yards that lie on their banks. Way up in the mountains, where many of the streams begin, the rains build up, filling the water tables and soaking the ground surfaces. Up there, the swelling is not noticeable, but by the time it reaches the valleys, it has become a roaring tide.

Such images graphically communicate what Amos the prophet meant when he wrote, "Let justice run down as waters, and righteousness as a mighty stream." God wants his world to experience a growing tide of righteousness and justice. Sometimes the little we can do to promote the right in this world seems to go unnoticed or promises little in the way of far-reaching effects. We are called to preach the gospel, and we are promised that Christ will build his church, but the scripture never promises the kingdom of God will gradually overcome by man's hand. Yet in God's plan there is a swelling in the currents of his will, and he plans to flood the sinful world with his righteousness some day, at the return of Jesus Christ.

Whether you and I are a part of that tide, or are swept away by it, depends on our relationship with Christ. Every person in the world needs to be confronted with the gospel and its pressing question: Do you know him as Savior and Lord? Are you living for him daily? Will his waters of judgment and justice bear you safely over into the presence of Jesus, or wash you away into eternal night?

Father, may the certainty of divine flooding prompt us to seek cleansing by the waters of your Spirit, through faith in Christ. Amen.

Some men's sins are open beforehand, going before to judgment; and some men they follow after.

All of us are sinners

Ever since Watergate, the political disaster that brought about President Nixon's resignation, people have been discovering more and more bad things about prominent persons. In fact Watergate seems to have marked the beginning of a time of relentless investigation and "dirt digging," for skeletons in the closets of every public person.

Most of us have been disappointed in someone we thought was beyond serious reproach. An official has been taking bribes; a politician is a homosexual; a star is a drug dealer; a community leader is a pedophile. On the other hand, there are many of us who think of ourselves, and others we know, as "good people." This is supposed to mean that someone is not guilty of any serious wrong. But you never know what may be found out. The Bible says we know some people to be scandalous sinners here and now, but will discover others to be so only in the by and by. The point is, although some are evident criminals or moral scoundrels, *all* of us are in fact sinners, and some of us who boast of our clean records might be scared to death to have our secret deeds published. But there is no way to hide them forever.

If any of us thinks to present himself to the throne of God recommended by our goodness, we may rest assured that our sins will trail behind us, and get there in time to testify for the prosecution. "A man is not justified by the works of the law, but by the faith of Jesus Christ" (Galatians 2:16). It is good to be reminded of this even if we already know it. Only by shifting our trust to the perfect righteousness of Christ—who will never be uncovered in a scandal-gate—can we experience forgiveness of sins and the power of new life. That applies not only to those coming to Christ for the first time, but to Christians seeking to live for their Lord every day.

Father, remind us that we depend upon the righteousness of Christ alone for acceptance with you. Amen.

He made the laver of brass, and the foot of it of brass, of the lookingglasses of the women assembling, which assembled at the door of the tabernacle of the congregation.

Stop looking at yourself

In reading the passages from Exodus 38 about the building of the tabernacle, one is struck with verse 8, which says that the great bronze basin near the tent of meeting was made from the mirrors of the women who served there. This basin was set on the approach between the tent of meeting and the altar. The priests were to wash their hands and feet as a sign of consecration when they went to minister there. This ceremonial cleansing was a very important part of their preparation to perform their duties. They, in turn, represented all the people as they carried out the sacrifices and other rituals signifying the people's approach to God.

It is fascinating that we are told the basin was made from the mirrors of the serving women. Their mirrors were bronze plates, highly polished sheet metal. Mirrors have always been a symbol of vanity, and surely were even more so for a nation of former slaves. Now, here are these women giving up the icon of their vain pursuits in order to provide for the house of God. In a sense their vanity was transformed into consecration and holiness. Whereas they had looked at themselves, now they looked to the Lord, to please him.

Today, the masses are turning the other way. The lyrics of a popular song a few years ago said, "You can't please somebody else—you got to please yourself." Every man for himself! The 1990s were known for this very quality of self-centeredness: the "me" decade. But God wants us to please him, to put him and his kingdom first. He wants us to take all those things in our lives that reflect only us and our concerns, and yield them to him, so that our lives may be spent in his service. Where are your bronze mirrors? Shouldn't they be in the melting pot to make something useful in God's service?

Father, too much of our time is spent pleasing ourselves. Help us to please you today. Amen.

What the law could not do, in that it was weak through the flesh, God sending his own Son in the likeness of sinful flesh, and for sin, condemned sin in the flesh: That the righteousness of the law might be fulfilled in us, who walk not after the flesh, but after the Spirit.

Learning to hate sin

There is such a disparity, sometimes, between our concern over things that don't matter much and things that do. One morning a writer was sitting at his keyboard when a small spot began descending in front of his forehead, hanging in mid air. Since he had just pulled a cobweb from the ceiling a moment before, he concluded this must be the "cob!" And it was: but it was rappelling from the man's head. Realizing that, he slapped wildly at it. Many of us upon walking into a spider web slap and brush ourselves instantly and thoroughly, and remain uncertain that something isn't crawling on us *somewhere!*

Isn't it interesting, however, that we will leave off attending to things that are far more threatening to us than little spiders. The spiders we crush instantly, while the big problems in us—our greed, laziness, lust, anger, intemperance, and the like—go unrebuked. These things that will cause us the most trouble. The principal reason for this irrational behavior is found in our basic attitudes. Many of us hate spiders, but do not, apparently, detest our own greed enough to attack it when it begins to show itself, or hate our own lust enough to arrest it when it bubbles up from beneath.

What is the solution? Paul says it is to let the Holy Spirit take charge in our Christian walk. When we name Christ Lord, in full repentance and sincere surrender, his Spirit can take full control. Then it is he who causes us to grow to hate sin, enough to react as strongly to it when it appears as we might to a spider—or a serpent.

Father, grant Christians the love of Christ and the hatred of sin. We confess they are really the same thing. Amen.

In my Father's house are many mansions: if it were not so, I would have told you. I go to prepare a place for you.

Looking forward to heaven

Some Christians are embarrassed to talk about heaven, perhaps because they have doubts about the spiritual world. Other Christians talk about nothing else but streets of gold and what we're going to do "over there." Perhaps for most of us, if life is not terribly burdened, we don't sit around longing to escape it. But when life does get tough, the thought of heaven is more attractive.

The Bible doesn't give a comprehensive description of heaven. But what it does say gives a varied look at an obviously diverse place. It is called Abraham's bosom, implying a place of comfort, like a mountain hideaway. It is called a city of great splendor, indicating God's intention to keep us in awe of himself and his works. In John 14, the evangelist tells us Jesus spoke of the many "mansions." The word in the original Greek language means "rooms," or "places to stay." When Jesus came to earth, there was "no room" in the inn. But when he comes again, there will be a place for every child of God.

Do you see in Jesus' promise the implication that heaven is what it needs to be for every reward, for fullest appreciation by all there? Often when the Bible refers to heaven, it implies the whole spectrum of places and states that make up eternal life. Numerous scriptures describe the new creation as having the best of God's creation preserved and intensified. There will be discovery and learning, exploration and wonderment. Eternal life will include excitement and fun, as well as peace and tranquility. There are glimmers of all this in the Bible. One thing is for certain: it will not be boring!

Edwin Hatch wrote in a poem about heaven, "In God's perfect heaven all aspirations meet; each separate longing is fulfilled, each separate soul complete."

Father, we pray to be content to remain as long as it is your will, and to be ready when it is your time for us to depart to be with you. Amen

Train up a child in the way he should go: and when he is old, he will not depart from it.

Raising children right

Many parents allow children to do just about anything they wish, in the name of self-expression or freedom of choice. Whether you are a parent, or a child, or both, the problem should be evident. The result of such unrestricted behavior is often a self-indulgent and wayward child and then young adult. Where did the idea of guiding children by principles of right and wrong, wise and foolish, go? Proverbs says parents are to "train up" their children, in what the New Testament calls "the nurture and admonition of the Lord." The resulting promise is a child who sticks with godly principles. The promise in Proverbs takes on new meaning when you know that "child" refers to a very young child, and "old" refers to a teenager. The verse means, 'If you raise your children right, as they grow up they won't go off the deep end.' There are exceptions, but godly parenting is our best promise of having godly, grown children.

Somebody wrote down some elements of effective guidance for growing children and youth: **Consecrate** your child to God at an early age. **Teach** him the joy of obedience. **Develop** in her the constant awareness that God knows everything she does. **Lead** him or her to accept Christ as Savior at an early age. **Give** him a sense of destiny and purpose in God's plan. **Guide** her to total dedication. **Train** him to discern character. **Saturate** his and her mind with scripture. **Support** him with fervent prayer. **Send,** or better still, **bring** him or her to Bible study and church. Some of these rules will require the parents, themselves, to go back to the basics.

Every observant Christian can think of some child whose parents have let him or her do anything he wanted. That child is on the road to rebellion and waywardness. Someone said that people, like rivers, get crooked by following the path of least resistance. Parents are to provide holy resistance.

Father, guide parents today, and may all of us—who are somebody's children—honor you. Amen.

Jesus Christ the same yesterday, and to day, and for ever.

Timeless truths

What would you do if you could travel through time? Many people would relive one or another event and do the right thing—this time. Some would take steps not to lose track of a friend. Others would want to observe things that happened before their lifetimes, or to be strategically located to find the answer to some longtime mystery. Some would want to peek into the future. Unfortunately, time travel is not possible. Science fiction has long depicted it, and supposedly Einstein's theory proposes it, but if not theoretically, then certainly practically, man is time bound, by logic, and by creation. We exist in a single moment. Now is all we have.

But there are some timeless things. One is God himself. His love is also timeless and unchanging, and the work of Christ Jesus, God the Son, is timeless. What he did on the cross of Calvary and in the empty tomb is something that continues to affect the lives of people every day. In fact, what he did nearly 2,000 years ago comes to life in the lives of humble, worshipful men and women here and now, as they trust him and allow him to take charge. The Bible says not that the cross *was* the power of God, but *is* the power of God unto salvation. It says not that Christ *was* able to save, but *is* able to save to the uttermost all them that call upon his name. It says not only that Christ *was* raised, but that he *is* risen—an accomplished and continuing fact that transcends time and promises power and transformation for your life and mine.

Across the years of time Jesus has remained the ever-present Christ, living through each age with each believer, "traveling through time" with his time-bound creatures, so that they might taste eternity while on earth and enter eternity when they pass from earth. Are you thankful to be part of that number of believers?

Father, today's time is fixed and short, and it's all we have to live in. May Jesus be Lord, whatever the time, for whatever time is left. Amen.

But we have this treasure in earthen vessels, that the excellency of the power may be of God, and not of us.

The tragedy of untapped power

A homeowner experimenting with television repair removed the set's chassis from its case and began tinkering. He removed a rubber cup attached to a large wire from the back of the picture tube and suddenly found himself on the floor, dazed. The wire was used to bleed static from the tube into a capacitor. Though the television had been unplugged, the capacitor was still full of charge, which flowed into the homeowner's hand when he touched the wire.

Some people discover power they didn't know was there. How much more typical, however, that people don't tap the power they *do* know is there. How tragic when the power of God, which he has caused to be in believers, is allowed to go unused. There is so much that needs to be done through it.

I have a little battery; it sits upon my shelf.
It isn't doing anything; it sits there by itself.
It isn't running lights or horns, or pocket radios.
It sits and waits for me to put it in someplace it goes,
And turn it loose to do the thing it once was made to do.
Just now, I have no place to use the battery—do you?

God is no mere battery. His power in us is immense and personal, and is not under our command. But his power does remain unused, though he has sent his Spirit into us for the very purpose of providing the power of resurrection and a new kind of life. How tragic when his power does not impel us in service, empower us in witness, or illuminate our lives with love and glory. How sad and dangerous when we stifle God within ourselves and do not allow him to work in the way he wants. Only when God takes charge will our lives operate as we were meant to.

Father, lead us to turn the power on, that our lives might shine before men. Amen.

Then Peter took him, and began to rebuke him, saying, Be it far from thee, Lord: this shall not be unto thee.

Contradicting God

A man walking down the street in New York saw Cary Grant. Knowing the face, but unable to recall his name, the man rushed up to Grant and stammered, "I know you! You're, uh, not Rock Hudson, uh, no, not Cliff Robertson—it's, uh—" and he stumbled on trying to say the name. Grant politely supplied the answer: "Cary Grant." "No," the man said, "That's not it."

If it didn't grieve him, it would probably amuse God that human beings would ever have the gall to contradict him. We might protest that we wouldn't dare contradict God. Most of us have read what Peter did, taking Jesus aside and attempting to correct him, and we have assured ourselves we wouldn't make the same mistake. We are appalled that he would have such nerve. But has God ever led you to do something for him, perhaps witness, make some contact, do some difficult thing, and you have come back with, "Lord, you know I can't. This is not my area of strength. Give me something else." What is this, but contradicting the Lord? What is it but telling God he doesn't know what he's saying or asking?

We should be horrified that we ever respond that way to God. It is far better if we are going to refuse the Lord's will to say simply, "I don't want to," than to say, "It's not the right thing." In either case, we have neglected his will, but in the latter we have also cut ourselves off from clear communication. By denying that God's will is "good, acceptable, and perfect" (Romans 12:2), we cast doubt in our hearts about the reality of his leading. We may deceive ourselves so thoroughly that we do not know *what* God's will is.

Make it a practice when God speaks, and you're confused, never to say, "Not so, Lord," but always, "I don't understand: help me to see your way."

Father, grant us the grace to be so aware of your awesome holiness that when you speak, we will not dare to say, "no." Amen.

Be not conformed to this world, but be ye transformed by the renewing of your mind...

Being different is hard

The idea of being different is attractive. Truck maker Dodge, Inc., advertised its product with the simple slogan, "Dodge: different." But actually being different is hard. The attraction of what other people are doing is strong. It is difficult to drive 55 when everyone around you whizzes by at 70. It is hard not to wear the latest fashion, even if it's immodest. It is easy to pick up the words and phrases the world is using, and use them yourself. It is difficult not to be affected by the moral—or immoral—thinking of the current generation. Thirty years ago, most people would have been offended by the use of curse words on television, or near-nudity on the streets, and certainly by open discussion of homosexuality. But all are common, now.

The average Christian has gone along with the trends, and his sensitivity to offensive things has been dulled. The average believer has largely failed to obey the implications of Romans 12:2, which warns us against conformity. The Bible states that the world is at cross purposes with God. To conform to the world—to be friendly with worldly ways—is to be God's enemy.

A Christian couple restricted certain toys in their home. As they raised two boys in the last quarter of the 20th century, they encountered many toys that were connected to demonism and witchcraft. One such toy was given as a birthday present to one of the boys, and the parents regrettably had to "disallow" it." A few days later, the young son said casually, "Boy, a whole lot of kids at school have those toys." After he repeated it, it was clear what he meant: though he was old enough to understand his parents' objection, it was hard for him to see others doing something, and not want to do it himself.

God calls us apart from the cravings of the sinful world. Will you yield to him, or to the world?

Father, help us decide for you, not against you, for we know we will be happier in the long run. Amen.

Lay not up for yourselves treasures upon earth, where moth and rust doth corrupt, and where thieves break through and steal.

What thieves cannot steal

A minister drove to his church office one morning and found a police car in the parking lot. Someone had broken into the building and had been trying to get into the office complex when he was frightened off by an alarm system. The minister shortly left to go to a church on the other end of the street, and there found not one but three police cars. Somebody, probably the same person, had broken into this church as well, and like Goldilocks, he had been caught at it.

Most of us find ourselves infuriated at the gall of someone to think he can violate our homes or offices, and take what is not his. But some people have little or no respect of others' property. Because of this, Jesus said, "Don't fall in love with things. Somebody will probably steal them. Instead, get rich on godly character and the joy of evangelism: nobody can take these away from you, ever." That's a loose translation of Matthew 6:19, and verse 33, which says, "But seek ye first the kingdom of heaven, and God's righteousness."

Somebody said, "When you search long and hard, save and scrimp, plan and arrange, and finally get what you want, somebody will steal it." That must be another corollary of the famous Murphy's Law. But it only applies to things of the earth. Because God's salvation and blessings, and Christian joy and character, cannot be stolen. In fact, the more of them you give away, the more of them you have.

When Jesus once visited Mary and Martha in Bethany, Martha complained that Mary was spending time with Jesus instead of helping with the work of hosting. He chided her: "Mary hath chosen that good part, which shall not be taken away from her" (Luke 10:42). This world's riches cannot be kept. But spiritual treasures cannot be taken away.

Father, what better insurance against theft than to lay up treasure where there are no thieves. Let our hearts be so directed today. Amen.

Praying always with all prayer and supplication in the Spirit.

Prayer changes ...people

There's an old Christian adage that prayer changes things. Maybe it would be more completely accurate to say that prayer communicates with God, and God changes things. But the simplified form sticks with us. It's a reminder we need constantly. For most of us, however, it isn't things that need to change so much as it is people—ourselves in particular. Prayer enlightens us with the revelation of God's will. Prayer encourages us by the experience of God's nearness. Prayer feeds us by the illumination it gives to God's word.

Every school child learns about photosynthesis: have you forgotten what it is? It is the mechanism by which plants make food for themselves. The leaves open up toward the sky to drink in carbon dioxide from the air and soak up energy from the sun. This energy works with the green pigment in plants to make the chemicals the plants "eat," so they can grow. A byproduct is oxygen, which we ourselves breathe. If the upturned leaves are denied light, the plant will die.

If a plant, to grow, must have leaves open to the sun, then Christians, to grow, must have lives open to the Son—that means prayer. Prayer is turning our lives upward to God, opening to him. It is the posture of a right relationship to the Lord. Something happens when we pray. To pray is to change. If you are unwilling to change, you will abandon prayer. This is a telling truth, isn't it! It often explains our irregularity in prayer, our excuses for the lack of it. This is why Paul counseled us in the Bible to pray always. It's a simple recommendation, but it's an extremely tall order. What it means is never to enter a phase of life in which prayer is not a regular and important part of your walk with God. Without prayer, there will be virtually *no* walk with God.

Father, we acknowledge we need to keep changing. Therefore, we need to keep praying. May we become disciplined to do it daily, and continually. Amen.

For whosoever hath, to him shall be given, and he shall have more abundance: but whosoever hath not, from him shall be taken away even that he hath.

Double blessing, double cost

The game of Scrabble has been around long enough to become a standard, like Monopoly. Many people enjoy it. But how the game is scored has always had its critics. It isn't difficult, but it seems a bit strange. The game ends when a player uses all his letters and there are no more to draw. That player has the value of all the other players' letters added to his score. But that's not all. They also have the value of their own letters subtracted from their own scores. It's a "double whammy." Critics have said this seems unfair. It seems especially so when one loses. But when one wins, apparently that's another matter. In fact, it is a part of winning strategies to be the first to go out, though slightly behind the leader, but win by acquiring the value of his letters.

It ought to strike us how biblical this model of scoring is. Jesus said in the parable of the sower that those who win by investing the resources God gives them, will get even more as reward, while those who lose by failing to invest at all will have what little they think is theirs taken away. What he meant was apparently connected to the individual's potential: what you have to start with you must use—it must produce fruit. If you waste your potential, your potential itself will be levied against you. If you produce, however, you will be given reward over and above even that.

There is a line somewhere that demarcates between the two, a point at which one stops being a candidate for loss and starts being the assured inheritor of gain. That point is the point at which you start responding to the gospel of Christ by surrendering your life to him and obeying him. Until then, it's a losing game.

Lord, grant us vision to see how our lives could be much more fruitful for Christ, and lead us to invest our whole selves in your plan. Amen.

Delight thyself also in the LORD; and he shall give thee the desires of thine heart.

Entrusting dreams to God

In a way, expressing a prayer is like taking a photograph. When you snap a picture, you have conceived an image you would like to see. On traditional photographic film, that image is only a *potential* picture. Then you take the film to a developer, and entrust your visual conception to someone who can make it a reality. Prayer has an interesting parallel. When you bring your prayer to the Lord, especially a petition, you entrust it with the God who can answer it. When your photographs are ready, your work and trust have paid off. When your prayer is answered, your praying and trusting have been rewarded.

But what about when photo finishers lose your film? That has happened to quite a few frustrated persons. Is there any parallel to prayer? Does God ever lose your prayers? Does he set aside your request or ignore it or fail to answer it? Some have prayed and never sensed or seen what they recognize as an answer. As a result, they have become discouraged in prayer, or doubtful of its purpose.

Not every request we make is granted, but in that some are denied, they, too, are answered—with a "no." How do we help insure a "yes?" Psalm 37:4 says the answer is to delight ourselves in the Lord. People who are basically antagonistic to the Lord and his will for them cannot expect that when they suddenly run into need and come to him, he will pour out a cornucopia of supplies. The person who ignores the Lord as a rule, but turns to him when things get tough, is not likely to experience the full measure of God's provision. But if you walk daily with the Lord, love him and look to him in obedience for your very life itself, he will honor that love for him with his richest blessings in answer to your prayer. Find your joy in the Lord! Grow to love nothing better than to know him and experience him daily.

Father, this day may we take joy in you, your truths, and your will. Amen.

One witness shall not rise up against a man for any iniquity, or for any sin, in any sin that he sinneth: at the mouth of two witnesses, or at the mouth of three witnesses, shall the matter be established.

Be slow to believe evil

In the news a few years ago was the story of a man convicted of rape, mostly on the testimony of the woman he allegedly assaulted. But after he spent six years in jail, she changed her story and said he didn't do it. The legal machinery worked in his favor, and he was released. There were curious facts about their relationship, and perhaps no one except the two of them will ever know the whole truth, but the incident brings up a principle. It is usually unjust to rely on the testimony of a lone witness, and nothing else, to convict someone of wrong. That's true in law, and it's true in everyday life.

You or I may never be judges or members of a jury, but we are presented almost daily with the personal decision whether or not to believe reports about people we know. Someone passes along a story about a friend or acquaintance being involved in something immoral or unethical: do we believe it? Someone tells us that he *knows* for a fact that so-and-so is rotten to the core, or is cheating, or whatever. In fact, it may be only an opinion or the result of his taking offense because of a chip on his own shoulder. Do we believe a report and form an opinion about some other person simply because we are "told" something?

The Bible says we must not! Gossip is prohibited. It is usually generated by someone who had a grudge, saw things wrongly, had a misunderstanding, or jumped to a conclusion that was unfounded. No matter how wide the rumor spreads, or how many sources you can quote as "knowing all about it," you know it probably comes down to *one person* who started it. In most matters, one is not enough to convict. Remember that. Don't believe rumors, and don't start any of your own.

Father, may we speak the truth in love, and believe in love as truth. Amen.

And these signs shall follow them that believe…

What proves you are saved?

It is normal for us to want evidence of our salvation, but unwillingness to take the promises of God by faith has caused many to look for proofs that go beyond what God offers every believer. Many, for instance, look for miraculous signs. Mark 16:17 listed some of the signs that would appear among believers when the gospel began to be preached. Some people would drive out demons, some would speak in languages they had not learned, and some would heal people with a touch. Eager to make these signs personal, some Christians have come to believe that every Christian should have some experience with speaking in tongues, healing and casting out demons.

But what about the rest of the verse, which says believers would handle snakes without injury and drink poison without effect? How many people go that far to prove to themselves they are really saved? Mark 16:17 cannot be taken as normative for every Christian in every generation: its prophecy was fulfilled in the first generation, and only then by representative groups as the gospel was introduced to the world. Even then, these signs were not meant to convince people that they themselves were saved, but to demonstrate the supernatural origin of the new message of the kingdom of God to the world that had never heard it.

It doesn't take a miraculous sign to prove to the individual Christian that he is saved. Our assurance of salvation is to be found in the promise of God: "Believe on the Lord Jesus Christ, and you will be saved" (Acts 16:31). The felt presence of the Holy Spirit then testifies to the fact that we are God's children. The change that comes about in our lives as we follow Christ proves to not only us, but the world around us, that we are born again.

Father, as we continue to trust your eternal security, may the real demonstration of our new lives be the one we give others—so they will believe, too. Amen.

And they continued stedfastly in the apostles' doctrine and fellowship, and in breaking of bread, and in prayers.

A triangle of necessities

There is an interesting triad of things the first Christians did, that helps explain the success of their churches. From Acts 2 come three words that are key: First, "fellowship." They wanted to be with each other. They were in a common cause, bound together by a deeper tie than any other social relationship. They made each other their fast friends.

Second, "steadfast." They devoted themselves not only to one another, but to the doctrine, the teaching, that lay at the core of their belief, and to the leaders who taught it. In essence, they were devoted to the church as the body of Christ. This means they participated. They were committed to this new enterprise, and they did what was needed to make it go.

Third, "giving." Acts 2:45 says their money and goods were not held out from their commitment, but were integrally a part of it. They were sacrificial.

The strongest geometrical shape is a triangle. Once put together, it cannot wobble or sag. Its angles are bound into one configuration. The building or object based on the triangle will be sturdy. In the church of living beings, that triangle is composed of these things: attendance, participation, and giving. Try having a church without these.

If you attend but do nothing and give nothing, you force a small group in the church to bear the load, and they may collapse under it. If you send in your check but do not attend or participate though you could, you help discourage the church into decline and death. If you take part in some peripheral activity but don't worship with the church or give anything, you fool yourself about your belonging, and you add dead weight to the body. The church lives and thrives on those who do all three: come, serve, and give. Which one needs help in your life today?

Father, make us aware of the state of our involvement in your church, and speak to us about what we need to do. Amen

For the good that I would I do not: but the evil which I would not, that I do.

Our repeating history

There are many memorable epigrams on success. One says, "If you want a place in the sun, you have to expect some blisters." Another: "Success is getting what you want out of life without violating the rights of others." Here's one that may grab us by our experience: "The measure of success is not whether you have a tough problem to deal with, but whether it's the same problem you had last year." That says it, doesn't it! So often we find ourselves tangling with the same problems. Sometimes, it's a certain weakness in ourselves. We tend to fall to the same temptations over and over.

One problem that could be at fault is external influences. We may not have done what we could to eliminate the source of temptation. Many of life's worst habits are sustained because we don't get rid of the stuff that tempts us.

But it might simply be that we have not dealt with that part of us on the inside that is open to temptation. We might not have surrendered that area of our minds or hearts to God. The result is like what Paul describes as the state of the man who is not under God's complete control. He has the desire to do what is good, but can't carry it out. He finds himself continuing to do what he doesn't really desire in his heart. The only solution is what Paul also expresses for us: "by the Spirit put to death the deeds of the body" (Rom.8:13). Self must be crucified and Christ enthroned.

We are taught the importance of studying history by the maxim: they who do not learn from history are condemned to repeat it. We learn a similar lesson about our personal lives: he who does not put sin to death is condemned to live through it all over again. We *can* break the cycle, by being broken ourselves—to the mastery of Christ Jesus through his Spirit.

Father, gently break us, so that we may be strong in the Lord. Amen.

I am made all things to all men, that I might by all means save some.

Adapting to circumstances

Driving across the United States, one witnesses a quaint phenomenon. Over thousands of miles of road, one stops at many a rest area. While some are just carbon copies of one another, in some states designers have taken a different approach. In Texas, Louisiana and Alabama, rest areas are often uniquely built. Some represent the part of the country in which they are located. One stop is built to blend in with the architecture of the other buildings in the area. The picnic tables at another in Louisiana are lean-to's. Some of the most interesting are in Texas, where at one stop the picnic tables are covered with a structure that looks like an oil well.

Here is an illustration of something Paul was talking about when he said he had chosen to become "all things to all people" so as to be able to "save some." Obviously, Christ does the saving. What we do is reach and touch people. It is that reaching and touching that demands that we adapt to circumstances. The Christian's witness is to be tailored to the person or persons whom he approaches with the gospel. The gospel itself never changes. But the way it strikes people, the way it gets to them, the way it needs to be presented in order to have its greatest and saving effect, *must* be suited to the life situation or contemporary needs of that person.

Paul was saying that we cannot go like robots and make people fit our conversational plan. We must find out where their hurts are, find out what their understanding is, find out just how their lostness before God affects them, and hit hard at those points, showing how Christ Jesus, the Son of God, is the Savior and salvation they need. If you have to become an oil well to talk to a Texan, then start pumping.

Father, witness is often ineffective because of failure to adapt. Help us to sense what people need most to hear about Jesus, that we might share his love successfully. Amen.

"Well said, teacher," the man replied. "You are right in saying that God is one and there is no other but him."

Agreeing with God

We all have a tendency to applaud what we agree with and boo what we don't agree with. This is not entirely bad, but when it comes to the word of God, we who call ourselves Christians must learn to say, "Amen," to all of it, not just the parts to which we already have conformed.

Jesus once taught about the resurrection saying that God is the God of the living, not the dead. The Bible says some of the teachers of the law said, "You are right." But a page over, it says that Jesus taught that same group that they must accept him as the one sent by God, and their response was that "they looked for a way to arrest him" (Mat.21:46). They said, "Amen," to what they liked, but, "Get him!" at what they didn't. But the same man spoke both things, and that man is the Son of God. God's word must be believed and obeyed *in total,* not just in part.

A preacher at a convention meeting bravely said to those attending that he noticed that during conventions people would readily say, "Amen," to the bell-ringers—speakers who said what we already believe with passion. But he also noticed those same people were strangely silent when a speaker began saying the difficult things, the troubling teachings of the Bible that find us out in our sin and demand of us our complete surrender to God.

It's like the little country woman who dipped snuff. As she sat in church one day, the preacher began talking about smoking, and she said, "Amen." He got onto drinking, and she said, "Amen." He condemned philandering, and she said, "Amen!" but when he came down on "dippin'," she said out loud, "Now you've quit preachin' and gone to meddlin'."

We are not given the privilege to pick and choose which part of God's standards we will live by.

Father, even when your word meddles in our lives, may we submit and say, "Yes, Lord." Amen.

Go to now, ye rich men, weep and howl for your miseries that shall come upon you.

The illusion of wealth

Bible readers may wonder if the writers of scripture felt it was nearly impossible to get rich people to believe they were really unfortunate. James warned rich but unsaved persons of their coming misery. He said they had lived in self-indulgence, fattening themselves for slaughter. They might have said to themselves, "Another poor man tasting sour grapes and trying to make us feel bad!" But was James just railing on riches because he didn't have any? No!

James pointed to solid evidence that earthly riches, while making us superficially happy, powerfully lure us into a dangerous spiritual condition of presumption. Additionally, this Holy-Spirit-inspired message hits hard at a point most of us don't like to admit: the "finer things of life" that come with a bit of affluence are deceitful. They are easier to lose than basic necessities, and frequently they are not really "finer" than the mere essentials.

A couple testing this theory spent time in several accommodations on a trip. They made a list of everything about the modestly priced motels they stayed in and also of the fairly high-priced hotels. While their findings were not scientific, or universally applicable, they were interesting: the more expensive rooms supplied them with a few more amenities, but the modest rooms usually had as much actual *room*. The real cost of the ritzy place was in providing the hotel with a bar and live dance bands, and with services which, while they might be occasionally needed by some people, cost extra anyway. The idea that the place was far superior to the "overnight motel" was mere illusion.

That's what James is saying: wealth is illusory. Don't be fooled. If God gives it to you, use it wisely for him and for your fellow man. But do not become inordinately attached to it. If you don't have it, don't crave it. In the end, you can't take it with you anyway.

Father, make us see how rich we are just to have what we need, and to know you through your Son, Jesus. Amen.

August 10 **Scripture Reading: 1 Thessalonians 5:16**

Rejoice evermore.

Lasting joy

1 Thessalonians 5:16 has both delighted and puzzled people. Rejoice always. That's all: there is no explanation as to how this feat is accomplished. What about when someone dies? What about when your car is wrecked, or when you lose your job? We could add dozens of other things that tend to dampen spirits. How do you have joy always?

Clearly there must be something referred to here that is not mere mirth, not just a surface attitude of happiness. It must have to do with a state of the heart that is not taken away by negative events in this world. The joy must be a spiritual attitude of deep peace and fulfilment in the Lord that overrides or underlies all other emotions. It is possible to grieve over loss and still be joyful. It is possible to be troubled over problems but still be full of joy in the heart. In fact, it is this inner joy that makes possible our conquering the emotional ups and downs of outward life.

Where does this joy come from? Paul does not tell us in this verse, but only because it is elsewhere unquestionably clear: the spirit of Jesus. Jesus said he desired "that my joy might be in you and be full." And Paul wrote, "May the God of hope fill you with all joy and peace as you trust in him." The key is to trust in God, to rest in the forgiveness, love and power of Jesus Christ.

Discouragement and depression are the result of responding to our troubles by believing the worst, doubting God, getting our eyes off the Lord's promises, forsaking prayer, abandoning praise. The cloud of our negative emotions may convince us there is no reason to have joy. Try repeating to yourself the blessings of forgiveness and eternal life and the repeated promises that God will supply all your need through his riches in glory in Christ Jesus. Repeat it again, from deeper in the heart. Continue until the joy rises gently and then fully into your heart.

Father, may our joy come from Jesus today, so that it will not be diminished by things that don't make us happy. Amen.

August 11 **Scripture Reading: 1 Thessalonians 5:17**

Pray without ceasing.

Continuing prayer

How exactly does one pray without ceasing? Modern translations often render this verse, "Pray continually." People have suggested various methods of putting it into practice. Some evidently believe that if you punctuate everything you say during the day with phrases like, "praise the Lord," it will constitute prayer. Others say that if you begin the day with, "Dear Lord," and don't say, "Amen," until you go to bed, that will accomplish it. The latter is pretty good advice, but Paul had something else in mind, we can be sure. This short and pithy verse means don't ever get out of the habit of prayer. Do it regularly and consistently, and often, each day, day after day. Don't give it up because of disappointment or busy-ness. It is your lifeline.

Some people make the mistake of believing that every time they pray it has to be a major speech. It doesn't. There should probably be a time of prayer each day that is fuller than others, but if you run out of things to pray, simply pause and take it up again later when things come to mind. Pray for one thing as it crosses your heart. It isn't necessary to have a minimum list of requests or praises. Breathe a prayer like breathing a breath. For prayer is just talking with God, and since the Spirit of God is with every true believer in Christ, there is no need to ask him to "be with" you. Simply speak to him inwardly, or out loud, and know that he is there and seeks the fellowship of prayer with you. One question is a prayer. One "thank you" is a prayer. Develop the mentality of communion with God. Practice the presence of Christ. Pray continually!

One discipline that will help you obey this command is to develop the habit of prayer as your first response. When someone tempts you to become angry, decide to pray instead. When a problem crops up, choose prayer instead of instantly worrying. When something good happens, before you celebrate with others, celebrate with God: thank him in prayer.

*Father, teach us **to** pray, today, all day. Amen.*

In every thing give thanks: for this is the will of God in Christ Jesus concerning you.

Pervasive gratitude

Christians who have thought any time at all about the instruction in 1 Thessalonians 5:18 have tried all sorts of ways to get around its message, but it stands there, forcing us to admit that complaining attitudes are spiritually immature. It takes a mature person in the Lord to fulfil the demand of this command. How can one give thanks when trouble is all around? Should one be thankful for death, loss, sin, temptation? Ah, but the verse says, "*In* everything," not necessarily "*for* everything." None of us should be thankful for sin, but the circumstances that bring temptation also have the potential of bringing blessing: it depends on how we respond. We are not likely to be thankful for tragic death, but God is not beyond using anything to get his message through to us, and for this we can and should be thankful.

It took real maturity, and grace beyond what many of us have, for the parents of a teen who had been killed in a car wreck to say, "We're thankful that the other boy wasn't killed." They found something to be thankful for. It preserved their confidence that nothing that happens is beyond God's redemptive purposes, and it opened the channel to God, who could help them in their grief.

The thoughts written by a housewife who walked in to face her messy house are memorable and instructive. She looked around, then set about putting order to things, and as she did she began praying: "Thank you God for these dirty dishes: they mean we have enough to eat. Thank you for the toys all over the floor: we have enough means to provide things for our children. Thank you for the noise and confusion of playing children: they are healthy and able to walk and tumble about. Thank you, God: you've been so good to us!" It makes all the difference in the world to be thankful!

Thank you, Lord, for whatever is ahead this day. If nothing else goes right, we have you to help us bear it, and for that, we're grateful. Amen.

August 13 **Scripture Reading: 1 Thessalonians 5:19**

Quench not the Spirit.

Inward fire

This pithy saying to the Thessalonian church is particularly important. We may have admirable qualities and live by high ethical and practical standards but lack the most important dimension of a Christian's life: spiritual control by the Holy Spirit. The Spirit has long been associated with fire: the burning bush through which God appeared to Moses; the fire that cleansed the lips of Isaiah; the fire burning in the bones of Jeremiah; the fire with which John said Jesus would baptize. God's Spirit is a fire that burns away impurities and creates energy within us to do his will. Passion for winning souls is holy fire. Enthusiasm for any area of God's will is an example of his fire at work within you. Power that comes from deep inside to resist temptation or speak up for the Lord, or be forgiving in the face of evil, is the fire of the Spirit. The Bible's instruction is: don't let anything put out that fire—especially in *you.*

The fire can be put out by piling up unconfessed sins; by shutting off the avenues of prayer; by stubbornly resisting the leadership of God. The fire of God's burning desires in you, and for you, can be quenched by worldliness, suppressed concern, or by procrastinating about immediate needs in your life in the spiritual plane. One of the surest ways is to get lax in reading the Bible.

Old-style hand warmers are one of life's mysterious little wonders and certainly a joy to have at a cold football game. You fill them with fuel, light them, let the flame burn out, then close them up and put them in your pocket. Yet they get hotter. A catalytic reaction explains it. Yet, they will burn out, if you don't keep them fueled. Forget about them, and they will be quenched, just like us—no fuel, no fire. No Bible, no passion. No influx of Spirit power, no spiritual fire. Don't quench the inward fire!

Father, remind us to let you stoke the fire today, at every opportunity, so we will burn hotly and brightly for you. Amen.

Despise not prophesyings.

Teachable heart

Before there were such things as kings in Israel, there were prophets through whom God directed and instructed his people. It isn't surprising that when Messiah Jesus came, he began his church under the leadership not of kings or presidents, but prophets. The Bible tells us God gave "some prophets" to the church. In the days before the New Testament was written, prophecy was especially important. Prophets' proclamations led the church; their teachings became the New Testament; eventually preachers would re-proclaim their message. Today's preachers have inherited the prophets' role, continuing to proclaim the message of Christ as it came down from the prophets, the apostles, and Jesus.

Therefore the Bible says not to despise, or show contempt for, prophesying—preaching. In fact, Paul wrote that God deliberately chose to use the "foolishness" (in the world's view) of preaching, to save those who believe what is preached. We are to respect and follow the genuine preaching of the word of God. There are many brands of preaching, and much difference of opinion. But in orthodox Christianity there is substantial agreement on the central teaching of the Bible. Our passionate disagreements on other things demonstrates that we know that understanding the Bible is important, and we care about proclaiming our understanding to the world.

Consequently, listeners should take heed. Preachers aren't perfect, but the Bible is, and God almost certainly has a word for you and me when the Bible is preached. This is the mystery of preaching: God uses it with all its flaws to send his word to those who need to hear it.

A young man was attending a service in a church other than his own. Responding to the preaching, he made a decision affecting his life greatly. He later realized the great weaknesses of the preacher who spoke in that meeting. But it didn't alter the fact that his own life had been changed by doing what the preacher said that was from God. God can use imperfect prophets to declare his perfect word to your heart.

Father, when many voices speak your word, let us not ignore them, but be teachable. Amen.

Ye know that after two days is the feast of the passover, and the Son of man is betrayed to be crucified.

Belief is a choice

It is hard to see why the disciples of Jesus did not understand that he would be killed. He spoke numerous times of his inevitable death. Sometimes the language was symbolic, sometimes very specific, as in Matthew 26: "The Son of man is betrayed to be crucified." How did the disciples miss it? Part of the reason may be that "the Son of man" was a title that enabled him to speak humbly. "The Son of man came to seek and save that which is lost." "The Son of man must suffer many things." "The Son of man is Lord of the Sabbath." He spoke of himself in the third person to demonstrate humility, and for another very important reason: to leave to the hearer the decision as to whether or not to *believe* he was the Son of man, and the Son of God, the Christ.

President Nixon presented an interesting case study of one who consistently separated his office from his person. He would speak of the President as if he were another person entirely. "The President cannot afford to do this; the President is responsible." He raised his office to a mysterious level at which he almost implied he was more than human when acting "in his office." This was not Jesus' case. But he did allow each hearer the decision as to whether the titles applied to him were true.

Do you believe Jesus was and is the Son of man, the Son of God, the Christ? God gives us the choice. What we decide doesn't change the truth, or create the truth, or change our accountability for rejecting the truth. It simply means God doesn't force us to believe. Our belief is a choice, and so it is with every Bible truth, every Bible promise. We can choose to believe, or not. In believing, our very lives and futures are changed.

Father, we know enough truth to change our lives. Grant us grace to choose to believe. Amen.

I would thou wert cold or hot.

Making up our minds

One thing about children that frustrates parents is the stage they go through when they are ambivalent—they can't make up their minds. A little boy with his parents at church told his father, "I'm going home with Mommy"—they had driven two cars that morning. So he gets in the car with his mother, then on the way out of the parking lot he has a fit to go with his daddy, instead. So the mother lets him out, and he climbs into his father's car, only to complain all the way home that he wanted to "go with Mommy!" It drives parents crazy.

But think of how we must look to the Lord. Christians ought to be making progress all the time, but we have our times of wishy-washiness—now hot, now cold for the Lord. This was a serious matter to Christ when he spoke through John to us all in Revelation 3:15, telling us to be either cold or hot. Pick which side of the fence you want to be on, and get there, but don't straddle it. Either be faithful to church or quit entirely. Either seek for and do God's will, or ignore it completely, but stop toying with God. It's incredibly dangerous. As Joshua said to Israel, "Choose you this day whom ye will serve" (Joshua 24:15).

Most of us have heard and been struck with the amusing wisdom of "Murphy's Law" and some of its corollaries. Here's one that illustrates our thought: "No matter which side of the door the dog or cat is on, it is the wrong side." A lot of us emulate our pets: we seem never to make up our minds. If we're out, we want in; if we're in, we want out. It probably comes down to our failure to be fully under the control of Christ, fully given to the Lordship of his Spirit in us. Until we are, we will imitate the see-saw.

Father, since life is no playground, but a proving ground for our commitment, teach us to make up our minds. Amen.

I follow after, if that I may apprehend that for which also I am apprehended of Christ Jesus.

Being fulfilled

All of us want to get the most out of life, to find what we were "meant for." But how do you do this? Do you slide by accident into a groove that was made just for you? Perhaps some of us do, but assuming this will happen is risky. It is better to investigate what we were meant for, inquiring from an authoritative source.

Christians believe that God made us and has a plan for us. No one knows better what we were meant for than him who designed all things, including us. Consequently it is of utmost importance that we find and do the "will of God," whatever that is. Paul talked about "pressing on" to take hold of that for which Christ took hold of *us*. If we really want to be fulfilled, we must take hold of God's plan for us, which he made us to fulfill.

For years, the great American broadcaster Paul Harvey advertised a certain brand of stereo system for specific models of cars. The stereo system was made especially for these few luxury cars, tailor fitted acoustically to them. The sound, said he, is the best it can be, because everything about the system is customized for the conditions. The same principle applies to any sound system for any media. It makes a difference what components are used in a unit. They need to be designed for one another. The input must match the source, the speakers must match the output, the cabinet must resonate with the speaker. When they do, the system will be as good as it can be.

You and I are designed for something. We don't fit anything else quite right. There are always gaps, tight squeezes, abrasions. But if we are in the will of God, doing what he made us and called us out to do in Christ Jesus, there will be harmony with him, and performance excellence by his standards. We will be fulfilled.

Father, bring fulfilment today by bringing us squarely into your will. Amen.

He that believeth on me, believeth not on me, but on him that sent me.

We must know Jesus

Some people try to skip Jesus on their way to God. Ask someone if he is a Christian and you will often hear, "I believe in God." That isn't the issue. Do you believe in Jesus Christ as God in the flesh?—That *is* the issue. Neither is it an optional issue. Jesus said, "I am the way, the truth, and the life; no man comes to the Father but by me." Before Jesus, faith could be placed in God as revealed in the scriptures, as preached by the prophets, as figured symbolically in the worship of the temple prescribed by God himself. But in all the Old Testament the Christ of God was forecast. Consequently, when God sent his Son in the flesh, in the fullness of times, he wanted us to accept him as our one mediator, God's chosen one. If we do not do so, we contradict God. How can we ignore God's Son, and expect God to receive us gladly?

Jesus said if someone believes on him, he is believing the Father. This is a deep truth with this obvious meaning: if one doesn't believe in Jesus, he or she doesn't believe in the *one true God.* Let that thought penetrate your mind and heart.

If you have trouble with the teachings of Jesus, you are questioning the revelation of God. If you doubt the sinlessness of Jesus, you are questioning the holiness of God. If Jesus is the express image of the Father, as Hebrews 1:3 says, then you can't skip him on your way to God. That's why it is essential that we concentrate on Jesus in our devotional lives. Coming to know God depends upon coming to know Jesus Christ personally. Today's challenge is to see how much you focus on Christ personally in your life, your thought, your witness, your prayer. If getting to know Jesus isn't what you aim for, you're aiming for the wrong thing.

Father, show us the Son, and it is enough. Jesus our Lord, show us yourself. Amen.

As the whirlwind passeth, so is the wicked no more: but the righteous is an everlasting foundation.

When trouble stirs

Rain is good, but it doesn't always come gently. Sometimes it comes in the torrents of violent storms. A storm will develop far out at sea, and be swept by mammoth currents of air to continents, where it wreaks havoc with coastlines and all that is built there, with people's lives and livelihood, with travel and safety. We sense we should thank God for rain if we have needed it, but we do not welcome the storms.

We, however, do the same things to other people's lives when we stir up storms of trouble. We affect not only the people we fight with or resent, but everyone around them as well. Sometimes we have no idea how far reaching our squabbles go. A whole church suffers when just a few people can't get along with each other. The whole fellowship is affected by the complaining of a small minority, by the disgruntled few who are never really pleased with anything.

God may allow storms in a fellowship or relationship just as he does other trials, for the purpose of weeding out the faithless and strengthening the obedient. Whether our trials are "acts of God," or acts of man, we should make certain the Lord is our foundation, and we should hold fast to him.

In the end, it is not those who stir up storms who get things done in a lasting way, but those who approach things with love, patience, redemptive attitudes, and commitment to Christ and his church. Those who boycott church or anyone in it, demonstrating that they have been offended, simply hurt themselves most in the long run. If they do anything *for* the church by their negative behavior, it will only be that by eliminating dead wood—themselves—the others will go on to greater heights. God knows how to enable his people to weather storms. For our part, we must determine not to cause them.

Father, forgive our impatience with others for their faults. They probably have at least as much trouble dealing with ours. Amen.

Blotting out the handwriting of ordinances that was against us, which was contrary to us, and took it out of the way, nailing it to his cross.

Christ cancels our sins

Every human being needs the removal of sin's condemnation from his life. The marvelous statement of scripture is that Christ does this through the his death on the cross. We cannot fully explain how it worked, but somehow God miraculously dealt with our sin through a sinless substitute. The love and power of God for us is such that he could and did do it, so that we might be forgiven and live forever with him.

Physicists have discovered the existence of something fiction writers have talked about for years: antimatter. This strange and hard-to-find stuff is the duplicate of matter, but with a different fundamental charge. If an atomic particle meets its anti-particle counterpart, the result is a release of pure energy, and the complete disappearance of those particles. Fortunately, if there really is antimatter for all matter, it's likely in another universe!

Like so many interesting things about God's creation, this tidbit from physics illustrates a spiritual truth. Jesus Christ was in every way like us but fundamentally opposite in that he had no sin. When he died on the cross, his sinless life canceled the debt of our sins. We are spared sin's condemnation by accepting this cancellation as a gift. But unlike matter and antimatter, which disappear by canceling each other out, we do not cancel Christ. He could not be kept dead. He arose. In this unparalleled event is the completion of our salvation. We accept the cancellation of sin, and then we receive new life through *his life,* which continues beyond this life, and never ends.

Avoid sin. Repent and be forgiven when you fail to avoid it. But you who are in Christ, rejoice today that your sins have been canceled, forgiven, done away with, by the awesome sacrifice of Christ.

Father, may Jesus Christ become the cancellation mark on someone else's sin today, through the witness of someone like us who understand it and can explain it. Amen.

August 21 **Scripture Reading: 2 Peter 2:10**

But chiefly them that walk after the flesh in the lust of uncleanness, and despise government.

Voting with our feet

Some say it's not polite—even that it's un-American—to ask a person how he is going to vote. Others don't mind at all, because it gives them an opportunity to try to influence people. As important as political elections are, however, spiritual voting is even more significant in the long run. How do you vote spiritually? One of the more effective ways to vote spiritually is with your feet.

The generation who rebelled against government in the infamous 1960's grew up to resist the authority of ideas, including teachings from the church. Their children, reared in this philosophy, are plagued with disbelief in moral standards, other than those moral concepts that make them happy. It's called moral relativism. Because of this condition, many churches have plenty of elderly people but the young are voting with their feet and staying away.

The moods and moral developments of any age are a concern to the church, and create crises and challenges. Moral relativism has created an especially dangerous crisis. In Romans, Paul says all authorities are designed by God, and to rebel against bonafide authority is to rebel against God. Peter describes social rebellion as "despising government," meaning the very principle of being under authority —especially God's. Peter says that those who live in rebellion against God's authority stand in danger of eternal consequences.

We vote with our feet. If we stay away from the church, we vote for its closure and for the world and the devil. If we go places and do things God commands us not to do, we vote for evil, for corruption of families, and destruction of lives. But if we go to worship, go to meet in fellowship with those who love God, we vote *for* the prevalence of truth and godliness. Going to church isn't everything, but it is a vote, and an important one, and every vote counts.

Father, may the divine poll show us joining many others in your kingdom who side with what is righteous, and the One who is righteous. Amen.

He that is of God heareth God's words: ye therefore hear them not, because ye are not of God.

The reason for unbelief

Some beliefs are persistent. They linger stubbornly in the face of all reason. This is why many people remain unsaved to their dying day, and why many who are saved remain in spiritual ruts all the time. Some of our errors we stubbornly refuse to see, and we pay the price for it. Jesus asked the Pharisees why his language wasn't clear to them, why it didn't get through. He answered his own question. The reason was that they didn't belong to God. Jesus puts eternal weight on hearing and obeying his words. We dare not resist the change of mind and heart that is required to believe and obey him.

A young psychologist believed that any mentally ill person could be cured by straight talk. He went to work for a mental hospital. He succeeded in helping many patients talk through their maladies. But one old man had been there for years, and was completely convinced that he was dead. No argument would convince him otherwise. The young doctor said to him one day, "Do you think a dead man can bleed?" The man said, "No." Taking a long pin, the psychologist plunged it into the finger of the patient as he sat there. He yelped and drew it back, and as the wound began oozing blood, he looked wide eyed at the doctor and exclaimed, "Well, what do you know—dead men *do* bleed!"

Some people will never be convinced of truth. They will twist it around to make it fit what they want to believe, which usually underwrites how they want to live. When the Bible says Christ is our only Savior who must be received, we should believe and obey. When the Bible tells the believer that loving the world makes you an enemy of God, he or she should believe it and repent.

Father, grant us humility to confess we do not know everything, and grace to believe and obey every word that comes out of your mouth to us. Amen.

Put them in mind ... to be ready to every good work.

Our need of reminders

There are some things which if told once, we should act upon and never forget. Some people, having had a close call in an automobile, never forget thereafter to wear a seat belt. Other things, however, we all forget, and need reminding of. The Christian should always fulfill his duty to worship, but occasionally some do require reminding. A host of other things get laid by the way as we go along, and someone needs to remind us to fulfill some Christian responsibility. It may be a reminder to give to support the church, to witness, to forgive, or to abandon practices which are immoral or unethical. Sometimes we are reminded to watch our speech or our thoughts. Sometimes we need reminding to spend time with the Lord in prayer and the study of the Bible. Often Christians resist the reminder and accuse the one doing it of sticking his nose into our business. But the duty of the preacher, the teacher, and any Christian led to humbly exhort another, is to call believers to live out their commitments to Christ.

Paul wrote that Titus should *remind them!* God puts people into our lives to prompt us to "every good work." We believers need reminding sometimes, perhaps frequently. Yet sometimes we clutter the reminders with objections that blunt the impact of the exhortation. A little poem goes this way:

I keep a little memo pad beside my bed to write
The multitude of thoughts and things that come to me at night:
Ideas rare are written there—reminders, and how I need them;
The only trouble is, of course, come morning, I can't read them.

That's futility, isn't it? God tries to get through with his reminders, using a friend, a broadcast, a sermon, a devotional reading, and we frequently make the handwriting on the wall illegible through confusion with excuses or defenses. Today, let us not ignore God's reminders. He sends them in myriad ways because he loves us and wants our lives to be pure, fruitful, joyful, and rewarding.

Father, be persistent with us today, and show us the way. Amen.

August 24 **Scripture Reading: Psalm 119:130**

The entrance of thy words giveth light; it giveth understanding unto the simple.

Where to find help

What do you do when you need help—specifically when you need guidance, wisdom, encouragement, or strength? Some people head for their therapist. They talk, listen to the professional say, "Mmm hmm," and then go home thinking they are better. Some people ask every friend they know what to do, apparently willing to let the majority opinion rule. Others talk to bartenders or cab drivers—and why these people should know what a stranger should do is anyone's guess. Sometimes people go to see ministers. They are usually pretty good sources of advice, but any minister worth his salt will refer people seeking help to an even better source of wisdom, and one people should think of *first:* The word of God.

Psalm 119:130 advises us that the real source of light is not the wisest of human beings, but the words of God. Understanding and wisdom begin with awe and respect of God, which come from a study of and acceptance of the word of God. In the New Testament, James counsels us, "If you lack wisdom, ask God." Going to the word of God is asking God. God inspired his word for exactly this purpose. When it speaks to you, it is God speaking.

The best companion to prayer for wisdom is a thorough study of the Bible as it speaks to your particular situation or problem. Try the Psalms for comfort, repentance, cries for help, testimony of deliverance, inspiration for worship. Go to Proverbs for practical advice on countless predicaments or situations. Look to the pastoral epistles in the New Testament for mature, spiritual guidance in interpersonal relationships. Read the gospels to draw closer to Jesus. Use a concordance to look up words that might help you find passages relating to your need. Spend time in the word of God. God gave it to you for a reason. It's where you will find help.

Father, just as our parents reminded us to listen to them when they said something, let us pay attention to what your word says. Amen.

Suffer the little children to come unto me, and forbid them not: for of such is the kingdom of God.

Children in church

Jesus had an affection for children, and more than once he told his disciples and others that his true followers must have some childlike qualities. Interpreters suggest that among other things, when Jesus said, "of such is the kingdom of God," he meant that children may become citizens of the kingdom as soon as they are able personally to trust God. Certainly, he meant that all of us should have a simple and easily expressed faith and trust in Christ to save us. But perhaps Jesus' statement also says something about the nature of maturity. Jesus was bothered by the stuffiness and false sincerity of the super-religious Jews. When he recommended childlikeness, perhaps he was telling them to "lighten up."

Something happens to most of us as we leave school and childhood behind in years. We leave childhood's unadulterated enjoyment of the moment and its innocent impulsiveness. It is not unusual for us to think that growing up requires us to give up joyful abandonment or carefree fun. This attitude affects not only the way we relate to friends and family, where it can stifle the atmosphere of happiness, but to the church of believers in Christ, where it can mean that worship is inhibited and youth are turned off. An educator coined the word, "dis-invited," for the process by which young people are turned off to learning or to involvement. Super-serious, stuffy ideas of maturity "dis-invite" the young, and make church out to be a place where imagination is taboo and enthusiasm must be restrained at all costs.

Be a Christian who enjoys God! Be a believer whose joy is so full, that her happiness, at least once in a while, cannot be restrained. Be a church member who keeps the slumbering saints awake and alive!

Father, make us young not only at heart but in spirit, by your Spirit in ours. Amen.

Strive to enter in at the strait gate: for many, I say unto you, will seek to enter in, and shall not be able.

Fitting through the narrow door

To the question of how hard it would be to be saved, Jesus told us to make every effort to enter by the narrow door. In Matthew's account Jesus adds that the way to destruction is broad. The concept is that living "just any old way"—the broad way—is a guarantee of condemnation, while being careful to live God's way—the narrow way—is the pathway to heaven. Some people think that any effort will be sufficient, that God will reward our nodding in his direction, or our generally good intentions, or our sporadic benevolence. But the concept of the narrow door implies that one's very life itself restricts entrance into heaven. In fact, God doesn't need to intervene directly to prohibit anyone's entrance. To use Jesus' metaphor, those who don't belong won't fit through the door anyway.

A woman grew up in a large church with many wings and interesting rooms and halls. Having been away a few years, she returned for a visit. Navigating her way through some obscure parts of the building she knew well in her youth, she tried to squeeze through a narrow passageway and found to her surprise that she had grown—sideways. She was embarrassed. Many of us have had similar experiences and know the problem. Many people have grown fat with pride, self-assurance, self-confidence, self-righteousness, and will not fit through the narrow door that leads to salvation. Jesus called it the eye of the needle.

What is the narrow door? It is the restriction and the requirement that you must confess to being a *sinner* in need of a *Savior,* and you must believe that *Jesus* is that Savior. He must become Lord of your life, before you may enter the narrow door. When you come to the narrow door, will you be embarrassed because you don't fit?

Father, grant the gift of humility and surrender to us today, that Jesus may be Lord, and we may enter life eternal. Amen.

They shall not leave in thee one stone upon another; because thou knewest not the time of thy visitation.

Recognizing God

Do you always expect God to approach you in a certain way? Do you think it will always be a dream in the night, a vision in worship, or a still, small voice? Do you always expect all the circumstances to point one way before you can be reasonably expected to confess, "This is God speaking to me?" God does not always come in the same way, or speak in the same manner. Sometimes we miss his leading entirely, because we have preconceptions about what his will is, and are not looking for alternatives.

Jesus said great calamity would come upon Israel because they didn't recognize the time of their visitation—the time God would present himself to them for salvation. God had not been deliberately obscure. He had not played a game with them, giving them clues but secretly hoping they would not figure out the messianic prophecies. Nor does he visit us with the revelation of his will, the uncovering of his answers, the sharing of his wisdom, but somehow disguise himself so we won't see and believe. The only things that keep us from understanding his voice are the veil of unbelief, the wall of sin, and the chasm of prayerlessness.

George Washington Carver, the agricultural chemist, was invited on one occasion to a Congressional hearing. He arrived by train and was to be met by someone. He stood alone, looking around, dressed as he usually was in a plain suit, dragging a heavy wooden case filled with important experiments. No one approached him. Finally he asked a passing redcap for assistance, and the man said, "Sorry, pops, but I've been sent down here to meet a very important man, a big scientist." Before Carver could identify himself, the redcap was gone.

Preoccupied Christians sometimes claim they are looking for the will of God, but they miss it when it stares them in the face.

Father, clear our vision so we can see your directing hand; help us stop looking around everywhere, so we can recognize Jesus. Amen.

August 28 **Scripture Reading: 1 Corinthians 11:1**

Be ye followers of me, even as I also am of Christ.

Models for our discipleship

Do you have a hero? Many people consciously or unconsciously pattern their lives after someone who represents what they are striving for. Heros are not all bad. But it is possible to get the wrong ones and wind up in error or confusion. It is also possible to misread our models, and become not like they really are, but like we think they are, which may be seriously mistaken.

Christians are permitted to have models, but they must be good ones. The best model is Christ himself. But Paul twice recommended to the Corinthians Christians that they use him as a model for developing their discipleship, and of the Thessalonian Christians he said, "You became a model to all the believers in Macedonia." How good not only to model after someone, but to be models ourselves. Christians are to "make disciples." This implies not just technical training, but personal influence. Christians are to be models of faith for each other and each new generation of believers. We must continue to present to people someone they can watch and if need be, imitate, in their goal to come to know Christ.

Art students sometimes have a person to serve as a model, who sits in the center of class while everyone draws him or her. What is fascinating is how people differ on what they see. One will see mostly rude form, another plays on the light, another stresses the mood. One may represent the model as more ideal, another will change the face to look beautiful when it is not. Another may distort the image so it can't be said what he was looking at. Christians are like that sometimes, even with the same ideal model—Christ. We don't all imitate him alike. Some of this is good: we are individual, with differing gifts. But we all should look like Christ in his love and truth. In these things, there is no room for disagreement.

Father, thanks for making us different. But make us all like Christ, and one in him. Amen.

> **Nay, in all these things we are more than conquerors through him that loved us.**

More than just success

Parents hate to hear their children say, "I can't do it." Fathers like to see their sons tackling big challenges and succeeding. Mothers like to see their daughters being brave and taking on the world. But little boys and girls have to grow and learn, and frequently they really can't do something. Dad's expectations may be too great. Mom's dreams may be too lofty. Sometimes parents forget that when they were children, they occasionally said, "I can't," and they really couldn't. Sometimes they could, but gave up easily. That's why *their* parents said to them, "Sure, you can." Even if there are things we cannot do, many of them we can do eventually if encouraged enough. When the time is right, we'll do them.

Paul told Christians that through the inward power of the Spirit of Christ, we are "more than conquerors." Our lives have the potential to go beyond merely meeting minimum requirements. In the face of trial, persecution, loss—anything that threatens our faith and our peace, we are possessed of a power to overcome by an overwhelming margin. There is nothing God sends us to do, nothing he expects of us as his disciples, that we cannot do through Christ our Lord and our power. He makes us able. Elsewhere Paul wrote, "I can do all things through Christ who strengthens me." This encouragement is very much like our verse. God promises not only that we can do it but also that we can exceed people's expectations of us and do it gloriously!

Often, it is encouragement that makes the difference. There is something about being told over and over, about being reminded of our potential, that makes us reach down inside for everything we have, lay it all on the line, take hold of God—to appropriate everying *he* has, and then, in his power, win. When we do, it makes us wonder why we are ever satisfied to say, "I can't."

Father, in Jesus name excite us to do your will, for we can—we CAN! Amen.

I will take heed to my ways, that I sin not with my tongue.

Watch your tongue

How many of us are really concerned about the way we live? This is a day and time in which people flippantly say, "Who cares," and do what they please. This is a day in which morals are being deliberately and flagrantly reversed to allow all sorts of deviance, because people crave it, and, this is a day of seemingly unrestricted filth flowing from people's mouths. People use the name of the Lord Jesus Christ as an expression of disgust, surprise, or contempt. Consider how many common epithets, even many not considered vulgar, are rooted in the name of Jesus or Christ. Sinful man seems addicted to the use of God's name for ungodly purposes. Nothing seems sacred.

In this moral climate, do you watch your ways, and keep your tongue from sin? Some people don't think it matters what they say, that it isn't possible for mere words to be wrong. We all grew up hearing that words could never hurt us. Some think as long as no one is hurt, consenting adults may do and say whatever they please. This is not what the Bible says about our speech, however. Do you recognize God's absolute laws, that warn us against all impure thought and speech, and particularly against the empty or vulgar use of his name?

Computer terminology includes the acronym GIGO. It means, "garbage in, garbage out." If you feed bad or mistaken information into a computer program, you get bad or mistaken information out of it. Likewise, if you feed yourself on the garbage of human activity, the trashy speech of humanity's gutter world, you will begin to reflect it. Your thoughts will eventually reveal themselves in actions. This is why the Psalmist said the righteous man is one who "walketh not in the counsel of the ungodly, nor standeth in the way of sinners." Sooner or later, your choice of friends and influences will come through in *you.*

Father, teach us the truth of the Bible's word of wisdom that bad company corrupts good morals. Amen.

Therefore we ought to give the more earnest heed to the things which we have heard, lest at any time we should let them slip.

Avoid drifting

The author of Hebrews urges that we pay heed to what the Lord has taught us because of the dangerous condition of the un-watchful life. If we do not remember, and follow, the teachings of Christ, we will "let slip," or "drift." The writer reminds us to be very aware of what is happening in our spiritual lives, and to carefully apply every spiritual lesson, every biblical preaching and teaching, to our conduct and thought, so that we will avoid the pitfall of drifting—slowly getting away from the heat of commitment to Christ. Drifting happens almost without our noticing it. We usually justify or excuse ourselves while doing it, and we rarely think we are in bad shape when we have drifted away.

Many a beach-goer has had the experience of lying out in the sun on a float, just beyond the breaking waves, and getting lazy. A bit of sideways drift doesn't concern him. But the farther out he drifts, the harder it is to tell that anything has changed, until a wave laps over his face and he sits up to realize he is in front of an unfamiliar shoreline and is a hundred yards out. That's one reason public beaches have lifeguards, to remind you that you are too far out, to keep you from drifting into danger.

The Holy Spirit is our lifeguard, to remind us to pay close attention to the Word, so as not to drift in commitment to Christ. He will use Bible verses you have read today or recently. If you have drifted out of regular scripture reading, he will use verses you read long ago. He may put someone in your way who unwittingly reminds you of the teachings of Christ. In some way, he will speak to you today about your relationship to him. Listen to him. It is for your own good.

Father, we really want to be close, and obedient. Help us to not ignore the Spirit's words today. Amen.

September 1 **Scripture Reading: John 9:27**

Wherefore would ye hear it again? will ye also be his disciples?

Giving in to God

The scene was Jerusalem. Jesus had just given sight to a man born blind. The Pharisees hounded the man to tell who had done it, and then they wanted to know how. Finally, as the man continued to tell them about Jesus, they demanded he give glory instead to God, for they said, "We know this man is a sinner." Once again they asked how it happened, and at this point he gave the answer in John 9:27. Did they want to hear it again so they could finally decide to follow Jesus? The irony was that they were very far from wanting to become Jesus' disciples—or were they?

There is a very fine line between resisting Jesus with all your might and believing in him with all your heart. Frequently the last barriers in us to belief are accompanied by the greatest force and anger, so that our hottest hostility towards something appears just before we break down and accept it. This was the experience of Saul on the road to Damascus. Many believers have experienced such conversions. It seems that sometimes what we know in our hearts is true we are the most unwilling to believe. Consequently, our strongest reactions are reserved for things we have the most flimsy grounds for rejecting. The gospel offends our egos. But our strongest resistance may well be just before our surrender.

We have heard the phrase, "The bigger they come, the harder they fall." The Christian may think of any number of persons in Christian history who illustrate this principle. John Newton, the slave trader, was struck by the message of the cross and converted. C. S. Lewis, the atheist, became one of the more influential Christian writers of all time. Why not pray today for some giant of un-belief. Who knows if his or her anger against God is the sign that the gospel will soon penetrate, and save!

Father, you can save anyone—you saved us. Win the victory in another life today, and let us join in the praise of you for it. Amen.

September 2 **Scripture Reading: Luke 8:46**

And Jesus said, Somebody hath touched me: for I perceive that virtue is gone out of me.

Touching God

Movies or television programs can deeply affect us. Motion pictures, in particular, seem to have the ability to define the mood of a year, or an entire generation, when they deal with a war, a political crisis, or some other social issue. Charities and other worthy causes are eager to make use of this emotional effect—people respond most generously and gladly when something touches them. The very phrase, "touches us" suggests a deep impact on the soul, an intensely personal thing. Something that touches us leaves us vulnerable but also motivated to action.

Jesus once said when a woman in a crowd reached out to lay hold of his garment, "Someone touched me." He was asked how he could identify a single person touching him in the press of a crowd. He repeated: "Somebody hath touched me." His explanation was that "virtue," or power, had passed from him into whomever touched him. The woman in question was urgent to touch Jesus because of her physical need. She sought him out, straining and struggling to reach through the bodies in front of her. Her reaching was the physical enactment of her prayer, the embodiment of her longing. She succeeded, and the touch evoked his awesome power.

The physical touch symbolizes the spiritual one in this passage. But Hebrews 4:15 tells us that Jesus isn't like merely human priests who cannot fully be touched with the feelings of our infirmities, but was instead able to empathize with us in everything, since he had experienced all our temptations and testings. As the incarnate Word, he experienced human life, and he knows our struggles intimately. Because he does, he is touched with our prayers and pleased to respond to us as we pour out our hearts heavenward. How wonderful to have a God who can be touched!

Father, we are truly glad you hear us, and care about the way we feel. We simply rejoice in your knowing compassion. Amen.

For meat destroy not the work of God.

The distraction of the less important

Some humorist observed that before you can do anything, you have to do something else. Many of us have been distracted from something that needed to be done by something that really didn't, at least not right away. Probably the most common reason people are late for appointments of any kind is that they are distracted by unimportant things.

Paul wrote the Roman church about several matters they debated as to their being allowed for the Christian. One had to do with eating meat—some of the Roman Christians were vegetarians for spiritual reasons. Paul clearly said they were mistaken—he called them "weak." But he went on to speak to the meat eaters, and generally to us all: Don't undo the work of God over food. It was a word about the relationship of one concern to another in the Christian life. All sorts of issues may arise in the course of our trying to live by the Bible and follow the Spirit. It is entirely possible, and in fact it often happens, that we are tempted to spend our energies haggling over things that are not essential to the faith. When we do, we jeopardize the spread of the gospel, and we endanger the discipleship of those who are still very immature in the faith.

Like winning the battle but losing the war, or not seeing the forest for the trees, we can become obsessed with minor issues and lose our focus on the major ones. This is not to say that there is no importance at all to issues other than evangelism and missions, or the deity of Christ, or other major doctrines. There are hundreds of subjects for Christians to address—biblical, social, or cultural—in their proper order and with the proper perspective. If, however, we are distracted by the less important, the most important— love and the gospel—may never get done.

Father, we get caught up in trivia sometimes, when there is no time for it. Help us see the main thing today, at each hour of the day. Amen.

God doth know that in the day ye eat thereof, then your eyes shall be opened, and ye shall be as gods.

The lure of false promises

Madison Avenue in New York is the proverbial home of advertising in America. Whether from there or Atlanta or Los Angeles, advertisers in the United States have made up many maladies for people to suffer from. Nobody had heard of iron-poor-tired blood before Geritol™ invented it in the 1950s. The condition existed, of course, but the famous name came from Madison Avenue. Immediately people began to fear they had it. Then there were Excedrin™ headaches, and "simple, chronic halitosis," again based on real and possible conditions, but picking up on the gullibility of many people to the idea that only one product can really cure what ails them.

Satan uses just that kind of lie when he comes to us and tempts us to sin. In the garden, he made up not a malady, but a supposed blessing, namely that Adam and Eve could be like "gods," and he tempted them with a condition that was purely fantasy. Eve bit. Then she bought. Then she fell, and she took her husband with her. The history of humanity is the story of the outworking of the complications and disastrous effects of that one, initial choice to buy a lie and spurn the truth.

Why do we believe Satan's Madison Avenue techniques? Is he that convincing? Indeed, he is. In addition to Satan's talent for deception, however, it is we ourselves who believe what we want to believe. Humanity is broadly convinced that our putting ourselves first will make us happy and that avoiding sacrifice will ensure our fulfilment in life. It is a lie. True fulfilment comes when we surrender ourselves to our Creator, who is the original and proper Lord of life. Any suggestion that God's way isn't the only way of true happiness is a lure to a false promise.

Father, give us yet another daily opportunity for surrender, so we may enjoy the blessing of being your children, not suffer the pain of trying to be our own gods. Amen.

September 5 Scripture Reading: 1 Thessalonians 1:9-10

Ye turned to God from idols to serve the living and true God; And to wait for his Son from heaven, whom he raised from the dead, even Jesus, which delivered us from the wrath to come.

No cheap Jesus

A few years ago near Christmas time, a woman in Colorado began manufacturing a baby Jesus doll. It had a glow-in-the-dark, detachable halo and a price tag of $31.50. It came in Anglo, Hispanic, and African models, in a wooden manger, with a card that said, "My name is Jesus. Jesus loves you. I am your friend. Please love me." The "inventor" said, "Anyone who is a Christian would want one." We know of several exceptions. There is something crass and superficial about the dashboard-doll approach to Christianity. All such things trivialize Jesus Christ. They are mere sentimentalities calling for a sappy form of piety rather than for broken wills, humble surrender and convicted love. Yet a great many people have this image of Jesus and this concept of religion.

Essentially, because it is a misapprehension of faith, it is a form of idolatry, an insidious form that lingers in cultural corniness and shallow religionism. It is an acutely *un*-profound fetish, giving vulgar significations to trinkets and tinsel. The Christian should avoid symbolism that reduces faith to cheap emotions. All of us should be sober, deep and thoughtful about the person of Jesus Christ. The effeminate Jesus seen in some pictures is a mythical figure. The real Jesus was a prophet, a compassionate but real man, a bloody sacrifice on a cross, and then a risen and glorified Lord, and he was one with the God of heaven. To view him as anything less is to toy with a deceitful form of idolatry.

Paul applauded the Thessalonians for turning from idols to serve the true and living God, waiting for Jesus Christ his Son, the crucified and risen Savior—a powerful person who will one day rescue us from the wrath to come. This Jesus is worth more than $31.50.

Father, help us not to trivialize Jesus in any way, but to enthrone, worship, obey and walk with him. Amen.

Whosoever is born of God doth not commit sin; for his seed remaineth in him: and he cannot sin, because he is born of God.

You live as you are

Most conservative evangelical Christians believe the Bible teaches"once saved, always saved." But even then, people can't "pull a fast one" on God. It isn't possible to deceive God by making a shallow confession of faith in Christ, then to live any way one wants but be allowed into heaven because of some "decision" made in church. If one lives like the devil, he must not be a saint.

Jesus said, "By their fruits you will know them." John the apostle picked up on this principle and wrote in his first letter that the "seed" of God's life in a true Christian will keep him from continuing to live a life of sin. We sometimes justify our sinful conduct by saying, "I'm only human." But God says if you are saved you are born of the Spirit of God, and you have the power not to sin. In fact, he says you will not continue in sinful behavior if you are truly born of God. That Bible proposition challenges our casual theology that one can walk an aisle, have a feeling, believe something in his mind, and get a guaranteed ticket to heaven. The Bible says we come to know we are truly born again, truly saved, not only by a decision made but also by a life lived. If it is lived for self, lived in sin, lived like the devil, then it must still be in sin, of self, and a slave to evil. For if God has made you new, you will be headed his way.

A popular band a few years ago sang these lyrics (perhaps insincerely): "I'll live like the devil until I become an angel." Another song went, "The angel in your arms this morning will be the devil in someone else's arms tonight." The idea persists, but it is disastrously false. You live as you are. What's really inside comes out for all to see.

Father, though salvation is eternal, help us to live out our new lives in Christ in the most deliberate and convincing way today. Amen.

That thou mightest know the certainty of those things, wherein thou hast been instructed.

Toward the knowledge of God

Statistics a few years ago from the National Technological Literacy Conference stated that a substantial part of the U.S. population is technologically illiterate. According to them, 70% do not understand radiation, 40% think rocket launches change the weather, and 80% do not understand how telephones work. One can argue that knowing these and many other things may not be absolutely critical to life, but it is curious that in as technologically advanced as our country is, so many of us are "technologically challenged."

Worse than that, however, is the fact that many people are theologically ignorant. According to Luke, he wrote his gospel specifically because people needed to know fully about the most important body of knowledge in the world: the life, death and resurrection of Jesus Christ. What, however, would the percentages be for these questions:

How many people believe specifically in the God of the Bible?
How many people believe Jesus is God the Son?
How many people understand what Jesus was doing on the cross?
How many comprehend that sin without salvation results in eternal death?
How many know what the gospel is?

The answers people might give to some of the questions above might reveal how willingly some people resist what churches proclaim; or, the answers might indict the church for not proclaiming successfully enough. The bottom line is that many people are not only theologically ignorant, but spiritually dead, and likely to physically die in that state and depart from God's presence forever. What does it matter whose fault it is? Let us share the good news that Jesus died for sin so that we might live with him!

Father, push us out of the nest of our comfort into the flight of gospel joy today, through a word of testimony to someone who needs it. Amen.

Ever learning, and never able to come to the knowledge of the truth.

The goal of truth

"News junkies" watch 24-hour news channels every hour possible, follow emerging details of every story, and lap up every gossipy tidbit. They may aim simply to be well-informed, but they may fail to realize that news consists of highly selective reports, and reports frequently contain editorial bias. Not all news is useful or truly educational.

Christians also may ingest a constant stream of "Christian" programs and devour stacks of books, and believe that as a result, they are simply being nourished maximally with divine truth. But sometimes Christians who are"ever learning" don't realize that some of what they hear, see or read is unsound or skewed. The "spiritual junkie" may also take in far more than he or she can really digest or put to use, and he may develop an attitude of pride for being an authority on all the latest truth and methods from Christian teachers.

When human beings take in more than their bodies can use, gorging themselves on every available morsel, the body turns the excess nutrition into fat. Theoretically, fat could be useful one day, if all one's food runs out. But typically fat just attracts negative attention, slows one down, and makes him or her less healthy all around.

Spiritual overload generally does the same thing: it provides us with information we can't assimilate, inspiration we can't follow through with thoroughly, teachings we can't properly evaluate in the light of personal study, and directions we may follow out of context and without wisdom. How much better it is to conduct an ordered and patient study of the scripture, to meditate on sermons and Bible studies, and to do as many parents and grandparents have advised their young ones: take small bites, eat slowly and digest thoroughly. *More* is not necessarily *better.* Wisdom is not found in the amount of truth we hear, but in how much of it we live.

Father, as we may read and hear your truth today, may it descend into our hearts and then make its way back into our lives. Amen.

September 9 **Scripture Reading: 2 Samuel 22:3**

The God of my rock; in him will I trust: he is my shield, and the horn of my salvation, my high tower, and my refuge, my saviour.

In God we trust

In 1956 the words, "one nation under God" were added to the Pledge of Allegiance. In 2002, the 9th Circuit Court of the United States declared the pledge unconstitutional, on First Amendment grounds. Congress immediately reacted with vociferous condemnation, the Senate passing a unanimous resolution against the Court's decision. The 9th Circuit is the most frequently overturned court because it is often out of step with the values of the country as a whole.

"Under God," in the Pledge, and the national motto, "In God We Trust," are evidence of the country's ties to its heritage. Try as some atheists might to change history, religion was a strong influence in the colonization of America. Most of the founding fathers were Christians, and both the philosophy of our government and the Constitution that enshrines it are derived ultimately from biblical principles. The Pledge declares the national sentiment that America is a nation whose existence and survival is due to the providence of God. But do we really trust in God, as our National Motto says?

The question cannot be answered for every American in general, or for every president, congressman or senator. The relationship of each person with God is an individual matter. But what about you? Do you trust in God.

When David spoke the words of 2 Samuel 22:3, he was not repeating a superficial saying or taking a perfunctory pledge. He was expressing his profound and energetic trust in the God who had revealed himself through creation, patriarch, prophet, history and law as the only God and the one in whom we must believe. He was putting into words what he put into deeds in daily living, demonstrating reliance and dependence on God to meet his needs, strengthen his arm, guide his heart, and win his victories. When we say we trust in God, are our words just as true?

God our Father, we trust in you, and as a man once said to Jesus, "I believe: help thou my unbelief." Amen.

September 10 **Scripture Reading: Genesis 22:12**

Now I know that thou fearest God, seeing thou hast not withheld thy son, thine only son from me.

Whatever God wants

The key to our having victory in life is for us to allow Christ to have victory in us. We can overcome temptation when Christ overcomes the flesh in us. We can experience victory in following the will of God when Christ has victory over our wills. Christians have not been given some inanimate power to conquer life: our victory is the product of our lives being conquered by Jesus Christ on a daily basis, and our consequently experiencing the power of his Holy Spirit.

Abraham heard God say to take Isaac his son and go slay him as a sacrifice. One can imagine the terror and heartbreak of his actions as he dutifully prepared to do as God said. But just in time, God prevented him, saying that Abraham had adequately demonstrated his deep, true worship of God by not withholding even his only son. Abraham had survived most of his adult life on the promise of this one son through whom God's promise would come. But when God himself seemed to contradict his own promise, Abraham did not say "no" to him.

Christians often make statements of promise to God, sometimes in moments of public decision, sometimes in private encounters of devotion. Frequently those decisions will be phrased to God in terms of "surrender," "consecration," or "full commitment." Hymns such as, "I Surrender All," and, "Wherever He Leads," express the desire and intention to give our lives totally to the Lord. Our decisions are commitments in principle; the real test, however, is what we do in practice. When God moves, leads, asks, and we come to understand that he wants us to go, speak or do, how do we respond in the moment? God may tell us either to take up something or abandon something. Are we quick and committed in response?

Florence Nightingale, heroic nurse of the Crimean War, was asked what was the secret of her success in life. Her answer was, "I never refused God anything."

Father, however your voice gets through to us today to show us your will at the moment, may we promptly say "yes" and cheerfully obey. Amen.

September 11 **Scripture Reading: John 16:2**

Yea, the time cometh, that whosoever killeth you will think that he doeth God service.

War against the true God

Jesus warned his disciples they would be the objects of persecution designed to wipe them from the face of the earth. People had hated him and would hate them because they were his followers. His prophecy began to be fulfilled within a very short time of the church's beginning, as Stephen was stoned and James was put to the sword. Before long, the Jewish authorities were trying to stamp out the new movement, and Saul was deputized to round up Christians for trial.

Throughout history various groups or authorities have tried to suppress Christians. Caesars, Emperors, and Fürers have tried; tyrannical oligarchies, paranoid dictatorships and oppressive communists have tried; people of other religions or no religion have tried. But Jesus said not only that his church would be the object of persecution, but also that his church would endure and overcome.

This is a message for each disciple as well as for the church as a group. Believers face many hardships, some designed by the adversary, Satan, to defeat them. Satan will acquire the cooperation of everyone from willing enemies of Christianity to unwitting agnostics. Then he will engineer events and circumstances in such a way as to threaten, discourage or frustrate Christians, hoping to cause them to turn away from Jesus Christ and become ineffective, or even better—for Satan—to become hypocrites who repulse the unsaved. Jesus' warning was meant to prepare his disciples for the fight ahead and steel their resolve to live for him no matter what.

In cultures where persecution is more subtle, it is still insidious. The world that serves the prince of this world is not content to let the Christian message be preached and shared without resistance, ridicule and open hostility. But Jesus said, "Be of good cheer: I have overcome the world."

Father of our Lord Jesus Christ, we will serve you today without fear, because all other gods will fall, and all your enemies will one day kneel before you, conquered. Amen.

Thou shalt worship the Lord thy God, and him only shalt thou serve.

No divided loyalties

When Jesus was tempted in the desert for forty days, the Bible records that the devil tried to get him to bow down to him, and Jesus responded with a quotation from Deuteronomy that forbids our worshiping or living for anyone but the Lord. If Satan had explained his temptation, he might have assured Jesus that he did not mean for him to switch his worship, only to share it. The answer Jesus would have given would have been the same: Worship God, and serve him only.

When it comes to who "calls the shots" in our lives, the answer is clear from God's word: it should be God and no other. We should be "beholden" to no one else. This means, in part, that we must not tie ourselves to other people or pursuits that may or likely *will* compromise our loyalty.

United States law does not prohibit persons being citizens of other countries as well. One may become a citizen of another country by marriage in that country, and immigrants to the U.S. may not lose their citizenship in their home countries by becoming U.S. citizens. But the United States does not encourage dual citizenship, because of the problems divided loyalty often brings. In fact, if a person actually applies for citizenship elsewhere, his citizenship in the U.S. may be revoked.

If you belong to Jesus, belong to him wholly. Fly no other flag over your life than that of loyalty to Christ. Pursue citizenship in God's kingdom, as strangers in this world. Develop the spiritual senses that enable you to detect your own wandering from total allegiance to Christ. Run from anything that pries you away from your devotion to the Lord and your witness for him. Cleave to Jesus. God wants it no other way, and the true joy of the Christian is found in selling out to him completely.

Father, grant us vision to see our little rebellions as well as great ones, and to surrender to you in them all. Amen.

Then said Pilate unto him, Hearest thou not how many things they witness against thee?

Truth on trial

When Jesus was tried before Pilate, he was accused by the chief priests and elders but gave no answer. Pilate was amazed, and asked him why, but Jesus didn't reply. He was accused of things entirely true: to those charges he pleaded guilty—"Are you the Son of God?" "I am." But he had also been accused of things entirely false: to these charges he made no comment. They had hired people to bring those charges, and denials would not affect them. The only opportunities he took to speak were to strengthen his witness of the truth. He didn't attempt to defend himself otherwise because he was not desperate to escape.

His accusers, however, were desperate. At all costs, they intended to deny the truth about themselves and about Jesus. Truth itself was on trial, and Jesus was the crux of the struggle. In a marvelously inexplicable way, God had determined to deal with humanity's sin through the crucifixion of a substitute—the Son of God, who would be perfectly faithful to the end. Jesus intended simply to be faithful to the truth, and he was.

Sometimes the most important thing is to be faithful to what is true and right, no matter what it costs us. The witness of that kind of integrity has potential far outreaching and outliving the benefit of a few more years to live, or a life without discomfort. We should not set out to make ourselves martyrs, but we should never avoid a cause that is right, just because we know martyrdom, in principle or in reality, may lie down the road. Had Jesus shied away from it, we would not have had forgiveness of sins. If we shy away from it, someone else may not have our convincing witness, and may not believe the gospel. Disciples who live by the rule of getting by with as little discomfort possible make little impact on lost people, or they may even turn them away. If faith is not worth some suffering, it isn't worth much.

Father, Jesus sacrificed himself for us, for which we love him. Grow us into his likeness. Amen.

Who comforteth us in all our tribulation, that we may be able to comfort them which are in any trouble, by the comfort wherewith we ourselves are comforted of God.

One reason for trouble

Theologians call it "the problem of evil." It is the age-old question of why there is natural or moral evil in the universe. The average person simply asks why bad things happen. We will not be able to answer that question to everyone's satisfaction in this life, but several good reasons can be articulated for the troubles we face. One of them is that through our own troubles, we become equipped to help others in theirs.

That may seem like begging the question. After all, if others didn't have troubles we wouldn't need to be equipped to help them. But there are other reasons for trouble, and as long as there are trials in our lives, they function in part to give us the experience and wisdom that will enable us to help the next one who comes along with similar difficulties. We are part of a chain of experience, passing down the comfort and the perspective that enable us to get through.

Paul told the Corinthian church that they should not pity him for his trials in being a missionary, because he had found that the things he went through enabled him to experience God and his sufficiency, and that in turn he had been able to pass on that comfort or encouragement to others. Paul didn't sit around saying, "Woe is me," about the persecution, death threats, arrests, trials, and other hardships he had faced for the testimony of Christ. He developed ways to make his experience available to others.

When you learn a lesson, pass it on. Pass on the help, pass on the comfort, pass on your perspectives, pass on wisdom, and pass on help God gave or revealed to you when you were going through something. Don't be impervious to your own education through trial, and when God helps you, you help someone else.

Father, the spirit of Jesus is to give and help. If we are his disciples—we get the picture. Amen.

September 15 Scripture Reading: Deuteronomy 10:17

For the Lord your God is God of gods, and Lord of lords, a great God, a mighty, and a terrible, which regardeth not persons, nor taketh reward.

How big is your God?

Concepts of God vary widely. Officially, of course, Christians believe that God is omnipotent, omniscient, and omnipresent. What counts, however, is not what we believe on paper but what we exhibit in practice. If God is truly omnipotent—he can do anything—do we allow that belief to shape our daily faith in him? If God is truly omniscient—he knows everything—do we live confidently as well as circumspectly? If God is truly omnipresent—he is everywhere—do we experience him daily, practicing the presence of Christ?

Sometimes our prayers suggest our God is too small. We may timidly ask God too little or only ask for a little help, not really having the faith that God is utterly powerful. We may explain our needs in profuse detail or defend our conduct with intricate excuses, not remembering that God knows our every need and our deepest thoughts. We may ask God to "be with us" or "go with us," unaware of what it means that he already is with us everywhere, all the time.

Moses had personal experience of God that shattered the limited concepts of the religions of Egypt, Chaldea, and every other nation and people. The God of gods, the Lord of lords, the creator of the universe who was not limited by anything and who was neither coerced by anyone nor beholden to anyone, had revealed himself to Moses, and then to the whole Hebrew people. On the basis of this revelation, he challenged the people to follow him, obey him, and know him.

God wants us to know him as the one who loves us sacrificially and desires fellowship with us personally. Yet as a divine friend, God wants us to realize that he is the infinite one whose purpose encompasses everything, whose will is sovereign, and whose power is limitless. We are to stand in awe of him and worship him, with words and with our lives.

Father God, and awesome Lord, we worship you, submit to you and wait upon you. You are great, and greatly to be praised! Amen.

And for Aaron's sons thou shalt make coats, and thou shalt make for them girdles, and bonnets shalt thou make for them, for glory and for beauty... And thou shalt make them linen breeches to cover their nakedness; from the loins even unto the thighs they shall reach.

Dressed for Worship

What is your concept of "church clothes?" In some quarters of the culture, proper clothing for church is still fairly formal. In other quarters, people have gone with the times and wear extremely casual clothes to church or just about anywhere.

When God gave the Israelites specific instructions about worship, he dictated that the priests were to wear formal garments. Even the rank and file of the tribe of Aaron wore a sort of uniform consisting of tunics, sashes and headbands. And God added that they must not forget to wear linen breeches. Quite literally, that was underwear.

Most of us wear underwear everywhere, but such has not always been the rule. Bluntly, why did God insist that the priests wear underwear? It was because they would be treading over the holy ground of the tabernacle and the steps of the altar. They were not to expose themselves to the holy places. The matter was entirely symbolic. Adam and Eve clothed themselves after their sin because their inner guilt expressed itself in embarrassment about the exposure of their intimate parts. Human beings put on clothes not only because of heat or cold but also because of the compelling urge to cover themselves. Some people rebel against this norm, but the laws and common practice of every civilized nation prove the rule: we need a covering.

Most of all, every person needs a covering to be able to worship. God provided that covering. In Eden, he provided "coats of skins." In Jesus Christ, God's covering goes to the core of the person and covers the sinful soul itself. Gal. 3:27 says the Christian has "put on Christ." He is the "robe of righteousness" of which Isaiah 61:10 prophesied. Whether your church expects suits and dresses or doesn't frown on jeans and T-shirts, dress for worship in the righteousness of Christ.

Father, thank you for providing a covering for my soul in Jesus my Savior. Let the glory of his righteousness adorn me more and more as well. Amen.

But we desire to hear of thee what thou thinkest: for as concerning this sect, we know that every where it is spoken against.

When bad news is good

The old expression, "No news is good news," means, of course, that if we don't hear anything from someone, we can assume everything is probably all right. Sometimes, however, bad news is good news, too. How so? There are times when bad press can get the Christian and the church a hearing when otherwise the world has stopped its ears to God's message.

Paul the apostle was taken to Rome under guard and had the opportunity to call a meeting with Jewish leaders there. They had not as yet gotten any negative reports about him, but about the church they had gotten an earful of bad press, and they wanted to look into "this sect." The critical reports about the Christian faith gave Paul the opportunity to witness, simply because the curiosity of Roman Jews had been piqued.

We never know when doors to witness will open. Sometimes they virtually fly open when the church or Christian faith is criticized, false rumors circulate, or detractors wax particularly offensive. But it doesn't matter what gives the Christian the opportunity to stand up for his Lord. Even if the chance to share a word about Jesus comes out of a situation of bad reporting, what has happened is good, because the Christian may be able to set the record straight to someone who may be more open than usual. Bad news becomes good news.

The old politician's adage goes: I don't care what you say about me in the newspaper, so long as you spell my name right. The Christian should likewise care less about those who criticize him and more about the publicity of his faith in Christ. When questions are raised about Christian faith, no matter who raised them or why, the opportunity may be pure gold.

Father, when others look for faults in the Christian or flaws in our faith, may we look for openings to tell them of the perfect Savior. Amen.

September 18 **Scripture Reading: Luke 11:13**

...Ye then, being evil, know how to give good gifts unto your children...

Our natural affection

When teaching about God's great desire to bless us, Jesus once compared our Heavenly Father to human beings who act lovingly as parents toward our children. God is far more inclined to be good to us than we are to be good to our children. But the illustration worked because sinful though we are, we retain some good impulses. Yet the scriptures teach that eventually even the impulses we would have thought were too deeply ingrained to be discarded may drift away like dandelion fluff. The Bible refers to this as being "without natural affection." The term refers to the loss of even a mother's instinctive love for her child.

Is this not what is behind the horrible statistics of abortion? Various coastal states protect the eggs of sea turtles by law, levying fines of $10,000 or more for their destruction. According to some scientists, the sea turtle is in danger of extinction, and the turtle, obviously, is in the egg. What, then, is in the womb of the mother—cells with no identity? No, human beings. A state may fine someone thousands of dollars for destroying a turtle egg that may or may not be fertilized in the first place, and which, if it did hatch, would have one chance in fifty of survival. But all over the U.S. it is legal to destroy human beings in the womb, more than ninety-nine percent of whom when born will survive. Something about the comparative values here is insanely twisted.

No matter what exceptions might be defensible for such reasons as medical necessity, the bottom line is that the vast number of abortions are sought for personal convenience, as a means of birth control after the fact. This is no mere political issue or matter of personal choice: it is a moral and spiritual crisis that demands the personal decision of every Christian, especially in a country where people elect those who make laws and appoint judges. Are we not glad our mothers did not abort us? Don't we desire the same love for all human children?

Father, lead us to defend those who cannot defend themselves, as we ourselves were once defenseless. Amen.

I have no greater joy than to hear that my children walk in truth.

The lives we owe others

Every generation must find out for itself what parenthood means. As much as fathers and mothers try to explain to their children how and why they love them, children have to become mothers and fathers themselves before they really understand. A person may barely understand the selflessness of his parents intellectually or even emotionally, until he becomes an adult and has children of his or her own. It has always been this way and it always will be.

The apostle John had a similar attitude about his children in the Lord. He wrote in his third letter to the church that nothing made him happier than to know that those he had the privilege of evangelizing were now continuing to grow in Christ. From a distance, he watched their progress and found deep contentment in their faithfulness. Their devotion to Jesus confirmed something about his own work, to be sure, but his great joy was found not in the proof that he was a good apostle and teacher, but in the fact that they, his children in the Lord, were being blessed in their Christian walk. John wasn't just happy for himself: he was happy for them. He was a parent taking joy in his children as they learned and grew.

Understanding something of this, it should be hard for us to knowingly disappoint our parents or our parents in the Lord. We have expectations to live up to. Our lives are not our own. First, we belong to God. But beneath that all-encompassing devotion we also have certain undeniable responsibilities to our families, those who taught us, those who instructed us in spiritual things, and ultimately to all mankind. We have the right to be individuals, but not to be islands. Everybody owes everybody the debt to love, and the greatest debt is to Christ, who died for our sins. If we live for him as we ought, we will not disappoint our parents in the Lord, or fail to love everyone he created.

Father, as your children, may we love and honor you today. Teach us something new about how to love others as you love us. Amen.

September 20 **Scripture Reading: Matthew 8:15**

And he touched her hand, and the fever left her: and she arose, and ministered unto them.

Serving the one who saves

The women who followed Jesus were wonderfully consistent examples of true discipleship. Women were in the larger group of disciples who followed him. Women supported him with their means. Women stood boldly near the cross. Women were first at the tomb. In Matthew we read that Jesus came to Peter's house to find his mother-in-law sick, and he touched her hand, making her well. Not to diminish whatsoever the awesome power of Jesus, perhaps Matthew's comment about what Peter's mother-in-law then did is the most interesting part of the story: she got up and began to wait on him. She did ordinary things for him, thoughtful things, needed things. It was her prompt and energetic response to what he had done for her.

Service should be our own response as well to the blessings of the Lord. Yet so often we take the blessings and run. We appeal to Jesus intensely when trouble comes, but when he works things out in our lives, we quickly forget our gratitude and go off living for ourselves again. We ought to be living for him.

Television's Andy Griffith Show included an episode in which Andy saved Gomer from some potential accident. Gomer, in his broadest drawl and with wide eyes began to say repeatedly, "You saved my life!" For days thereafter he tagged around after Andy trying to do everything for him. The show made fun of his gratitude just a bit, and he did get rather silly about it, but a subtle point came through. This simple fellow saw that he had been the recipient of a life-saving deed, and the appropriate response was equally simple to discern: he should be thankful.

Jesus Christ died for you. Are you living for him?

Lord Jesus, give us today as an opportunity to get up and serve you, for all you have done for us. Amen.

... show me the dream, and the interpretation thereof ...

Discerning God's will

Knowing the will of God can be one of the most difficult things in the world, or it can be a delightful quest with a confident end. In other words, you may think you will never know what God wants from you, or you may have no doubt at all about his direction in your life. It depends on the source of your knowledge.

Nebuchadnezzar once had a dream that troubled him, and he called his advisors and said, "Tell me the dream and interpret it for me." He expected them to know not only what his dream had meant, but to know what the dream was in the first place—when he had not recounted the dream at all. However, a godly, praying young man named Daniel successfully told him his dream as God revealed it.

Some people think knowing God's will presents a similar problem: his will is in his mind, and he hasn't given out any hints as to what it is, but he expects us to discover it anyway. Is that the way God works? Does God expect us all to have the prophetic gifts of Daniel?

Happily, the message of the Bible is that God works through myriad means to unveil his will for us. Sometimes he uses circumstance, other times he provides illumination in the Bible, or occasionally he gives visions. But consistently he imparts the knowledge of his will to those who by pure living and continual prayer seek to know him intimately.

People sometimes say, "Guess what?" to which you say, "What?" and they reply, "Guess!" You have no idea where to start! If knowing the will of God were like that, we would be constantly discouraged. But God is not like one who says, "Guess what?" He says, "Listen!" If we come close to him and listen, living in obedience to him, he will tell us what his will is and how to interpret it.

Father, may your will be done in our lives today, as we hear it from your own heart and obey it. Amen.

September 22 **Scripture Reading: Psalm 69:1**

Save me, O God; for the waters are come into my soul.

Turning to God in emergencies

The Psalmist often cried out in desperation. In Psalm 69:1, he reveals to us that his situation had become most urgent. The Hebrew word translated "soul" in the KJV literally means "throat." The waters of his trouble had come up to his neck—things couldn't get much worse.

When we are really in deep water, we know we need help. Perhaps most of us have a way of letting ourselves get in over our heads before we are willing to make a point of turning over everything in our lives to the Lord. But it is interesting that the Lord often treats us no differently in those times than he would have if we had come to him sooner. This is the nature of his grace, mercy and love. He is not an "I-told-you-so" God.

Trust the Lord for every need. Go to him before you get in hot water or deep water. But don't fear to turn to him in emergency situations. Even if you neglected to consciously seek his leadership, wisdom, strength, and providence earlier, do not allow guilt to keep you from seeking him when you realize how dependent upon him you really are.

It is proverbial that a captain goes down with his ship. Many actually have, though surely not all do. A few years ago an English cruise ship foundered in the North Sea and the captain was the first to climb into a lifeboat. Perhaps the reason some captains stay with their ships until the bitter end is not so much for the sake of honor but because they don't want to be shamed later for bad decisions leading to disaster.

When you come to a strait in your life, lest you think, "I'll handle this alone or I will go down with my ship trying valiantly," remember that as a Christian you are not the captain. Christ is. Make your report to him. Cry out that the waves are rising, that the reefs are looming, that the storm is bearing down. Call on the captain for his help. For Christ, our captain, does not intend for the ship to go down at all.

Father, we trust you—we really do. So remind us today to call on the captain of our souls, for what he alone can do. Amen.

September 23 **Scripture Reading: Romans 10:12**

For there is no difference between the Jew and the Greek: for the same Lord over all is rich unto all that call upon him.

God disregards color

One of the more common notions of human beings is that "our kind" is better than "their kind." The attitude may come from cultural snobbishness, educational advantage, racial difference, or some other thing. Many of us struggle continually with the temptation to discriminate. Such attitudes are part of the legacy of sin in humanity, and God calls us to a higher way in Christ. The word of God tells us that God makes no distinction between persons in any of those areas in which we often compare one another. Each of us is a unique individual, but all of us are on level ground before God.

In Romans 10, Paul wrote that when God sent Christ to die for our sins, he didn't set forth one way for Jews to be saved and another for Gentiles. He boldly declared that the same Lord saves anyone and everyone who calls upon him. The implication of that verse is sweeping. We must do more than say we love all people; we must reflect it in our lives and our church's ministries. We must do more than say we have warm church fellowships; we must expand our friendships to include persons of all ages and economic strata, whether they are "our kind" of people or not. Christ offers salvation to all without regard to type or color. All in Christ have been made one body.

Color photography is possible only because light is a mixture of colors. Just as the eye sees how different things absorb various colors of light and reflect the rest, so film reacts to various colors of light. How well the colors work together! Think of the rainbow, which displays the variety, but the sun, obliterating the visual recognition of any difference, burns brightly with the unity of all, bringing life to the earth.

Father God, for whatever way we have thought ourselves better, we ask forgiveness, and the gift of your vision of us all, as the recipients of Christ's love. Amen.

... your faith, being much more precious than of gold that perisheth ...

God values faith

Occasionally, events in history prompt the United States to direct its Mint to make special coins. The 1984 Olympics spawned coins that were quite beautiful. They included both silver and gold pieces. The Mint also produced a U.S. Constitution bicentennial coin set in 1987. The silver dollar in that set cost $28 at the time, and the $5 gold piece cost $222. The Mint regularly makes gold pieces that are legal coinage, but worth far in excess of the face value. The simple beauty of these proof-quality coins is obvious to anyone who sees them. There is just something about gold!

Yet God says there is something more precious than gold. It is faith. 1 Peter 1:7 says that God allows trials to purify our faith, just as gold is purified by fire. He wants our faith to be genuine and adulterated, which means we trust him simply, purely, fully, and continually. Your faith—your capacity to take God at his word, trust him for his provision and obey him in everything—is more valuable than gold. People have killed for gold, but gold will not last. Your faith should be of more value to you. You ought to value your ability to know God, your ability to grasp the promises of God, your ability to trust Christ. Think of the multitudes on earth who cannot bring themselves to trust Christ, or who simply refuse to. Faith in Christ, your belief in God, is the conduit of God's saving and delivering grace. It is a precious gift, and an invaluable possession.

Is there a struggle going on in your life, a trial in which despair, disillusionment, or discouragement loom up and threaten to consume your joy and dissolve your hope? In the hands of God it is a refiner's fire. It is treasure in the coin of pain. Faith is God's gold, and he keeps testing it, and purifying it, until "the day when our faith shall be sight, and the clouds be rolled back as a scroll."

Father, train us through hardship to value our faith relationship with you over all money, power, and possessions. Amen.

Ye have been called unto liberty; only use not liberty for an occasion to the flesh, but by love serve one another.

Use freedom for good

A few years ago in a state that has a government operated lottery, a man won a tremendous amount of money. Within the hour he identified his winning ticket, he notified the gaming authorities. The same day, he decided to celebrate. He went to a bar and bought drinks for everybody. He got himself exceedingly drunk, walked outside, and stumbled into the street, where he reeled into the path of an oncoming truck and was killed—all in the same day.

That story preaches its own sermon. Here is a man who has just been freed from the drudgery of years of hard labor by an astounding, liberating windfall, and he forfeits his newfound freedom through indulgence in foolishness. Regardless of what one thinks about the morality of gambling, here was a man whose blessings were great, but whose unworthiness was devastating.

The Bible says the salvation of Christ is the greatest blessing of all. It is possible to squander that blessing and shame the Lord, even if one does not do so as publically or outrageously as another. Paul wrote in Galatians 5 that Christians were called to liberty, but he warned them not to use their freedom to indulge themselves. Instead, they were to go out and see how much they could do for each other, in imitation of the spirit of Christ. Jesus had freed them from the fear of judgment and given them the riches of eternal life. He expected them to use that rich freedom to seek the good of one another and the expanse of the gospel.

Satan tempts Christians to take for granted their eternal security, and to relax their standards. If we fall prey to that temptation, we will come under the disciplinary action of God.

Have you spent too much of the blessing of freedom on yourself and too little on carrying out God's purposes for your life right now?

Father, renew today and every day our sense of freedom in Christ and our sense of duty to Christ. Amen.

Jesus said unto him, If thou canst believe, all things are possible to him that believeth.

Faith brings good things

Have you ever noticed that nothing good happens where you are until you leave it? That's not really true, of course, but sometimes it seems that way. The college doesn't build the arts building, the student center, or the better housing, until you graduate. The city doesn't improve the roads, develop the downtown, or build the shopping center near your house, until you move. The church doesn't overcome its inertia, reach the neighborhood, or begin growing gloriously, until after you leave.

You wonder if your being there had anything to do with things staying static, dull, boring, backward, or dead. It's possible, of course, and we must all consider how we play a part in things not changing for the better. But more likely than not, we just didn't recognize the changes that occurred while we were there. We ignored or took for granted the good things that were happening. After we leave, we notice.

We need to accentuate the positive and make the most of the good things God is doing among us. This is part of what Jesus meant when he said that all things are possible to him who believes. Believing is more than intellectually admitting the potential; it is emotionally and willfully proclaiming the requested. We ask God to do many things. How many of them do we really expect him to do? In church we pray for renewal and revival. Whether he will grant the request may rest on our willingness to trust him for it. If in reality we doubt that good things are going to happen, they probably won't. If we believe, they probably will. The greatest reason Jesus could do no great work in some places he visited was the lack of faith on the part of those who were there. God, interacting with our faith, likes to do things that we notice and praise him for. His plan is to do good in and through our lives.

Father, teach us in some crucial way today how faith brings good things. Amen.

Finally, my brethren, rejoice in the Lord. To write the same things to you, to me indeed is not grievous, but for you it is safe.

Better safe than sorry

Constantly preaching the gospel is necessary even among the Christian community. Some people join churches without having really experienced the saving grace of God. As years pass it becomes harder for them to come to Christ, because in their heads they think themselves Christians already. One of the goals of gospel preaching is finally to reach these "head believers" and for them to be saved.

A makeup instructor was teaching actors in a play to make artificial beards. He showed them how to put spirit gum on their faces and then to apply stage hair in layers. After the adhesive had dried, he told them, "Now tug at the beard. Root out all that isn't stuck. If it can't stand tugging now, it won't stay on later. Eventually it will fall out." More fibers always went on than stayed on.

The same is true with most churches: not all who attend are really rooted in Christ. One function of the continued teaching and preaching of the gospel is to tug at the roots to test the genuine faith of those who call themselves believers.

The repeated proclamation and explanation of the gospel also benefits those who truly are saved but have grown indifferent, or who have struggled, failed and given up. The message of the cross—the price Jesus paid for our sin—may move the indifferent back into consecration, and the message of grace—God's undeserved love and forgiveness—may lead a struggler back into victory. The genuine Christian should appreciate continual reminders of the basic gospel message: Christ died for us that he might bring us to God.

Father, may the gospel bear new fruit of gratitude in us today, as we recognize the wonderful gift of grace. Amen.

Wherefore let him that thinketh he standeth take heed lest he fall.

Humble about what you know

When Paul wrote the Corinthians to "take heed," lest they fall, he did not mean that one may never be certain of his salvation. Other scriptures—many of them from Paul's own hand—assure us that we can know for certain we have been saved beyond ever being lost again. Paul's meaning was not that we shouldn't be certain of what *Christ* has done, but that we must not be dogmatic about what *we* are going to do—or never do. Paul is warning us to beware of falling when we think we are unshakable in our stance.

We are not to be boastful in our ability to climb the ladder of godliness—if there were one. Overconfidence removes us from the realm of faith in God. If we believe that we can function on our own without God's grace and strength every minute, and if we rest on our own stability or strength, eventually we will fail miserably and bring disgrace to the church and to Christ.

An Arab proverb says:

He who knows not, and knows not that he knows not, is a fool: avoid him.
He who knows not, and knows he knows not, is simple: instruct him.
He who knows, and knows not that he knows, is asleep: awake him.
He who knows, and knows he knows, is wise: follow him.

Researching that proverb yields many variations on the order and the translation of the four phrases, but on one thing all agree: the person who really doesn't know, but claims he does—is a fool. We should never boast that we *know* we will never commit this or that sin, because we don't. Nor should we say that we *know* that we will always be faithful to Christ. If we're going to boast, may it be only in what Christ has done.

Father, may we rely fully on Christ Jesus, precisely because we know we cannot rely on ourselves. Amen.

And he did that which was right in the sight of the LORD, according to all that David his father did.

Being like our Father

Being like your daddy is good—or not. The Bible says of Hezekiah that he was like his father David—really his great, great, great grandfather—in that he did right in the sight of God. That's good. But of Ahab, Jeroboam, Jehoash and many other kings the Bible records they were just as wicked as their fathers had been. Some fathers are good role models, and some are not. What a blessing to have one who follows the Lord!

But is being just like your father, or your mother, for that matter, a justification for anything? The long and short is that if we follow their good examples, we're wise, but if we follow their bad examples, we're not, and we've no one to blame but ourselves. One of the most scathing rebukes uttered by Jesus was that some individuals were "of their father the devil." Sometimes it is disastrous to follow a forebear's example.

The way to make sure we do well in our imitation is to make sure we have the right father. While we can't change the one we were born to, we get another one when we're born *again.* Our earthly fathers may or may not be fine examples, but our heavenly Father is perfection itself. When we become the children of God by faith in Jesus Christ, God is our Father not only by creation but by adoption. When he is, we can see him clearly to imitate him. What glory if we were all to grow up to be like our heavenly Father!

A company marketed a Father's Day card that pictured a lighthouse and a beach and footprints in the sand, and the caption, "Dad, I'm proud to follow in your footsteps." If you live like your Father in heaven, he'll be pleased with you, too.

Heavenly Father, today we would be like you, so tomorrow they may say good things of us. Amen.

Jesus answered them, Have not I chosen you twelve, and one of you is a devil?

God is so very gracious

After all is said and done, some of God's actions remain a mystery to the limited human mind. Jesus chose twelve disciples, and apparently he selected one of them knowing full well he would not work out. John records that Jesus had Judas Iscariot pegged from the beginning as a devil—a person filled with evil and eventually possessed by the prince of evil. Why did Jesus select this man? Was he facilitating his own death? We do not otherwise have a picture of him manipulating his destiny that way. Perhaps it had something to do with the impenetrable purpose of God's grace, which offers the best of opportunity even to those who most certainly will squander it. Beyond that, we may not understand.

People sometimes say, "I know plenty of church members who don't act like Christians!" They identify some bad apple, a notorious backslider, some person who is clearly associated at least in his past with a certain church, but who really ruined his witness and his character in a terrible act or a major turn of life toward evil. It may even have been a minister. Why did God ever call such a person into the family of believers if he knew that he or she would ultimately cause such hurt to the kingdom?

Of course, the extent to which that person may hurt the kingdom, and the extent to which we ourselves may hurt it when we sin, differ only in degree. How much have we done to stunt the growth of the kingdom? Put another way, how much have we done to promote it? Have we always done things honorably and pleasing to Christ? Maybe the grace Jesus showed Judas is meant to humble us; for God is clearly so very gracious to have us around, too. For we are all sinners, and those who are saved are saved only by God's amazing grace.

Father, thank you, thank you, for choosing us to be disciples of Jesus Christ. Amen.

If any man preach any other gospel unto you than that ye have received, let him be accursed.

The evil of deceit

Paul the apostle used disturbing language in Galatians when he wrote that if anyone presented a false gospel he was surely under a curse. It doesn't sound very gracious, and wasn't meant to. In fact, it sounds very much like what Jesus said: "Temptations to sin are bound to come, but woe to him by which they do come: it would be better for him to have a millstone hung around his neck and be cast into the sea." Better than what? Paul said it: than to be "accursed"—eternally condemned.

God provides his sternest penalties for deceivers. Even they may repent, of course, but deceit and deceiving are such infernal and entrapping sins that they constitute the hardest errors to see through or get out of. The enormity of the sin of deceit is found in the fact that it affects not only the one who perpetrates it, but all those trapped by it.

When the Titanic was sinking in 1912, after a few hundred people filled the insufficient number of lifeboats, there were many left on board the ship. Some were locked on lower decks without access even to the rail. Others had two choices: jump overboard, or stay. Either way, they faced death. If they jumped, the icy waters would soon cause hypothermia. Many jumped anyway in the last moments, as the sinking ship tipped up and went down lengthwise, most likely creating a sucking vacuum that drew in debris and swimmers around it.

Religious deceivers are like that destructive vortex, sucking in the credulous, seducing those desperate for easy answers or instant relief. That's why the deceiver's condemnation is great. Don't be deceived: it's dangerous. Don't be a deceiver: it's the deadliest of all.

Father, lead us in truth today. Let us not be deceived, and let us not lead others astray. Amen.

Jesus answered and said unto him, What I do thou knowest not now; but thou shalt know hereafter.

God is always up to something

What parent has not said something like, "This is going to hurt me more than it hurts you"? Children almost never believe that. First of all, they don't understand it. They can't, because they're not parents. They don't know what it is to punish while hurting inside because it must be done. All they see is the appearance of anger. All they feel is the sting.

Many things have to happen to us that we don't understand. A six month old baby was taken to the hospital for a hernia operation. He didn't understand what was being done to him, the shots, the wooziness, the unfamiliar people, the scary surroundings. His parents held him and felt deeply sorry that he was so confused. But it had to be done.

Jesus once washed his disciples feet. Peter balked at first, because he thought he was unworthy and that it humiliated Jesus somehow. But Jesus told him that though he didn't realize what he was doing at the moment, later he would understand. Pressed for some reason, any reason, Jesus said, "If I don't wash you, you have no part with me." Hearing that, Peter wanted the whole bath! But he still did not understand exactly what was going on. It was enough to know that it was of God and was good.

Would that we could be that way about God's discipline, that we could even welcome it because we knew that God was up to something beneficial in our lives. Like the Israelites in Sinai, some Christians experience great periods of wilderness wandering, the reason for which was their earlier unfaithfulness, but the purpose of which is God's benevolent redirection. The desert does not seem pleasant while they are in it, but it is just a lesson away from the edge of the promised land. God doesn't have hurting, but helping in mind, in all he does toward his children.

Father, if we really trust you, then let us grow to accept whatever you send, even when we don't understand. Amen.

Because that for his name's sake they went forth, taking nothing of the Gentiles.

Giving is special to God

John complimented the churches that they had sent out evangelists with the support that kept them from needing to solicit funds from other sources. Today, John would take pride in churches that support their mission not by selling things, but by committed giving. Even when one can justify another means of financing church work, by saying, "It was Christian people buying the cakes or car washes because they wanted to help a worthy cause," the difference remains. The difference is not that some money is "tainted" while some is not. It is rather that the involvement of those who support the cause is based on godly commitment instead of conditional interest—the interest that says, "I'll help if I get something tangible in return for my dollar."

There is nothing actually wrong in this kind of fund raising: many charities use it. "For your pledge of $50 or more, we will send you this beautiful coffee mug." The issue is not what is *wrong,* but what is *best.* The Bible teaches that God will best bless the work done with the gifts of his people.

A woman made a habit of stashing money. Occasionally she would find one of her stashes and consider it a windfall and would spend the money right away. But Christmas and birthday gifts of money were quite different. She would stash those, too, with notes that reminded her who had given them. She said, "I can't spend that money for just anything: it was a gift from so-and-so." She held on to some gifts for years before doing something really special with them.

God regards Christian gifts as special, too, and will bless the loving gift as he does no other resource—though all things are his.

Father, work the grace of loving giving in us, with no thought of reward, that we may be like Jesus. Amen.

And put a knife to thy throat, if thou be a man given to appetite.

Getting tough with sin

Many Bible proverbs are pungent. The recommendation that one deal with the sin of gluttony by putting a knife to his own throat is pointed, to say the least. But it's no more severe than the recommendation Jesus gave us. He said that if your eye offends you—causes you to sin—pluck it out. If your hand gets you in trouble, cut it off. That's severe! But what do these sayings mean? Are they to be taken literally? Muslims take them that way. In some Islamic states, for instance, rulers cut off thieves' hands. But did Jesus mean for governments to be cruel or for people to mutilate themselves? No.

Jesus meant not to be soft on yourself. Rigorously discipline yourself, and root out the deep, internal causes of sin—the fleshly nature, the heart of sin itself. Don't just spray antiseptic on your sinful life: do surgery on the heart.

A man who really did not like going to dentists avoided seeing about a tooth that was clearly decaying. He thought to himself that eventually he would seek a simple filling, but not just yet. Eventually, reality caught up with him. One evening while relaxing he was suddenly jolted with throbbing pain. As he inspected the tooth for the umpteenth time, he realized he could no longer fool himself. The pain had changed his procrastination into urgency. The dentist said, "You know it will have to come out." And the man answered, "That's what I *want!"*

Sometimes we aren't ready to get rid of the root of some sin when it first begins to trouble us. However, like toothaches that make us believe in the need to remove decay, or fat that finally takes its toll on our lives and health, the trouble wrong living brings will eventually convince us we need to get tough with our sin. It won't go away on its own.

Father, I'm ready to get serious about leaving sin and learning righteousness. Amen.

Saul took a sword, and fell upon it ...Saul died for his transgression which he committed against the LORD.

The hand of God

We can look at life from many angles. Some give a better perspective than others. Some give a more meaningful viewpoint. The Chronicler reports that Saul fell on his own sword. He killed himself because he was afraid that now wounded, and the battle with the Philistines seemingly lost, he would be dishonorably treated by his enemies. But in the next paragraph the Chronicler says that Saul died because he had been unfaithful to God. Which is true?

Both are. The first statement tells us only that Saul killed himself, and how. The second statement tells us what events led to his demise and why. The armor bearer with him might not have seen it that way, and the Philistines surely would not, but the Chronicler and many others realized that God had brought Saul to this ignominious end because, though he had been the Lord's man once, he had wandered far from the Lord. God finally had to direct things so that Saul was taken from the scene, and another could come.

You and I may think of our predicaments as the result of chance, or the evil of others, or our stupid mistakes. Perhaps our difficulties are the result of God's moving to test or chide us, or even as a prelude to blessing. The key to discovering God's best for us is to see life from the perspective of his moving in and through it. Many of us can see God's hand long after the fact, but faith sees it before and during, and acts accordingly. Despair would come less often or not at all if we learned to see the hand of God in our lives right now. If we cannot see it clearly, at least we should confess it, because we know it is true.

Father, we know your hand is at work in our lives. May our ability to see it grow today. Amen.

The Lord is not slack concerning his promise, as some men count slackness; but is longsuffering to us-ward, not willing that any should perish, but that all should come to repentance.

God always keeps his promises

A survey of the Bible reveals multitudes of promises. If you were to list them all, you would discover that many of them have to do with the ultimate reward of those who love God and follow Christ. The New Testament in particular contains hundreds of variations on God's promise to end evil, punish sin, and save and reward those who repent and trust Jesus Christ.

As much as we human beings would like to keep our promises, we sometimes fail to do what we assure others we will do. But there is one who will do all he promised to do. The apostle Peter wrote that Christ was not stalling or forgetting his promise, but simply being gracious to the nth degree, so as many who would repent, could repent. But then Peter added, "But the day of the Lord *will* come."

God hasn't forgotten. He is waiting patiently for his own purposes. What should people be doing in response? Those who hear the gospel should realize that time is short. However long it may be, its duration is uncertain, and people need to respond while they still have the opportunity to turn from sin and receive Christ. As well, Christians need to ask themselves a question: what would you do if you came to a railroad track and found a man lying on it unconscious, and the express train was due? You would pull him off. Similarly, the lost person is lying on the tracks of destiny, and God's judgment express is due. While we eagerly anticipate his salvation for ourselves, we should be urgent about warning others to be saved while God's longsuffering persists.

Father, if Jesus is coming—and he is, then help us get going—as we should. Amen.

...Give me neither poverty nor riches; feed me with food convenient for me: Lest I be full, and deny thee, and say, Who is the LORD?

The danger of wealth

Agur was a wise man. In one of his proverbs he recorded what may have been a repeated prayer that God would spare him from being poor, but on the other hand that God would by no means make him rich. He feared the temptations and curses particular to either situation, especially having great wealth. Consequently he asked God to provide him with "convenient" food, which means just daily bread. Agur knew himself well enough to know that having much more than he needed would constitute an immense temptation to feel less and less need of God, until at last he would think himself to be a "self-made man."

Have you ever noticed that the most effective and lively churches generally consist of folks of average means? Affluent churches tend to cater to those who, like them, have money, rather than following the Lord sacrificially. Paul said in 1 Corinthians that some, but not many, influential or powerful people are in the church. Jesus said bluntly that it is hard for the rich to get into the kingdom of heaven, because the lure to make a god of money is so strong. Money whispers a lie in the ears of our souls that we can buy happiness, even perhaps the lie that earthly happiness is all there is.

Because of the insidious deceitfulness of wealth, Paul advised us that if we have food and clothing—in other words, our basic needs—we should be content. Circumstances and culture create differing levels of need here or there, but most of us know when we have passed the level of need and have begun to approach the realm of affluence. Is anything wrong with having more? Not in itself, no. But Agur's caveat echoes in every age. Wealth contains its own temptation. If God grants you wealth, devote its use to him.

Father, you know best how to bless us. May we use all we receive to serve you. Amen.

I have wounded thee with the wound of an enemy, with the chastisement of a cruel one, for the multitude of thine iniquity; because thy sins were increased.

God's chastisement

A great misinterpretation of the scripture is the idea that all trouble comes from Satan and can be escaped through prayer or miracle. The Bible says otherwise. Hundreds of passages tell us that God tests people with hardship or punishes them with trouble. Hebrews 12:6 gently teaches us that God chastens those he loves. The Old Testament is a bit more abrupt: God sometimes responds to our serious or continued sin by wounding us the way an enemy would.

It is important for us to avoid exaggerating this perspective on God. He is not hard, angry, or unloving. God reserves his toughest treatment for the toughest cases. Occasionally the only way he can get our attention is by thrusting us into difficulty. God *does* discipline us, and he is never unfair. He brings things into our lives to chasten us for rebellion, to redirect us from spiritual harm, or to purify our motives and our methods.

Still, the idea persists that every difficulty should have an immediate solution. For the credulous who seek miraculous answers to all their trials, there are sufficient charlatans who hold out the promise of such miracles for a price.

The tendency to believe that problems should go away immediately in response to some prayer or act of faith is intensified by the fast-food, drive-up, online, email, text-messaging day in which we live. But there is not always a quick fix for tough times. Sometimes, the time spent in the tough time is the one way God has of convincing us to put a stop to some self-destructive sin. Perhaps there is some adversity in your life today that contains a message.

Father, we don't like trouble, but you don't like our sin. Help us avoid the former by abandoning the latter. Amen.

To the praise of the glory of his grace, wherein he hath made us accepted in the beloved.

God's acceptance

One of the most glorious thoughts of all is that God has chosen to make persons acceptable to him through his Son Jesus Christ. It is not something God owes anyone, but something he wants to do because of his great love. Ephesians 1:6 praises God for his amazingly gracious plan to send himself in the person of the beloved Son, through whose life of perfection, death of propitiation, and resurrection of power, we can be accepted by a holy God. It is Christ's worthiness, not ours, that makes us acceptable, and in this confidence we can approach life without anxiety and face eternity without fear.

A toll taker on a long river bridge manned his post through hot and cold weather alike. One snowy late afternoon, when a blizzard had motorists trying to hurry but feeling themselves held up by the toll booth, the taker took a lot of flack from drivers. One man, however, decided to assure him that all motorists were not so disagreeable, and he told him not to feel discouraged. The toll taker seemed unflustered anyway, however, and answered the kinder driver, "That's all right, mister; the man in the front office thinks I'm okay."

After all is said and done, what matters is that we are accepted not by man, but by God. If we are okay with God, we are okay indeed. If we are declared by him to be acceptable, then we are—period. What a glorious thought with which to begin or to end a day, and to carry us through every day.

Father, thank you so much for your acceptance in the beloved, Jesus. May our lives and lips praise you now and forever. Amen.

...Being predestinated according to the purpose of him who worketh all things after the counsel of his own will ...for by grace are ye saved, through faith.

God's choice and our choice

The Bible presents the marriage of many seeming paradoxes. One verse says that we were and always have been chosen to be saved, by the eternal plan of God. Another verse says we express our faith in the gracious, saving act of God in Jesus Christ, and as a result we are saved. In other words, one verse says our salvation is God's decision, and another says salvation depends on our decision—for faith is a deliberate choice. Both verses are true. In fact, the verses are in the same book and were written probably within a few minutes of each other. The way it works is this: In eternity, God chooses us to belong to him specially. Then in time, he works on our hearts by his Spirit, and as a result we choose him.

Look at the right and left halves of a zipper. They are identical. Yet they are opposite. They are identical in form, and opposite in position. When you pull the joining tab, they intermesh and become one. Predestination and free choice are something like that. Both are true, yet they stand on opposite sides of the gemstone that is the salvation of God. They are, in fact, different facets of that stone, viewing God's wonderful mercy from two perspectives, God's and man's. God is concerned with his sovereign plan; man is concerned with his free choice. God provides for both.

Which is more important, the right or the left wing of a bird? Likewise, God has settled in heaven everything that takes place on earth. Yet not a single solitary human will is violated. It is a miracle. But then, that's how God is used to doing things, isn't it?

Father, praise to your name for your wonderful way of working. May we work in harmony with your way today. Amen.

October 11 **Scripture Reading: Ephesians 2:19**

Now therefore ye are no more strangers and foreigners, but fellowcitizens with the saints, and of the household of God.

Belonging to God

A man needs a home. Male or female, *man* needs a home. That need is why God made both man and woman and brought them together in the beginning. But even the fulfilling partnership of marriage and the home that union creates is not enough to fill the ultimate need of *man* the creature. Man needs not just a dwelling: he needs belonging. God knows this and at the very beginning he provided that belonging in a relationship with him. Man was "in touch" with God. It was man who ruined a good thing by sinning. But God has done something about it. He has given man access to himself through the Spirit, who indwells us when we surrender our lives to Christ. Once having this access to God, Ephesians says we aren't strangers anymore, but citizens—we belong. What a wonderful blessing God offers, that we should not wander around in loneliness, but have a caring, loving heavenly Father, a very present Lord through his Spirit, and belonging: we are settled and at peace with God inside us.

At the turn of the 20th century Edward Everett Hale wrote a story about a man who was treacherous toward the United States and was stripped of his citizenship and forced to sail the seas. No country would receive him. How awful to think of tossing endlessly on the ocean, with no homeland to go to. Only death could relieve that man. But the opportunities are more promising for man as he stands before God. If a person obeys the gospel, he can stop wandering, and stop fearing the future and eternity. In Christ, we come home to God.

The old hymn says, "I've anchored my soul in the haven of rest; I'll sail the wide seas no more …in Jesus I'm safe evermore."

Father, thank you from the deep waters of our hearts for the gift of heavenly citizenship in Jesus Christ, and continual access to you by him. Amen.

But I say unto you which hear, Love your enemies, do good to them which hate you.

Love non-selectively

Loving our neighbor seems reasonable as long as our neighbor is relatively like us. But enemies are enemies precisely because they are not like us: they don't value the same things, they have contrary manners, they have conflicting goals, they want to harm us or take from us, or in some other way they clash with us. How can we love them?

It is easy for us to create in our minds a scene in which some ogre of a person mistreats us and we respond with heroic but humble grace by forgiving him and saving his life or some such wonderful thing. In our best imaginings, we look good. But what is hard is living out this principle with real human beings. Jesus was not referring to some faceless world of "enemies of Christ," but the very personal world of individuals around us. Someone said, "I love humanity: it's people I hate." It is quite possible for us to be guilty of such sin.

We Christians can be tempted to select whom we will love, and to love those persons until it becomes obvious that they are not going to return that love. At that point, we tend to transfer our love to people who will respond in kind. This behavior is logical. It is "only fair." It is good business practice. But it amounts to loving only those who love us. It limits Christlike love to a "probation period." Christ's love, on the other hand, starts out by accepting the fact that in some cases love will never be returned. That's hard. But that's what he taught. The only way we can love in that way is by letting God love through us. Perhaps it will help to consider how unlovable we ourselves are at times, and to remember that God keeps on loving us anyway.

Father, this teaching is hard. With man it is impossible, but with you, anything can be done. Help us love like Christ. Amen.

And I say unto you my friends, Be not afraid of them that kill the body, and after that have no more that they can do.

Worth living ...and dying for

Early in the Christian experience, there arose a principle that was expressed in the immortal words of Polycarp, "The blood of the martyrs became the seed of the church." Try as it may, the world will not wipe out the church. That principle holds true on an individual level, too, where believers mean business about their Lord. When it comes down to it, they realize their commitment to Christ and their relationship with God are more important than possession of earthly things and even physical life itself. Jesus said his followers must learn not to fear those who can destroy bodily life but cannot go beyond that.

In the Soviet-Afghanistan war, the Soviets targeted Christians for their military draft, sending them for duty in that conflict. As a result there were—what do you think? fewer people willing to become Christians in the Soviet Union? No. Evangelism experienced an increased rate of success during those years. Interestingly, the result of sending Christians to Afghanistan was that there were more than twenty prayer and Bible study groups in that country started by Christian Soviet soldiers. The Russians thought their efforts would help wipe out Christianity by sending men to their probable deaths in a bitter war. Instead, the Christians became missionaries.

That's just like a Christian, don't you think? Is it like what you would do? Do you take hardship as an opportunity to shine for Christ? Do you take danger as a chance to show what true believers believe in? Do you take persecution as a chance to demonstrate deep commitment and to advertise your faith?

Father, may we turn the pressure of crisis into progress for Christ today. Amen.

Then Peter said, Silver and gold have I none; but such as I have give I thee...

What we have

We are not responsible for doing what we cannot do or for giving what we do not have. We are, however, responsible for doing what we can and giving what we have.

Some churches are large and prosperous and some are small and struggling. Some Christians are well-to-do while most are not. Sometimes Christians are tempted to believe that prosperity, rapid growth, burgeoning attendance and phenomenal budgets are proof that a church is spiritual. In other words, Christians sometimes get stuck on the first part of Peter's words, and lament merely that "silver and gold have I none."

But Peter's statement to the lame man looking for a handout demonstrates conclusively that what is far more important for a Christian or a church to have is the presence and power of Jesus Christ. We need to move on to the crux of Peter's message to that needy man: "Such as I have, I give you." What we have is a Christ who saves and delivers.

A do-it-yourself-er hunted in vain in the largest home improvement stores and the national chain electronics stores for an odd item to repair an appliance. After exhausting the places where everybody goes, he discovered a hole-in-the-wall shop off the beaten path. There he found not only his part, but a wealth of fascinating and useful items for future projects. The shop owner said he knew what it meant to have unusual and obscure needs, and his goal was to provide them.

Only one thing can change people's lives, and it isn't money or things. It's the saving gospel of Jesus Christ. *That* we have. That, therefore, we must give.

Father, as we go, may we give what we have, that others may know how to live forever. Amen.

He retaineth not his anger forever, because he delighteth in mercy.

Good to be forgetful

One of the marks of maturity is the ability to resolve anger. All of us become angry now and then, and if there is a just cause anger itself is not wrong. What is wrong is to let anger sit, suppressed, repressed, unresolved, brewing and stewing, and motivating evil thoughts and plans of revenge. What we should do is communicate the anger without malice and attempt to resolve the issues over which the anger was aroused.

God is described by the prophet Micah as one who doesn't stew in his own juices. God goes all the way from being angry to being merciful, to the very people whose disobedience and immorality has made him angry in the first place. This is a challenging thought to ponder. We need to learn how to imitate God in this progression toward a redemptive attitude of life.

Two little boys were playing with each other happily one day when a disagreement arose. They were suddenly pitted against each other as if great enemies. The mother of one observed their shouting and hostility, and intervened briefly. A while later, she noticed they were again playing together without a hint of the argument. "I thought you boys were not getting along," she said. But the older boy replied, "Naw. Me and Roland is good fergitters."

Along with all the other things we are prone to forget, let us deal with the things that make us angry, so that we can forget them, too, and get on with life.

Father, show us your nature, and make it our own through the indwelling Spirit of Jesus. Amen.

The LORD is nigh unto them that are of a broken heart; and saveth such as be of a contrite spirit.

Don't worry, be humble

An old adage says that worry is like rocking in a rocking chair: you can do it all day and it doesn't get you anywhere. It's hard not to worry, however. Things happen suddenly and upset us, and worry seems automatic. The answer to worry is best found in having someone who is able to take care of our needs. This is why the Lord Jesus Christ is so precious to the Christian in times of stress and difficulty. God promises to make himself real and come to the aid of the humble petitioner who seeks him.

The Psalmist's term "brokenhearted" describes those who are in great sorrow, but it also depicts the result of profound worrying. One who is upended by a terrible threat or crushing conflict in his life may experience physiological consequences: the chest aches, the head throbs, the stomach churns, food isn't interesting, and sleep does not come. Worry, tension, distress! It's hard to turn off, but God will help.

The Psalmist declares two important truths in commenting on those who are "brokenhearted." He says that God is near them, and he declares that an attitude of contrition or humility is vital to experiencing God's help. It is vital for those crushed by worry to remember that in the midst of their crisis—in a sense perhaps even because of their crisis—God is near. It is equally vital for the believer to realize that often worry is the result of falling for the temptation to believe that we can do God's job for him. Instead, claim this promise from the Psalms, that God saves those with crushed spirits. Rest in him. Pray much. Rejoice in advance for God's answers.

Father, break like sunshine over any dark clouds of the heart, and bring your confidence. Amen.

October 17 Scripture Reading: 2 Corinthians 11:28

Besides those things that are without, that which cometh upon me daily, the care of all the churches.

Someone else's shoes

A song a few years ago called, "Walk a mile in my shoes," took off on a Native American proverb, only the Indians originally said "moccasins." When we realize the pressures others face, we understand their attitudes and actions better. Trials in our own lives keep us sensitized to the needs of other people.

This was part of Paul's point in 2 Corinthians 11. After listing all he had been through—floggings, prison, stonings, shipwreck, being a fugitive everywhere he went, laboring without sleep and so on, he said that the external difficulties were only part of his stressful situations. The other part was his continual responsibility for caring for all the churches. Just because Paul was not the pastor of a single church doesn't mean he was carefree. He had a heavy load of leadership and responsibility and assumed a personal, spiritual responsibility for every church he had begun. The implication of what he told the Corinthians was that before they boasted about all they had gone through for the Lord, they needed to walk a mile in his shoes.

Philippine dictator Ferdinand Marcos and his wife Imelda lived extremely lavishly. When Marcos was deposed in 1986, it was discovered that his wife had collected more than a thousand pairs of shoes, many of them ridiculously expensive. The story prompted no end of jokes, including a comment by a woman who said she was not going to criticize Imelda Marcos until she had walked a mile in each of her pairs of shoes. It's possible to take a proverb too far! But perhaps the point is well made that we should be exceedingly kind in our assessment of other people, because we do not always know how it would feel to be in their shoes.

Father, through our troubles teach us to understand and be patient with each other. Amen.

I found Israel like grapes in the wilderness; I saw your fathers as the firstripe in the fig tree at her first time: but they went to Baalpeor, and separated themselves unto that shame...

Drifting away from God

Every Christian has had at least one beautiful experience of grace, love and power in which he felt intensely close to God through Jesus Christ. In language we can understand, the Bible says God also remembers such moments with his people. The prophet Hosea said God regarded Israel like grapes in the wilderness, a refreshing find in a world turned against him. But the high moment did not last. In essence, the Lord says that with Israel it was "love at first sight." But the beloved lost interest in the lover from heaven and went off to pursue other delights.

Things like that happen with us. Most of us do not turn on God or renounce the faith, but we often cool off, become uninterested in spiritual things and get out of touch with the Lord. This can happen when we fail to repent of some sin. Stubbornness builds a wall between us and God. It can happen when we slowly yield to the constant temptation to rest on past progress and we give up the discipline of prayer and the study of the Bible, or we become infrequent in worship. With some, the honeymoon is so quickly over.

In a cartoon of three panes representing a progression of time, a wife and husband are at the breakfast table. In the first, she says, "May I pour you more coffee, honey?" In the second, she says, "I forgot the coffee. I'll get it later." In the third, as he rises she says, "While you're up, get *me* a cup." The story could be told as well with the roles reversed. The point is, affections change.

Have you stopped loving God as you once did? Is there distance between him and you? If so, guess who moved?

Father, forgive your children wherein we may have strayed. In our return, warm our hearts. Amen.

...Whilst we are at home in the body, we are absent from the Lord.

Experiencing Christ

Paul taught the Corinthian church that the Christian's present experience of Christ is not as great as it will be eventually. As long as we are in this earthly body, we are "absent from the Lord." That statement by Paul not only prefaced a remark about eternal life—a truth we cling to in times of grief—but it also says something about life in the here and now. It says that presently we are not with the Lord. But wait: didn't Jesus tell us, "I am with you always?" Isn't that true? The answer is yes, but no.

We are absent from Jesus; it is the Spirit of God who is with us. Technically speaking, Jesus is not in our hearts: the Holy Spirit is. Now, the Spirit is the spirit of Jesus, so in that sense Jesus is in us. But Jesus, the God-man, the incarnate word of God, the one who walked the earth and ascended, is now at the right hand of the throne of the Father. The person of God who is in us is the Holy Spirit, who makes Jesus real to us. The distinction may be fine, but it is important.

Where this truth comes into play for life today is that we must be aware that the Spirit is real, and that his purpose is to make Jesus known to us and to reproduce the person and character of Christ in us. Daily we need to be surrendering to him so that this purpose may be fulfilled.

How do you surrender to an invisible presence in you? First, realize he is in you. Repeat the truth, confess it, meditate upon it, and speak to him. Next, articulate your surrender—say it. Repeat it. Mean it. Then practice it. When any decision comes up, consult him within, and listen. Go with the flow of what you detect as his movement. Practice makes perfect. Then one day, we will be absent from this body of uncertainty and will be present with the Lord. Until then, practice the presence of Christ by his Spirit.

Lord within, take control and let us both feel and know you as we yield to you. Amen.

And they departed thence and passed through Galilee: and he would not that any man should know it. For he taught his disciples...

Apart with the Lord

A "hiding" motif runs through the word of God. The Psalmist often spoke of hiding in the Lord, taking refuge, being hidden by God. We read about being "in secret" with the Lord. Consequently our hymns contain great phrases such as, "Hide me, O my Savior, hide, till the storm of life is past," "There is a secret place," and others. Many of these hymns speak of times of trouble, but there is a secretive gathering with Jesus not related to trouble. In Mark 9:30 the evangelist records that Jesus didn't want anyone to know he and the twelve were in Galilee because he was engaged in a time of teaching and wanted them to be apart, without distraction. The sheer logistics of his ministry demanded that they have some private time. He intended to leave to the world disciples who truly knew him and were fully trained. That took time; so occasionally he had to hide away with them.

All believers need time to hide away with Jesus. Most of us cheat ourselves of that time, and as a result we limit what God can do with us. We need time away from the world, from other concerns, from other people, just to be with the Lord. This is true for every individual, but also the group of believers needs to retreat in worship, or prayer meetings, or other special times, to focus their collective attention on Christ the Master, and to listen to him and experience his teaching ministry. If we are to carry on as his body, we must learn from him constantly.

An old Persian story has it that a common grassy plant was asked one day why it smelled so sweet. It replied, "I have been living near a rose." If we believers expect to have the proper impact on our world, we need to spend time in secret with the Rose of Sharon, the Master we represent, soaking up his character and taking on his personality.

Our Father, as we spend time with Jesus today, let nothing come between. Amen.

Woe unto you that are full! for ye shall hunger. Woe unto you that laugh now! for ye shall mourn and weep.

Mindful of the giver

Jesus' warning to those who are well fed is part of the sermon in the plain. It and his caveat to those who laugh sound like James's assertion that the rich should howl in misery: if taken bluntly, Jesus would seem to say that being blessed with abundance is cause for future punishment. We know enough to realize this is not the case. Clearly Jesus has in mind: those who have enough and don't care about those who don't; those who presume that God will provide for them no matter what their state of obedience to him; or those who simply do not count God into the equation at all. The presumptuously satisfied are the ones who should watch out.

All of us would do well to remind ourselves that God is the giver of every gift, and without his sustenance there would be no plenty, and not even a sufficiency. Something about suddenly being thrust into hunger or other dire need has a way of focusing our attention on our need of God.

A pastor ate supper one night with a farmer after a downpour that seemed to announce the beginning of the end of a long drought. The farmer said to him, "I believe this drought has helped us all, even while it hurt us. You know, farmers, like nobody else, see the ultimate dependance on God's grace to provide for us. For all we do, if God doesn't grant the rain, the increase will not come." The two men gave true thanks for enough to eat that night. Woe to us if we lose a clear and specific sense of gratitude to God for our sufficiency, or fail to care about the need of others. Helping them to have enough is one way to ensure that we do not fall into a precarious position of judgment.

Father, keep us from the carelessness of contentment, and teach us the generosity of gratitude. Amen.

October 22 Scripture Reading: 1 Thessalonians 5:21

Prove all things; hold fast that which is good.

Getting the whole truth

God used a multiplicity of sources to providentially complete his written revelation. It took all the God-appointed historians, story tellers, priests, singers, prophets, evangelists, missionaries and visionaries to give us the entire picture in the word of God, Old and New Testaments. During the first century, God blessed the church with prophets who through the Holy Spirit gave them authoritative directions. The apostle John exhorted believers to "try the spirits," so they would not fall prey to the deceitfulness of false prophets. On the other hand, Paul exhorted believers to put spiritual teaching to scriptural test, and finding prophecy to be of God, to hold fast to it. Clearly Paul, John and the other apostles understood that God could and would speak through many messengers. Believers and churches were not to disregard all but their favorite prophet. But neither were they to swallow everything passed off as prophecy.

Neither must we choose one man, one church, one superstar of preaching or teaching, and make him the standard by which the authenticity of every other voice is tried. The only one who is the source of all truth is God, and he has many prophets and witnesses whose testimony conforms to his Word. Don't be surprised if you get something new from each one of them, and don't resist the truth from any of them.

There are numerous true stories of persons who for racist reasons refused blood transfusions and consequently died. Refusing to hear truth from anyone God sends our way is just as tragic. God sometimes purposely sends unlikely messengers with urgent instructions.

Father, teach us however you will today, and help us to have open ears. Amen.

October 23 **Scripture Reading: Matthew 27:66**

So they went, and made the sepulchre sure, sealing the stone and setting a watch.

The certainty of God's promises

The authorities who had Jesus crucified attempted to make certain he would not be taken from the tomb where he had been buried. A seal on a stone and a detachment of soldiers were their "insurance" that Jesus would remain dead. Some insurance. We know the story: nobody came to steal the body; nobody had to tell any lies. Jesus simply rose, disregarded the walls of the tomb and disappeared into the realm between here and glory, reappearing at will to his disciples. A seal on a tomb, a guard with a sword—some insurance!

Insurance policies do not promise we won't experience accidents, fires, injuries or death. They merely promise to pay us or other people money if and when we encounter those undesirable incidents. The money helps, but nearly everyone would rather not get hurt, be robbed, or die. The fact is, we cannot prevent bad things from happening anymore than the soldiers could prevent the greatest thing in the world from happening. God wanted it to happen, so it did, in spite of all the insurance, the seals, and the guards.

God's promise that Jesus would rise the third day was the master promise that enables Christ in his saving grace to enter our lives and deliver us from darkness to light, hell to heaven. Every other promise of God is just as certain. If God in his unconditional will intends for something to take place in your life, it will. If God gives a promise with conditions, when you comply with the conditions his promise will be fulfilled, no matter how much the world around you may want to prevent it. What makes that a certainty is not the strength of your faith, but rather the faithfulness of God. Count on it. Count on *him*.

Father, thank you for your precious promises, those fulfilled already, and the rest, that will be. Amen.

October 24 **Scripture Reading: Mark 10:38**

Ye know not what ye ask.

Praying wisely

Drought had stricken the foothills near the Blue Ridge Mountains for months on end. Water tables were down, and prayer levels in churches were up. A pastor and his family went for a vacation to a mountain campground. While they thought recent trends meant they would have clear weather, just as they arrived it began to rain. It rained four days, and only cleared off as they were beginning to leave. But none of the campers dared pray the rain would stop. It would have been selfish and short sighted to ask for relief from what people back home needed so badly.

Sometimes we pray for what the world around us needs until it interferes with our personal convenience. Then we pray selfishly. "Lord, make an exception in my case. Hold off until I get out of the way. Don't bring judgment if I am going to get caught in it, too."

Jesus heard his disciples James and John arguing and asked what they wanted. They asked to be put in a position of honor and power. Jesus said, "You don't know what you are asking." There was more to his answer, but that first part of it contains its own general lesson: Often when we ask God for things, we don't realize the full extent of our requests. We may be asking for a burden to be lifted that is there to keep us close to the Lord or to turn someone else to him. We may be asking for a blessing that would be too great for us to handle and would ruin us. We may be asking for clear skies when we need rain in our lives.

How do we learn to pray more wisely? We do it by living more in the will of God, walking closer, and just plain practicing. The more we pray and see how God answers, the better we get at discerning how we should pray in the first place.

Lord, teach us to pray ...better. Amen.

October 25 **Scripture Reading: Jeremiah 9:3**

They are not mighty on the earth because of truth; they go from one evil to another, and they do not know me. (RFS)

When evil seems to triumph

In a perfect world, crime would never pay. In the world we actually have, things are different. The Psalmist lamented, "Lord, how long shall the wicked triumph?" And Jeremiah the prophet of God observed that many evil people are in power all over the world. One of the believer's problems has always been reconciling this troubling fact with the goodness of God.

At least part of the problem is our failing to place human events into their eternal perspective. If we look at a few years or even a lifetime only, evil does seem to triumph sometimes. Some injustice seems to prevail for generations, and worsen with time. But what about the end—either of an evil life or an evil age? Don't discount the reckoning of all things!

Jesus said in a parable that evil would continue to grow and come to fruit along with good, but that the day of judgment would rectify all wrongs and reward all right. If that seems like weak consolation against the suffering of injustice now, it is only because our perspective is inadequate. If this life is all there is, the prospect of future vindication would be no substitute for relief here and now. But this life is only a brief moment compared to eternity, and it is not to be the chief focus of our hearts, especially as incapable as we are of conceiving the things to come.

When a child comes to a parent and says, "Johnny took my toy," some parents say, "Take it back." Even more parents would call out to Johnny, or go to him and make him give it back. But probably better than either is to say to the first child, "Yes, Stevie, Johnny is being ugly. You be nice. If you can't get it back nicely, I'll make sure you have toys and that Johnny gets what he deserves." That's good advice for the Christian, too. Some things will have to wait for God to make them right. Until then, be patient.

Father, it's hard to bear up under wrong and wait for reward. Help us see how it can be done patiently. Amen.

He that blesseth his friend with a loud voice, rising early in the morning, it shall be counted a curse to him.

Careful of our motives

It is possible to say you're doing good when you are doing its opposite. It is possible to do what looks nice when its effect is to hurt or insult. The proverb writer draws us a verbal cartoon to make the point. His observation is not only a practical piece of advice about being too boisterous around people who have trouble getting up in the morning. It is actually aimed at those who mask mean spiritedness with sweetness and light.

How many times have Christians gone to other Christians and said, "I'm telling you this in love," and then they proceed to launch attacks characterized by judgmental thinking and based on gossip or personal dislike or hostility. They claimed to be baring their hearts, but were actually venting their spleens.

A girl once followed Paul the apostle as he preached in a certain town. She was saying that he was a man of God and that people should listen to him. After several days of this, Paul turned around and ordered a demon out of her. What? Her testimony sounded like compliment and praise. But Paul knew she was after something else. She didn't want to be noticed as a girl possessed by evil, so she feigned the part of a believer. She realized that if people saw her as part of Paul's ministry, she would ultimately profit, to the expense of the confusion of the gospel of course, since she served the devil.

Sweetness can easily be a cover for wrong motives. Be certain that your motives are pure.

Father, you know our hearts. So show them to us, and guide us into honest lives. Amen.

...and, lo, I am with you alway...

Always with us

A movie poster a few years ago advertised a film whose theme was the existence of life on another planet. The picture on the poster depicted the visitation of earth by alien beings, and the caption was simple: "We are not alone." People differ on whether we are alone in the universe or there is life elsewhere. Arguments on one side are often based on mathematical probability and rooted in an evolutionary concept, while arguments on the other side are usually theological. Whether or not there is human-like life or any life at all, anywhere other than the earth, may be unanswerable on any basis at present.

But no matter what the answer, we are still not alone. Even if there is no other planet where there is created life, there is a creator, and he is not distant, but right here. The Christian, in particular, is never alone. Not only does he have the general presence of God in the world near him, but a specific presence of the Son of God by his personal Spirit. Matthew 28:20 gives us Jesus' amazing promise.

There are times when believers are more sensitive to the need of the presence of God than others. Smooth sailing can engender a sense of self-sufficiency that displaces the consciousness of one's need of God. But stormy weather brings the believer back to his need to know God is with him, and at work in him. The Christian has the companionship of Christ as a promise because of his new life in him. The unbeliever has no such companionship, because of his continued rebellion against God. Neither person is alone, because God is everywhere. But the presence of God is a reminder to the believer of God's favor, while the presence of God to the non-Christian is an indication of impending judgment, until and unless he accepts God's offer of deliverance through Christ.

Lord, May your presence be a comfort today as we find ourselves in right relationship with you. Amen.

How is it that ye sought me? wist ye not that I must be about my Father's business?

Where to find Jesus

On Jesus' *bar mitzvah* trip to Jerusalem, he stayed behind when parents and friends had left for home. When they came back for him, they finally found him in the temple. What were Jesus' words? "Didn't you know I have to be about my Father's business?" Other versions say, "in my Father's house." The Greek phrase literally says, "in the [things] of my Father." Evidently Jesus had already set a pattern of love for the house of God so that they should have known where to go right off.

Likewise people today should know where to look for Jesus, but often they don't. Many people create their own image of Jesus and insert him into their religious inventions as a prophet or a good example, but not as who he said he was. People looking for meaning in life are looking for God, whether they realize it or not. This search, too, takes place in strange places: meditation, philosophy, drugs, or generic "spirituality." Why do people look everywhere except where Jesus can be found? —in the house of the Father! In the things of God—the church, yes, and the Bible, but Jesus is also to be found in the Christian's life and witness, in the believer's encounters with people in need, and in the gospel preached around the world.

Vance Havner, an evangelist who died in 1986, used to say when people told him they were sorry he had lost his wife, "I didn't lose her. I know exactly where she is—in heaven with Jesus." Let's be clear on where to find Jesus, too. He is not lost somewhere in the world amid speculations and mystical signs. He is in the heart of every believer by the Holy Spirit. He is in his Father's house and can be found in worship with Christians anywhere. He is in the truth of the Bible. If you want to find Jesus, look where the things of God are.

Father, may we really want to find and know Jesus, and may we help others find him, too. Amen.

When they heard this, they were pricked in their heart, and said unto Peter and to the rest of the apostles, Men and brethren, what shall we do?

What pricks the heart

One way or another, God finds a way to turn the hearts of people toward him. Luke, the first historian of the church, tells us that after Peter preached the first Christian sermon on the subject of the crucifixion and resurrection of Christ, people were cut to the heart, and urgently asked what they could do to respond in such a way that they would be saved. They were anxious about their spiritual condition, and eager to find a solution to their predicament.

Unfortunately, these days many an impassioned sermon is ignored. People become calloused by their carnal defenses to the friction of frequent preaching. When that happens, God can use other things to make the preaching of the gospel suddenly more interesting. An article in a metropolitan newspaper a few years ago said this very phenomenon was taking place in that city. It said that single adults had decided that bars provided no fulfillment and that STDs and AIDS were scaring them away from sexual license. Instead, as the solution to their search for something solid to found their lives on, they were going back to church.

It seems that God is using the dead-end streets of sexual profligacy to bring some people to the point of hunger for real fulfillment. He is using the fear of disease resulting from perversion and immorality, and the fact that all sinful lifestyles lead to confusion and disillusionment, to bring people to long for something that brings peace and purpose.

Even in lives where there is already Christian commitment, God uses what he must to make us keep our eyes on him. The key to joy is to pay attention to God's discipline, not ignore it; to learn from his lessons rather than to run from them. When God uses whatever he can to prick our hearts, we need to learn to say, "What shall we do?"

Father, turn our cities and our nation around. Keep Christians faithful to the gospel of hope, power, faith, and love. Amen.

O Lord, thou hast pleaded the causes of my soul; thou hast redeemed my life.

God is for you

One of the finer decisions of our government has been to mandate the appointment of legal counsel to persons who could not afford it but had to have it. The advice or defense of a lawyer is almost indispensable in this country of complicated laws. Yet their price is prohibitive for many people. Justice demands that all should have the privilege of defense. But with no defender, many would suffer who might not be guilty.

God's even more wonderful provision is that although every one of us is guilty of sin, God has not only tried us and found us wanting, not only pronounced sentence, but has also provided a defense for us, a counselor, an advocate who pleads for mercy. This defender does so not because of our worth or our redeeming qualities, but because of his own substitutionary worthiness. The defender requests mercy from the judge because of his—the defender's—own righteousness.

1 John 2:1 likewise says that if we sin we have one who acts as our advocate before the Father: Jesus Christ. He does this in his role as the one who died for those very sins on the cross. Yes, we committed the crimes, but Jesus says, "Penalty already paid."

Jeremiah, who wrote Lamentations, did not know of Jesus, but he knew of God's character, and he sensed God had himself stepped in to redeem him. Somehow, he knew that the Lord was his advocate, not just his judge.

God is for you, not against you. Sin is what God is against. His warning about sin and its condemnation is meant to help you. His judgment is necessary only if you resist him and rebel against him unto the last. Turn yourself in. Christ will take your defense, and forgiveness will be yours.

Father, thank you for seeing to our redemption. We could not afford it ourselves. Amen.

Whatsoever things are true ...whatsoever things are pure ...if there be any virtue, if there be any praise, think on these things.

Can bad things be good?

Many people defend unbiblical practices or traditions as "harmless." The Bible, for instance, condemns witchcraft, divination and attempts to contact the dead, because they all involve communication with demonic beings. Yet today many people think witches are good and think mediums and spiritualists are valid sources of truth. At Halloween, people fall in with the crowd and have fun basically celebrating the existence and activity of demonic spirits, making light of ghoulish things and fixating on death and evil. But, they reason, it's harmless.

Celebrations vary widely, of course, and perhaps the focus of some is innocuous. But the interests of others are not. Curiously, many Christians fail to consider how their actions align with biblical standards. Can sinful things gradually lose that status over time, just because a culture embraces them? Can evil become "harmless?"

Consider the issue from the opposite perspective. Can we apply the standard of Philippians 4:8, for instance, and actually call sinful things "good?" Many a Christian, confronted with the question, "Is witchcraft true, pure, or virtuous?" could not in conscience answer, "yes." Neither could he say a seance was worthy of praise. On the basis of Paul's direction to the Philippian Christians, the things that occupy our minds, and therefore our actions, are to meet these criteria. Studying the existence, the evil role and the insidious nature of Satan involves us in the truth of God and arms us against temptation. But focusing on Satan for entertainment or to learn how to connect with his power is deceptive and ultimately destructive and idolatrous.

The question every Christian should ask himself or herself is not, "Is it harmless," but "Is it holy?" And can we think about things that are true, pure, and virtuous, and about the ghoulish, ghastly and ghostly at the same time?

God our Father, keep our minds on holy things, and give us a thirst for what is true and right. Amen.

If I do that I would not, it is no more I that do it, but sin that dwelleth in me.

Constant warfare

Try as we may or try as we might, we often do wrong when we mean to do right. We all have the problem of having good intentions that do not prevail in the presence of other desires. Every dieter knows the problem: you want *not* to eat, but you do. All of us have tried to reform our conduct in some way but have run headlong into our own stubborn resistance. This is why self-reformation in spiritual terms is impossible: our nature is against it. It's frustrating.

Paul dealt with this frustration and God led him to write about it for our sakes. He talked about the inner warfare constantly taking place, and then he said that it isn't he who is sinning, but *sin* itself, in him. Note that he did not say, "The devil made me do it." What he said is that there was a nature within him which, while it did not operate independently of him, did have great, internal power. He blamed that nature for the sin, and implied that the new nature in him, the one given him by God when Christ became his Savior and Lord, was not doing the sinning. As for Paul, so for us a constant warfare takes place between the old and the new natures.

Judith Martin, whose syndicated-column name is Miss Manners, responded to a letter asking if a woman could tell her friends of how she had turned down a marriage proposal. Martin replied that it was against all rules of etiquette for her to do so, but added, "It is against all rules of nature for her not to."

How like our situation. We know we shouldn't, but we do. We know we should, but we don't. What is the answer? Paul gave it: "Through Christ Jesus our Lord." Or we might translate it, "through having Christ Jesus be Lord." The solution is to turn each struggle over to God and to let Christ have his way. Unless we do, we will experience one frustration after another, as we try to whitewash our sinful natures.

Father, let Jesus take control and win the battle today. Amen.

Out of the same mouth proceedeth blessing and cursing. My brethren, these things ought not so to be.

Conflicting claims

A plant employee was trying to hang a four by eight foot poster on the company cafeteria wall. A fellow worker saw him struggling with it and offered to help. "No, no," he said, "I can do it myself." Another coworker later repeated the offer. "No, really," said the first, "I can do it." After much solitary effort, his job was finished and the banner proudly proclaimed the company's motto for the month: "Together, we can find the answer."

Sometimes our actions belie our words. Sometimes our methods don't fit our message. We may speak of love and practice indifference. We may pray with praise and thanksgiving, and then live in criticism and bitterness. Which is the real "us?"

James, writer of scripture and the brother of Jesus, caught hold of this troubling truth of the conflicting claims of our lives, and he "gave them down the country for it." He said we use our tongues to praise God, and then we wag them in censorious criticism of fellow human beings, when all of us are made in the image of God. James's summation? "Brethren, these things ought not so to be!" In modern, casual vernacular, "Don't do dat."

Earlier, James talked about being "doers of the word, not hearers only." The same principle is involved. When our lips make one claim but our lives make another, we may defend ourselves by saying we just slipped a little in our follow-through, but we really can't blame the world for noticing the conflict and branding us hypocrites. Far too many Christians say holy things but live unholy lives. The impact that changes the world, one life at a time, is made by Christians whose words and lives give the same witness.

Father, may we apprehend the grace that enables us to not only confess our faith but also live it. Amen.

There is therefore now no condemnation to them which are in Christ Jesus...

The banner of Christ

During the Iran-Iraq War (1980-1988), Kuwaitis were having trouble getting their oil out of the Gulf of Oman. Iran wanted to interrupt that oil flow, especially what was headed for Iraq. The United States finally proposed that the Kuwaiti tankers be "re-flagged," taking on the Stars and Stripes and sailing as if they were our ships. The idea was that under our protection, they would be safe, since to attack them would be to attack the United States. The U.S. believed Iran would not dare to risk war with America.

A similar situation exists with Christians. The Bible says we are "in Christ," and that there is therefore no condemnation upon us because of that fact. Jesus has "re-flagged" our lives. We live under his protection. We carry his banner. When God considers us now, he sees us as he would see Jesus: as righteous and holy, because Christ has flagged us with his own righteousness. Nothing can eternally harm us now that we fly the flag of Christ.

Becoming a Christian does not mean the cessation of all sin, though we would stop sinning once and for all if we could. Giving our lives to Christ means we leave the direction of sin and set our sails in God's direction. God does two thing for us in this regard: first, he forgives our sin and covers us with the righteousness of Christ; and second, he gives us his Spirit to help us resist temptation. We fly the banner of Christ and operate under his divine blessing, and by the winds of his power we sail the embattled straits of life. We are *in* Christ, and in him there is not, and never will be, any condemnation.

Father, thank you for the salvation and protection of Christ. May we sail today in your power and grace. Amen.

Speaking the truth…

Truth matters

The Ninth Commandment tells God's people not to "bear false witness against thy neighbor." The prohibition was specifically concerned with dishonest statements that were intended to harm them. More generally, the commandment implied God's people were not to lie at all. However, nothing can be more direct than the statement of Ephesians 4:15, which not implicitly but explicitly says to tell the truth.

We have all sorts of rationalizations for not speaking the truth. We sometimes reason that we told part of the truth and are therefore not entirely in breach of God's law. We may say that people don't need to know the truth, or that it would not be kind to tell the truth, or that someone would be harmed by the truth. Indeed, there are times when it is not our responsibility to tell what we know, but there are times when not to speak would be to imply a lie. In any event if we must speak, we should speak the truth, and not attempt to deceive.

Sometimes, forays into dishonesty are more than minor. The temptation to lie comes at us with particular persuasion when the truth would cost us. At an airline ticket counter, a small boy four years old accompanied his mother. She told the agent he was two. The agent looked at him suspiciously and asked, "Do you know what happens to little boys who lie?" The boy said, "Yes, they get to fly at half price." Sometimes, indeed, they do. But eventually, lies have a way of catching up with us. All of us learn one way or another the value of telling the truth. Sometimes, it's the hard way.

How much better to be truthful, and to sleep well.

Father, make our hearts honest, and then our lips will not deceive anyone. Amen.

Looking unto Jesus, the author and finisher of our faith…

The one who leads us

Election time is fascinating, isn't it? It's marvelous to see all the candidates who care so deeply about us and our safety and comfort, appearing on our streets, mailboxes and email, holding such personal conversations with us via radio and television, hoping to garner our trust and vote so they can serve us. There are altruistic politicians, of course, but isn't it interesting how many causes that go un-championed most of the time suddenly find dedicated, self-sacrificing spokesmen around election time? It calls to mind Brown's Rule of Leadership: The best way to succeed in politics is to find a crowd that's going somewhere and get in front of it.

Jesus Christ was not such a person. The one who leads us did not find causes to espouse or crowds to get in front of. He lived as he lived and said what he said because of who he was and whom he lived for. The Father God directed his life. If he attracted a crowd, it was because he was the truest of leaders with the most worthy of all causes. Unlike many politicians who cosign bills for political currency, Jesus Christ originated the kingdom of God and made the way for us all to become its citizens. Hebrews tells us Jesus is the author of our faith—he blazed the trail, conceived the glory, and made the necessary sacrifice to make it reality.

Some non-Christians are willing to concede that Jesus was a great man. But the Jesus the Bible describes was infinitely more. He was the only incarnation of God. Likewise his mission was and is unparalleled: to die on a cross for our sins and rise from the dead for our regeneration. He did not pander to crowds: he called people to follow him in self-denial and on to glory. Those who know and follow him would elect him any day, but they don't need to. He is the Lord of all already. Are you following him?

Lord Jesus, we will follow you today because you loved us and gave yourself for us. Amen.

For if I yet pleased men, I should not be the servant of Christ.

Soldiers and ambassadors

Many Christians are afraid of the inherent militancy of Christianity. A popular concept is that a Christian is one who gets along with everyone, no matter what. But the Bible concept is much different. It says people who put their stress on pleasing other people have already abandoned pleasing God. Paul wrote the Galatians that if his priority were "getting along" he would not be the servant of Christ. While much of the time we can, indeed, live harmoniously with most people, we must never compromise principles to avoid disagreement.

We live in a world of ancient rivalries such as the British with Northern Ireland, the various groups in the Balkans, and the Jews and Arabs. Negotiated agreements in some international or inter-cultural conflicts would be beneficial, but they may never be reached. During the Cold War involving the U.S. with the U.S.S.R., there were talks about this and talks about that, and an occasional agreement that neither side actually trusted the other to keep. Diplomacy is valuable, but in its extreme it is little more than a nice way to say very little. What would happen in some of the world's currently stalemated conflicts if someone on each side, untrained in diplomacy but streetwise in how to stop a fight, were to sit down and try to settle matters? Progress would probably result. But if not, it would be because when it gets down to brass tacks, people have radically different and unnegotiable goals.

The Christian has conflicting goals from the world's. He wants the lost of the world to come to see things God's way, but if not, he must not come over to their side. We are soldiers of Christ as well as ambassadors. Let us not forget that loyalty to our Commander in Chief is more important than anything else.

Father, let our praise of you today be the way we live solely for your glory. Amen.

And what is the exceeding greatness of his power to usward who believe...

Where is the power?

Are there times when you wonder where the power of God is? There is a part of us that would like to see miracles suddenly take place to correct all our mistakes and facilitate all our fondest wishes. Perhaps that's laziness or just frustration with human inadequacy, but probably all Christians would like to see more overt power of God displayed in their lives than they usually do. Ephesians 1:19 refers to the incomparably great power of God displayed in the lives of those who believe. Where is that power to be found?

It is to be found in the ability of the mind of a Christian to say yes when the Spirit of God says to the inner man, "Do this." It is found in the ability to say, "I'll obey, Lord," when the Spirit whispers to do or not to do something. The power of God is to be found in the emotional and spiritual stamina that seems to well up out of the depths when stress comes and you think you will break. It is to be found in the faith that makes you say to yourself, "I know God is going to work in this situation," when there is no circumstantial evidence at presence to indicate he will. It is to be found in the earnestness of your heart to reinvest yourself in the work of the Lord when you are most disappointed and disillusioned. These things are the power from God, the power in you because of God.

Come to think of it, these things are something of a miracle after all, aren't they? For they are all the outworking of what Jesus said: "With man it is impossible, but with God, all things are possible."

Father, do some more miracles. We need your power to show in our lives today. Amen.

Look not every man on his own things, but every man also on the things of others.

For others

Paul urged the Philippian Christians to continue to develop the kind of spiritual maturity in which they were as concerned with the good of others as they were with their own—or even more. This principle applies to the public lives and prayer lives of modern Christians just as well. The prayers of many Christians, while saturated with scriptural language and offered with deeply felt emotions, are frequently mostly if not solely about themselves. Our lives, our attitudes, our actions, our comprehension of the will of God, our growth in Christ, our searching, our struggles, etc., are certainly valid objects for our prayer, but where do others fit in? When we go from prayer to daily life, we need to keep the same perspective: we must develop a concern for others.

A lady took a Red Cross course in first aid. The day she graduated she went walking down the street and saw a bad wreck occur right on the street corner where she was standing. Hurt, bleeding people were lying in the street—it was a gory scene. Talking about it later, she said, "It was awful, but I knew just what to do. I sat down on the curb, put my head between my legs and didn't even get sick!"

Winston Churchill said, "We make a living by what we get, but we make a life by what we give." Christianity is certainly about what we get from God: forgiveness and eternal life. But it is also about what we give: the love of Christ and the gospel, God's eternal first aid. We share Christ with the dying that they, too, might live.

Father, let the spirit of Jesus, who came to this world for others, dominate us today. Amen.

Having spoiled principalities and powers, he made a shew of them openly, triumphing over them in it.

The testimony of scars

When we're going through difficult times, it is hard to think of them as the emblems of our victory in Christ. But they can be just that, if we let God work in them the way he wants to.

Colossians 2:15 says that Jesus disarmed (spoiled) the powers of evil and held up his victory on the cross for everyone to see. Satan hoped that by the crucifixion of Christ he might forever be rid of the eternal Son of God; for he did not realize what would happen after the cross. But though the incarnation of Christ was a "risk, "in a sense, because it made Christ vulnerable to death, the risk was eliminated by the utter faithfulness of Christ to the will of God. In his perfect fulfilment of God's will to the very end, including the cross experience, he earned the vindication of God in the resurrection. Thus, the cross represents the peak of temptation and the essence of holiness to God. All Jesus' life was about the cross, and he won, because even in the cross experience he did not give in to sin. He did not curse God, leave God, become faithless, complain, or give up. He endured it and blessed God, winning his own victory—and consequently, victory for all of us who will believe on him and receive his life.

The cross was the acid test of Christ's obedience to the Father. Since he passed the test, we can pass it as well. Placing our faith in Christ and surrendering to his Lordship results in his making his abode in us through the Holy Spirit. When life gets tough, we have the enormous privilege of calling on the Spirit within us, in all his divine power, to sustain and enable us. As much as our trials hurt while we go through them, when we emerge intact because of the Lord, our scars become part of our witness. We can tell others how God upholds and strengthens us and makes himself near and known to us, in life's dark and treacherous hours.

Father, thank you for the victory Christ won on the cross. May he himself be our victory today. Amen.

Wherefore by their fruits ye shall know them.

The proof of our claims

A man who considered himself a semi-vegetarian applied for membership in a vegetarian's society because of the discounts they got at a local health food restaurant. On the application form, however, he admitted that he ate fish and poultry "on occasion." The reply from the vegetarian's society soon came, and it said, "Your membership has been approved, but you cannot vote."

Many things we do because of the advantage in them, the social acceptance, the connections, or just to get someone off our backs, but our hearts are not fully in them. It is a fact that a great number of folks who say they're Christians say so not because they love Jesus Christ with all their hearts and have surrendered their lives to him as Lord, but simply because it was convenient for some reason to do so, or it seemed appropriate at the time. Maybe they even felt some emotion about a "decision" they made. But their lives subsequently have failed to prove their claims, as anything at all takes them out of church, worship, and fellowship. They neither study the Bible nor live by Christian principles. Their fruits, in other words, demonstrate a superficial alignment with Christian ideas, rather than a deep commitment to Christ himself.

Jesus said, "By their fruits you will know them." The test of genuine Christianity is whether or not the life of the claimant is productive for Christ. God is not obliged to receive into heaven every person who repeats some words or has some feeling. He needs no proof of the genuineness of our claims: he knows already. But we ourselves need to produce fruit so as to "make our calling and election sure" (2 Peter 1:10). Others need to see that fruit, lest we validate the world's favorite reason for rejecting the gospel: There are too many hypocrites in the church.

Father, let the root produce the fruit today, that we may rejoice in salvation, and prove our faith in the eyes of the world. Amen.

It is God which worketh in you both to will and to do of his good pleasure. Do all things without murmurings and disputings.

Cure for complaining

A book about various keys to success contained a chapter urging the reader to stop complaining about everything that he believes is keeping him from success. "Excusitis" is a condition in which one complains that circumstances beyond his control, or people who have it in for him, are responsible for his leaving things undone, or for his failures. Many people excuse themselves for not being Christians by complaining about Christians they know, and some who are Christians excuse unfaithfulness by complaining about hardships or the failure of others to give them a good example.

Complaining produces tension and leads to defeat. If you want to continue to fail, complain. If you want people to dislike you, complain. Nobody likes a whiner, but many of us are whiners. Whining, however, is not caused by problems themselves. Many persons have had your problems and have not complained. What makes the difference? For one thing, it is a determination to look on the positive side, to make up your mind that you are not going to let life defeat you. That is a purely human thing, and anyone can do it.

But the Christian has an even better way. When Paul wrote about God's working in us to make us want to do—and be able to do—his will, he connected this thought to the previous one about being productive believers. But he followed with the challenge to live without complaining. Since God is at work in the heart and life of the Christian, he should be motivated and empowered by the Lord, not defeated by a negative spirit. The Lord always wills victory, and always offers the power to have it. The reason Christians do not experience victory is not that it is not available, but that they do not appropriate that power.

Lord, may your victory in Christ be replicated throughout our experiences today. Amen.

When ye see these things come to pass, know ye that the kingdom of God is nigh at hand.

Knowledgeable expectation

A California preacher announced the "end of the world" would take place on May 21, 2011. The predicted hour came and went with no event. The preacher joined the sad history of self-proclaimed prophets who believed they knew when Christ would return as he said.

Most of us have heard it said that nobody knows when Christ is coming back. Technically, that's true. 1 Thessalonians 5:2 says, "For you know very well that the day of the Lord will come like a thief in the night." What people have ignored, however, are verses like 1 Thessalonians 5:4, which says that Christians should not be surprised as others will be. Jesus gave some very clear signs of his return to the earth and said that by such signs we would know that it was near.

Paul says faithful Christians, who study the word of God, should not be shocked by the second coming. He comes short of saying that guessing a date will be possible, but he definitely says that one walking with the Lord will sense it is around the corner, and will be ready for it. This is why signs were given to us. If we were not to have some idea, the signs would have been cruel deception on God's part.

Leila Morris wrote a powerful hymn of the Christian's expectation of Christ's coming:

Jesus is coming to earth again—what if it were today?
Coming in power and love to reign—what if it were today?
Faithful and true would he find us here if he should come today?
Watching in gladness and not in fear, if he should come today?
Signs of his coming multiply; morning light breaks in eastern sky;
Watch, for the time is drawing nigh—what if it were today?

That every day brings us closer to Christ's return is an obvious truth. But when Paul said, "Our salvation is nearer than when we believed" (Romans 13:11), he was really saying, "Watch and be ready!"

Father God, send Christ soon to make all things new, and may we be ready. Amen.

Give to him that asketh thee, and from him that would borrow of thee turn not thou away.

Careful charity

Jesus' words are occasionally troubling. Some things he said require constant interpretation in light of our circumstances. His meaning does not change, but the way we must apply that meaning sometimes does. Take what he said about charity, that we should give or lend when asked. What did he mean? It seems clear in a way, but when you realize that all sorts of requests come to Christians and that some are unworthy or fraudulent, you realize you have to interpret Jesus' statement case by case.

Suppose a man comes to your door and says he is poor and wants a car. Would you give him yours outright, and give him the contents of your pantry, or turn over your bank account? The suggestion is absurd. Are we under obligation to open our car windows at a stoplight and put money in a plastic bucket that says "Youth Missions," even though we don't know either who is sponsoring the collection or if there really is any youth mission? Obviously, this is not what Jesus meant when he said "give to him that asketh of thee." Yet if we take his words too literally, that's what they would demand.

What Jesus was aiming at was our tendency to be hard hearted. What he wanted to engender in us was compassion. Yet, both the person who is habitually hard hearted and the one who is mindlessly soft hearted are guilty of folly. You can be warm hearted without being soft headed, and you can be carefully charitable without being cold hearted. That balance should be our goal.

A Moody Institute staffer told of being met in an airport by a girl soliciting for "National Bunny Week." She used a crafty trick of softening the heart by showing furry little bunnies. The cause was somewhat unspecific, however. The staffer did not bite. He said later he felt a little guilty, but that's what the girl wanted him to feel. Later still he saw her counting the day's haul, and he didn't feel at all bad about not giving. Sometimes, saying no is the right thing to do.

Father, we want to have the heart of Jesus. Grow us in compassion as well as sensibility. Amen.

November 14 **Scripture Reading: Malachi 4:5**

Behold, I will send you Elijah the prophet before the coming of the great and dreadful day of the LORD.

The importance of repentance

Paging through your Bible, notice where the Old Testament ends and the New begins. Think of the closure of one division of revelation from God and the opening of a new one. Think about the transition from an old way to a new way, the turning of a page from an old life to a fresh, new one. Think of the saying, "I'm turning over a new leaf," and how appropriate it is that as the leaf turns from the Old to the New Testament, the closing words of Malachi say that God would send the prophet Elijah before the great day of the Lord comes. Malachi wrote that when Elijah came, he would turn the hearts of fathers to children and vice versa.

Immediately when the New Testament begins, the new Elijah does appear, whose name is John. Jesus identified him as such. John's message was, "Repent, for the kingdom of heaven is near." To repent means to "turn," and just as the page turned to a new era of God's grace in Jesus Christ, so to experience God's grace requires us each to turn. If the old is to be gone and the new is to come, we must change in heart. If old ways of despair and defeat are to end and new ways of power and victory are to begin, we must be done with the old, and ring in the new. We must turn from sin to the Savior, from law to grace, from works to the Holy Spirit, from mere morality to Jesus.

God wants us to experience something supernatural and new that will begin to, and continue to, characterize our lives from now on. Not only are we to repent so we may be saved, but daily our lives need to reaffirm that repentance by our turning from the nature that tugs relentlessly at our weakness, and turning to the nature that is bound up with the Lordship of Jesus.

Father God, Jesus our Redeemer and Deliverer, Holy Spirit our power, make us new daily in you. Amen.

November 15 **Scripture Reading: Luke 8:39**

Return to thine own house, and shew how great things God hath done unto thee.

The heart of evangelism

Many people are fearful of witnessing. Even the word *witnessing* or its sister *evangelism* is enough to prompt some people to excuse themselves from a church meeting. This is troubling in view of the Great Commission, which places every believer under the responsibility of witnessing. But witnessing need not be some highly structured activity that only professional people can handle. In fact, it is a simple activity that everyday believers can and should be engaged in every day.

Jesus once healed a man—by casting demons out of him, to be specific—and then told him to go home and tell how much God had done for him. There it is in a nutshell: witnessing is telling people what God has done for you. By implication, as opportunity permits, the witness should also explain the gospel in clear terms and invite persons to receive the salvation and blessing of God. The specifics of leading someone to Christ can be added and tailored to the situation. But most Christians need to get over the initial hurdle of learning to talk about their faith.

A young boy growing up in the 50s got a job going door to door to sell light bulbs. He got a lesson in selling from one of the people in his neighborhood. The man told him, "Son, if you want to sell any of those things, you have to do something other than say, 'Mister, you don't want to buy any light bulbs, do ya?'" In sales as almost nowhere else, it is vital to believe in the product, believe people need and want it, and not apologize for offering it.

The same goes for sharing Jesus Christ. Embarrassment about witnessing actually may be due to not knowing Jesus Christ personally. But for those who know they have received him, reluctance may be the effect of a strained relationship with Christ. Fix what ails your spiritual health so that you will be able to naturally and enthusiastically engage people in conversation about the Savior you love.

Father, as we are fully sold on Jesus Christ, you can use us today to persuade others. Amen.

But every man is tempted, when he is drawn away of his own lust, and enticed.

The devil *didn't* make me do it

The widow of a man by the name of John Mark Galbraith sued the R. J. Reynolds Tobacco Company, because John died of lung cancer, which has connections to cigarette smoking. She lost the case, as well she should have. This conclusion isn't a defense of Reynolds or praise of their product. It is simply a recognition of individual freedom. Tobacco is a product whose demerits have been spoken of in public for decades, taught in schools, and warned about in the media. People who freely make a choice to use a product they know is linked to disease should have no right to blame tobacco companies for the sad results. As the carnival barker says, "You pays your money and you takes your chances."

Sixties comedian Flip Wilson portrayed a character of a woman named Geraldine who couldn't control her shopping, and then defended herself to her husband: "The devil made me buy that dress!" Most of us similarly want to blame someone else for our wrongdoing or have someone else bear the cost of our foolishness.

The Bible makes it clear, however, that we are tempted when our own internal desires get hold of us. James does not mention Satan. He describes temptation entirely in terms of innate desires. To be sure, Satan introduced sin into creation, but we now have enough sinful nature in us to continue on our own steam. Sometimes Satan is personally the source of a specific temptation, but we cannot blame all our temptations on him. Put another way, if Satan were to leave us alone entirely, we would not by any means attain perfection.

We cannot blame our parents, our friends, our enemies or our environment for our sin, and to be sure we cannot blame God. Sin is our fault, and ours alone. That's why salvation is a personal matter that God provides through Jesus Christ. One on one, Christ provides forgiveness for sin and power to overcome further temptation.

Father, I know Jesus is my remedy for sin today, as I own up to my own actions. Amen.

It is not good to eat much honey: so for men to search their own glory is not glory.

Searching and self-indulgence

The love of sweets must be in the genes. Except for the most disciplined souls among us, most of the rest know how luxurious it is to eat candy and sweet foods until our stomachs get sour and we suddenly feel bad. Still, sometime in his life, which of us hasn't indulged in something and paid for it later?

The Proverb writer with great insight from God connects two ideas: overeating honey, and indulging in self-aggrandizement. When we take too much time pleasing ourselves or spend too much energy promoting ourselves, the indulgence tends to turn sour down inside our souls. It may take a while, but pride after a while transforms into punishment. For all our filling ourselves full, we find ourselves tragically empty.

The human race is never free of a generous supply of egocentricism. It's good, for instance, to be the right weight, but bad to worship thinness. It's good to look nice, but bad to preen and spend a small fortune on looks. It's good to be psychologically healthy, but bad to be so absorbed in "knowing yourself" (whatever that means) that you effectively suggest that the focus of man should be on himself. God says our focus should be on him. One of the gems of John 1:4, "In him was life," is that the very source of our true identities is to be found in the one from whom we derived our unique human kind of existence: the eternal Word of God.

In fact, the written word of God says that we really begin to live only when we stop looking at ourselves and start looking to Christ, and when we stop trying to live unto ourselves and begin living unto God. The problem in trying to find yourself by looking into yourself is that you find only someone who still hasn't been found. Try looking into the Lord. There you find what he made you to be.

Father, be our mirror today, and show us who we can be. Amen.

Therefore speak I to them in parables: because they seeing see not; and hearing they hear not, neither do they understand.

How we see

An old expression says that some people look at life through rose colored glasses. It's true that some don't want to see things as they are, so they filter everything through the emotion of some experience or through the innocence of their upbringing. But it is equally true that some people imagine that life is worse than it really is. As another saying goes, the optimist believes this is the best of all possible worlds, while the pessimist fears this is true.

Fishing glasses can be quite interesting. In one style, the basic tint is amber, which increases the contrast of scenery. Then there is a purple tint to parts of them, and finally the tops and bottoms of the lenses are very dark, to screen glare from both sky and lake water. The overall effect is that about one fifth the normal light reaches the eye, and everything looks like it is on the verge of sunset, even in the middle of the day.

To those who take a dim attitude about life because they view everything through the dark glasses of despair, doubt, or disenchantment, life is just as falsely perceived as to those who use rose colored glasses. Both are like the people Jesus described in Matthew 13. Though they see, they do not see. They have physical sight, but inadequate spiritual sight. Some see the world, but not as God sees it, which is the way it truly is. Some see reality, but through the glaze of past experience or unrealistic dreams, and so they don't really see reality at all.

Where does the Christian fit in? God calls us in Jesus Christ to see things the way they are, and then to grasp a vision of faith, and to confess both. The believer does not think life is hopeless, but neither does he lie to himself that it is already perfect. He simply sees what God wants it and him to be, and lives for that purpose in the power of the overcoming Christ. Seeing, he sees.

Father, by the Light of the World let us see, believe, and live in divinely given hope. Amen.

Wives, submit yourselves unto your own husbands ... husbands, love your wives.

Love each other

If people would follow God's rules of relationships, they would get along. Divorce rates illustrate the difficulty many people have in solving problems together. People sue each other over next to nothing. Jobs are lost over problems that should never have existed. Friendships are strained over petty things. All could be prevented by doing things God's way. The chief rule is to love your neighbor—friend, workmate, boss, wife, husband—as yourself. In applying that rule to marriage, for instance, Paul the apostle spoke of the attitudes of wives and husbands toward one another. The master rule was given in 5:21: "Submit yourselves to each other." And in general he taught us all, "As much as is possible, be at peace with one another."

We talk about "give and take" in relationships, and surely both are important. But Paul talks only of the giving. To submit is to give respect; to love is to give self and life. If more couples would submit and give of themselves, there would be less marital discord. But all relationships thrive on the same principle. Brothers and sisters, friends and coworkers, church members and leaders, all get along better when they put each other first and give, give, give.

Syndicated columnist Sydney Harris once said, "Incompatibility as grounds for divorce has always struck me as an insufficient reason. All people are incompatible to start, being different. ...Marriages are not made in heaven, but on earth by two people who labor and sweat, love and sacrifice, for something bigger than and beyond themselves." The same goes for all relationships. It's a proposition of give and give. Help keep families together. Help keep friendships together. Help make workplaces pleasant, neighborhoods warm and cities inviting: love one another.

Father, we pray to love as Christ did, and does, by giving, then giving some more. Amen.

...they were fishers. And Jesus said unto them, Come ye after me, and I will make you to become fishers of men.

The nature of God's calling

Jesus was walking by the Sea of Galilee when he spotted Simon and Andrew casting nets. When he called them, Mark says they left their nets at once to follow him. One of the more interesting things about this encounter is how Jesus appealed to these brothers at the point of a very real interest of theirs. He grabbed hold of that interest by saying that his calling would make use of the very skill or inward fascination that made them good fishermen. We know they loved fishing, for later they went back to it temporarily as a familiar and apparently restful retreat. So Jesus called on that inward motivation that made them love fishing and he used it as bait for his own calling. They would fish for men. Note how quickly they responded.

The Lord does not automate Christians or fit them into an unnatural mold. He always has a particular purpose for each individual, that makes use of each person's strengths and invests him with other strengths to get the job done. God has made us, he knows us, and what he gives us to do in his kingdom is bound to reflect some inner motivation and appeal to desires and skills—if only latent ones—that he places within us.

Looking at the various uses of shells at the beach is interesting. Some people take shells and pour handfuls of them into glass jars and make lamps. The shells are just *there,* as filler. But other people let the shell be the lamp, determining the shape of the base, even serving as a housing for the light, or a filter of a nightlight. The shell is very much a part of the product. God does something similar. Christ calls us to be uniquely a part of his kingdom work. He uses what we are, what he has made us, what we have become in his providence, to get the work done, and to bless lives.

Father, thank you for making us unique and for calling us into roles only we can fill. Amen.

November 21 **Scripture Reading: Genesis 34:2-3**

Shechem...saw her, he took her, and lay with her, and defiled her. And his soul clave unto Dinah the daughter of Jacob, and he loved the damsel.

The power of sex

Certain species of animals, such as monkeys, mate for life—when boy meets girl, it's permanent. How come? It may be an automatic bonding that takes place during mating. Certain animals of higher intelligence apparently respond that way to physical intimacy. Man is very much like the other creatures in God's world. It should not be surprising that he, too, finds that physical, sexual intimacy produces a bond he cannot deny.

Genesis records that Shechem raped Dinah because he found her exciting. But then he fell in love with her. However the other details of the story unfold, the account demonstrates that sexual intimacy makes a man and a woman one in a deep and undeniable way. Today's rejection of the sexual morals of the past is based on the assumption that people can sleep around and never suffer any consequences. However, there *are* consequences, not only in the way of physical diseases, but also in the emotional ping-pong casual sex plays with a person who tries to deny what intimacy does to the spirit, the heart, and the mind.

Sexual purity before marriage is the highest guarantee of an undefiled relationship with your spouse. Sexual purity and faithfulness in marriage is the basic provision for uniqueness and wholesomeness of intimacy throughout life. Even toying with the temptation is dangerous. Lustful thoughts wean a person away from his or her mate or weaken the purity of singles.

Why let some animals show us up in the matter of courtship and marriage? If you're unmarried, reserve sex for marriage. If you've already sinned there, repent and minimize the damage. If you're married, become and remain utterly faithful to your mate. Remember that God is gracious and both can and will give you a new start when you come to him for cleansing and renewal. Be pure, moral and holy in your body!

Father, grant strength today for continuing physical and mental purity, and faith for spiritual holiness. Amen.

November 22 **Scripture Reading: Joshua 6:26**

And Joshua adjured them at that time, saying, Cursed be the man before the LORD, that riseth up and buildeth this city Jericho.

Re-sinning

As bad as it is to develop a wicked culture, it is worse to rebuild it after God has judged and destroyed it. We say we study history to learn lessons from it. Why do we not learn, as a society, that the moral degradation that typified Roman culture, Greek society, and other cultures that fell, will destroy modern cultures as well? The parallels have often been drawn: it seems that Americans and Westerners in general have not learned from history. But our fall may be even greater than some wicked cultures of the past.

In Joshua 6, the Bible describes how "Joshua fit the battle of Jericho, and the walls came tumblin' down." Joshua then warned everyone against rebuilding the city. He went on to prophesy that if people rebuilt Jericho, it would be at the cost of their children. The lesson is powerful: God often increases wrath upon those who stubbornly rebuild what he has thrown down.

The application in personal life is just as clear. God sent his Son to die so that the power of sin would be broken. If we become intent upon redeveloping the ways of life that we once abandoned to follow Christ, we risk greater consequences. Sinning brings discipline, but "re-sinning" may well multiply that discipline, as God must use more and more stiff measures to turn us around and convince us to live for him.

When God saves us, he breaks the power of sin in us. He means us to be free of things that hurt others or keep us from doing his will. If we lay again the foundations of sin in our lives after Christ has come to break them down, we risk heartbreaking consequences. God wants us to be holy unto him.

Father, may we experience the Holy Spirit's penetrating power today, to rid us of sin. Amen.

November 23 **Scripture Reading: 1 Kings 12:28**

The king took counsel, and made two calves of gold, and said unto them, It is too much for you to go up to Jerusalem: behold thy gods, O Israel, which brought thee up out of the land of Egypt.

Too hard to obey God?

In the divided kingdom after Solomon, Jereboam was afraid he would lose the struggle to Rehoboam, king of Judah. So he made two gold calves, put them in Bethel and Dan, and told Israelites to spare themselves the unreasonable expectation of attending worship at Jerusalem by staying closer to home. Many scholars believe the calves were not intended as idols, but as pedestals for the invisible presence of God. Either way, Jeroboam was defying God, who required all his people to appear before him at the temple. Jeroboam led the people of Israel in a lie.

Hebrews 10:25 indicates that the Christian has the similar obligation to worship and fellowship with his church. When a believer develops a pattern of forsaking the assembly of worshipers, even if he substitutes a TV church to assuage his guilt, he is treading on dangerous ground. Satan knows if he can keep Christians out of worship, where they are challenged to love and serve God, they will likely be neutralized as to any godly impact on the world. Televised religious programs have a place—as a supplement to live worship, as a ministry to the truly incapacitated, or as an outreach to the unsaved. But for Christians to become unfaithful to their churches is sinful.

We don't belong to ourselves; we belong to God, who created us, and he has the right to expect our all. He does not ask too much in commanding us to love his church, to obey him, to live morally, and to serve others in love. It is not only right, but prudent, for us to give God his due, surrendering ourselves in loving obedience. Far from suffering a loss for the time we spend, the inconvenience we experience, or the money we give, we will be blessed many times over.

Father God, sin in us resists worshiping you, but Christ in us wants to. Let him prevail. Amen.

The law of the Lord is perfect, converting the soul: the testimony of the Lord is sure, making wise the simple. The statutes of the Lord are right, rejoicing the heart: the commandment of the Lord is pure, enlightening the eyes.

The worth of the word of God

The Psalmist's assessment of the worth of the word of God is expressed in Psalm 19 and in other psalms with compounded superlatives: he can't say enough about how great and perfect it is. In the four statements of Psalm 19:7-8, David describes how turning from our self-directed ways to God's eternal principles under the leadership of his Spirit will straighten out our lives. Notice the four practical results of living by God's word: (1) spiritual revival—new life; (2) the accrual of wisdom; (3) joy of heart; and (4) insight.

When we try to solve our problems with the best of human wisdom only, we may achieve a certain level of satisfaction, but something is always missing: life is hollow and ultimately pointless. But following God's principles brings a sense of life, a definitive wisdom for the future, abiding joy in the heart, and insight that lends assurance.

A father labored feverishly into the night on Christmas Eve, trying to put together a bicycle for his daughter. Well into the morning hours the derailleur gears and complicated brakes defeated his attempt to assemble the bicycle by following his instincts. Instead he validated the old saying, "When all else fails, read the instructions." His daughter was delighted Christmas morning.

Many simple tasks can be tackled successfully without instructions, but the more complex the assembly, the more we need the maker's manual. Life is the prime example. Life is indecipherable and its challenges insurmountable without the Maker's manual—the word of God. God gave us the Bible through inspiration and providence so that by studying it we might find him, discover his way, know his principles, and follow his leading.

Lord, lead us back again and again to your word, so that life, while amazing, will not be a mystery. Amen.

If thou hast run with the footmen, and they have wearied thee, then how canst thou contend with horses?

Pray to be faithful

We may pray for God to enlarge our influence or responsibility even though we may not be ready for it. God, however, knows what we are capable of; he is not likely to give us opportunities we are certain to botch. God apparently makes a habit of giving his important responsibilities to persons who can be trusted with them. This is not to say that God never gives us a job when he knows we will fail, but only that he rewards prior faithfulness.

Jesus said that those who are faithful in little will be the ones who are faithful in much. Though we might like to skip the learning exercises and go on to the great privileges, it doesn't work that way. God told Jeremiah that the difficulty of his task as a prophet so far was small compared with what lay ahead. If the footrace tired him out, he would certainly never outlast the horses. God did not mean to discourage Jeremiah because of his weariness or even past failure, but to challenge him to continue to run the race faithfully.

A couple in a church complained that they were not asked to do anything. Finally they were asked to take important team responsibilities. They first demurred, suggesting that someone else might be better, but finally they accepted. One of them never showed up for a meeting, and the other was unreliable. They were not asked to serve thereafter.

Before we pray for greater things, we should ask ourselves honestly if we are ready. Have we proven our faithfulness? Is God likely to entrust us with something if we have quit or reneged before? As with Jeremiah, God's purpose is not to discourage us but to challenge us to be faithful. We do not know how great his plans for us are, but we know we have a task today. God's standard of success for that task is simply that we be faithful in accomplishing it.

Lord, we have all been unfaithful before. Teach us the importance of the smallest opportunity from your hand. Amen.

Be not deceived: God is not mocked.

Don't fool yourself

No kidding, we kid ourselves about as much as we kid anyone else. People have a way of talking themselves into believing things they say that simply are not true. But they tell themselves these little lies—sometimes these big lies—because they are embarrassed by the truth.

When a person says Sunday is his only day to rest, and he gets up at dawn to go fishing, or spends hours on a jet ski, whom is he kidding? When someone says church is uncomfortable and too long, but then he drives two hours to a stadium where he sits cramped for two hours in drizzle, whom is he kidding? When someone says he cannot afford to tithe, but he can afford a comfortable house, a nice car, plenty of food, a closet full of clothes, and frequent entertainment, whom is he kidding? When a person says, "I don't have time for church," but does have time to spend hours in front of a television or in the mall or on a hot golf course, whom is he or she kidding?

The "art of the spin" is the technique of twisting a story to make it more complimentary to the one telling it. The danger is that eventually people may begin to believe their own spin. Just as Paul reminded the Galatians, while we may fool ourselves, we never fool God. We reap what we sow; if we sow lies, we will reap shame in discovery. God knows the score. Down deep, we do, too. For the most part, we do what we want and no one forces us to do otherwise. While each of us can think of someone else who needs this reminder, let it be personal in whatever way it applies. Today, tell yourself only the truth, and if anything needs changing, act accordingly.

Lord, if you who said, "I am the truth," are in control of me, I will have no trouble being honest with myself. Amen.

And they told him, and said, We came unto the land whither thou sentest us, and surely it floweth with milk and honey...

Recognizing abundance

Often, contrast helps to identify God's blessings. The Hebrews in slavery in Egypt and then wandering in the wilderness had no trouble realizing that the land of Canaan was God's blessing: it was a land flowing with milk and honey.

But the contrast may be more subtle. After suffering persecution, danger on the sea, death from disease and cold, and the hardship of carving out life in a new land, the pilgrims who first came to America saw the end of winter, their embattled survival, and the cautious friendship of a few Indians as God's blessing. They proclaimed a time of gratitude to God, setting a precedent eventually enshrined in our Thanksgiving day. Yet we often confess that we have spent much of the year insufficiently aware of our blessings. Maybe we lack contrast.

Perhaps Americans need privation to awaken us to the vast sweep of our national bounty. September 11, 2001 made Americans realize how secure we have been on this continent. The blackout of much of the northeastern U.S. reminded millions just how wonderful electricity is. It often takes drought to make us fully appreciate rain, and sometimes sickness is required to make us pause to thank God for our health. How much better it would be if we searched the landscape of our lives for the purple mountain majesties of God's continuing blessing; if we inspected the fields where we live and work for the fruited plains of the Lord's unnoticed benefits; if we looked with hearts untarnished by cynicism and saw the spacious skies of his mercy, and the amber waves of grain in the Living Bread.

God could force us to recognize his blessing by taking it away. It is far better for us to open our eyes daily, see the milk and the honey, and say, "Surely, we are blessed."

God our Father, thank you for your abundant blessings, in this world, and in Christ Jesus. Amen.

Who is blind, but my servant? or deaf, as my messenger that I sent? who is blind as he that is perfect, and blind as the LORD'S servant? Seeing many things, but thou observest not; opening the ears, but he heareth not.

Recognizing ruts

God speaks sobering words through Isaiah, who puts his finger on the sore spot of Israel and shows them that they are, indeed, the people of God, but they are being obtuse and dull towards him. Isaiah does not deny that Israel is the Lord's people or that they are in some sense committed to him. He only says they have gotten to the point where they can listen to the preaching of the word, read the scriptures, and see the living message of God in history all around them, and still they are sitting like bumps on a log doing nothing—certainly not obeying.

The church of the Lord Jesus needs to be reminded constantly not to get into this kind of rut. Yet it is just this kind of rut that we slip into regularly. It may be the pattern of prayerlessness or neglect of worship. It may be a ditch of discouragement, a gully of griping or a treadmill of tradition, and it isn't the other guy who is at fault. We know who it is. What does it take to get you and me out of the ruts we fall in?

A frog hopped down the road and fell into a rut. He tried to jump out several times, but gave up shortly. Sitting in the bottom of the rut he heard a frog friend say from the ledge above, "Why don't you jump out?" He answered that he couldn't. The next friend who came along asked the same, and was answered the same. Finally, the frog decided he rather liked the rut. He didn't have to go anywhere. Besides, he 'couldn't' get out. But a truck came along and he did get out.

May we not wait as long as the frog. Heedless habit eventually renders us unproductive in living and ineffectual in witness. God wants us to be fulfilled ourselves and helpful to others.

Father, we need not stay in the rut until completely useless to you. May we be scared out or helped out today. Amen.

Come, and let us return unto the LORD: for he hath torn, and he will heal us; he hath smitten, and he will bind us up.

A time to rend, a time to sew

In a speech to America on the subject of South Africa, President Ronald Regan quoted a poet who said those hurt by others often do harm themselves. He was speaking about the temptation to retaliate. When we are attacked or wronged, we may follow up a bad situation by making another one, this time with ourselves at fault. God is not like that. Yet sometimes, mysteriously, he must bring what all of us would call hurt into our experience in order to divert us from destruction, or teach us wisdom, or keep us in the way of fruitfulness to him. He did that with ancient Israel. He rent the nation of Israel so they would return to him to be sewn together again.

What a mysterious and marvelous thought about God. Ultimately he allows "bad" things to happen to "good" people, but he doesn't do it for bad purposes but for good. Evil men are sometimes turned from evil by calamity; good men are usually purified by trial. God must chasten to correct.

When the Southern states of the U.S. seceded in 1860, the Union, led by President Lincoln, fought aggressively to squelch the confederacy. Lincoln was certain that the departure of the South would destroy the dream of America and that only the union of us all would keep us on the right track. He waged a destructive war to reach his goal. Hundreds of thousands of men were killed. Finally, Lee surrendered to Grant, and the Union was preserved. The South was beaten, but did Lincoln and his successors enslave it as punishment for rebellion? Did he demote it, or forever subordinate it? No, the South was built back in what we now call the Restoration. After much war, it was time to heal.

God treats us this way. Because of sin we may have had to suffer, but the same God who ordered our bitter bondage heals us when we return to him.

Lord, we return for healing. Thank you for restoring our unity with you in the bond of peace. Amen.

He must increase, but I must decrease.

The increase of Christ

A girl once performed a science project in which she put the scraps from her plate each meal in a contraption that fermented them and produced gas, which in turn inflated a man-sized, man-shaped balloon. She had been conducting the project for a week and it had not gone well, because—as she was a hefty girl—she didn't leave many scraps on her plate in the first place. Finally, she decided to diet, and the scraps became more numerous. When she began to see the difference in the project and her own figure as well, she said to her mother, "It's just like the Bible says: He must increase, and I must decrease!"

That's not exactly what John the Baptist meant when he said the words, but it illustrates the truth. The purpose of Jesus' presence in our lives is to increase as we decrease. That means not that we disappear, lose consciousness or become mindless robots, but that attention is directed away from our own accomplishments and focused instead on the Lord we serve. Our sinful wills must grow less dominant, and his character and purpose must shine through. In order for this to happen, we must renew our surrender and our submission regularly. If we do not decrease, he cannot increase. If he does not increase, we will not grow and mature spiritually.

We must never worry about God's directing our lives so as to prevent fame and fortune. If he does so, he may simply be burying our egotistical tendencies. If he denies us success by the typical measure of worldly acquisition, he may only be instructing us in the godly standard of success, which is faithfulness. After all, his purpose is not that we might be seen for being something in ourselves, but that Christ might be seen in his glory in us.

Father, hide us, and take the limelight yourself in the person of Christ Jesus in us. Amen.

Nevertheless the centurion believed the master and the owner of the ship, more than those things which were spoken by Paul.

Saving yourself shipwreck

Acts 27 records in vivid detail the experience of Paul on the ship voyage toward Rome. Luke writes that the centurion in command made an unwise decision. Paul said they should stay in the harbor where they were, instead of sailing on. He insisted that if they left the harbor—which, interestingly, was named, "Fair Haven"—the ship would experience trouble at sea. The ship's pilot and owner, a man trained to predict weather accurately and sail a ship safely, believed the small chance of trouble at sea was worth leaving the inconveniences of Fair Haven as a winter port. Instead of taking the word of a preacher, the centurion decided to take the advice of an expert. They sailed on. A hurricane-force storm promptly met them on the way, and the ship was destroyed. By the providence of God, the men were all saved.

Non-Christians for certain, but Christians also, can invite destruction by plotting their course according to something other than God's will. When we are driven by worldly, self-laid plans, almost invariably we make the wrong moves. Even the most expert human advisors, if they are not plugged into the wisdom of God, can mislead us seriously. God tries to direct our paths, sometimes through persons we neglect to hear because they are "nobody important." Our subsequently making wrong decisions almost always leads to loss. But God frequently spares us for another try, because he has a purpose for us yet. Nevertheless, we could spare ourselves much grief by moving only when he says to move, and staying put when he doesn't speak.

Children play a game teaching this lesson: Simon Says. "Simon says take a giant step. Simon says stop. Go. Ah! I didn't say 'Simon Says.'" We must learn this lesson about God's leadership. God says go. God says stop. Save yourself shipwreck: listen for the voice of God.

Father, I am listening today. No giant steps, or even little ones, without your word. Amen.

December 2 **Scripture Reading: Romans 16:20**

And the God of peace shall bruise Satan under your feet shortly.

Relief from resistance

God's promises and warnings are often contained in the same verses. Paul told the Roman Christians that Satan and all those who join him in resisting God's truth and righteousness in the world would soon be crushed. This assurance implies a promise for every Christian: that God will enable him to overcome the temptation that is embedded in every trial or persecution. God will defeat the temptation to sin when we appropriate his power made available through the Spirit of Christ, who broke the power of Satan through his cross. But this verse also includes a warning: all those who persecute believers and reject Christ will be included in the punishment of evil, unless they turn and surrender to him. People who make war against God and his kingdom, are fighting for a losing army.

The same loving God promises deliverance and heaven to those who receive Christ and warns of judgment and hell for those who to their dying breaths reject him. God shows his love for the believer by saving him, and also by separating him from persecution and evil forever. Some who reject Christ complain that they can't believe in a God who would send anyone to hell, but in the matter of condemnation, sin is the culprit, not God.

A man who awakes in the night to find an intruder with a knife about to kidnap his son not only has the legal right to use lethal force against the intruder if that's what it takes: he has the moral obligation to do so. A man who will not protect his family when the choices are so very clear is not demonstrating love for them. Similarly, God in his love eventually must choose to bless the beloved by judging the beloved's enemies. Even this warning is an implied promise: we believers will not have to endure opposition forever. Soon we will participate in the final victory that will deliver us eternally.

Father, we're glad to be on your side. Crush the tempter soon, and keep him under today. Amen.

And be not drunk with wine, wherein is excess; but be filled with the Spirit.

Under the influence

People—even many Christians—debate whether the Bible's overall message concerning alcoholic beverages is one of abstinence or one of moderation. Some who choose abstinence don't know how to interpret verses that seem to treat wine as an acceptable beverage. But many who choose moderation are not aware that in Bible days respectable people always highly diluted wine for table use. The fact is, no alcoholic beverage today corresponds to the reconstituted wine used at meals during the times the Bible describes. All modern alcoholic drinks in a typical, single serving have a measurable effect on the human body, loosening the tongue, breaking down even helpful inhibitions, and depressing the nervous system.

There can be no debate, however, that the Bible sternly warns us against any degree of drunkenness. We should always be in control of our faculties and should never surrender ourselves to the control of alcohol. Drunkenness leads to irresponsible acts and foolish decisions. We should never drive or do anything else "under the influence" of alcohol. But Paul uses the vivid image of drunkenness to illustrate another kind of influence all of us should always be under. We should always be filled with the Spirit. God's Spirit should have the kind of influence, control and Lordship over us that result in our living in the flow of his strength and the river of his joy.

There is to be no moderation at all as we drink in the presence and power of God's Spirit. He is in us that we might experience constant companionship with God, effectiveness in our efforts of righteousness, and faithfulness in our following of Christ. Imbibe the Living Water through his word. Let it well up in you continually. Live under the influence—of God.

Father, may our hearts be merry and our lives be fruitful through the wine of the Holy Spirit today. Amen.

December 4 **Scripture Reading: 2 Thessalonians 3:4**

We have confidence in the Lord touching you, that ye both do and will do the things which we command you.

The power of positive expectation

The Bible teaches the Christian how to help others become all they can and should be: use the power of positive expectation. Paul wrote the Thessalonian Christians that he was sure they were already doing and would continue to do what he instructed them as an apostle of Christ. Note his approach: he used the word "command;" he was certainly an apostle with the authority to issue such authoritative instructions; and he had the right to expect them comply. But in this case, he chose to emphasize his confidence in them, implying that they had acted without the need of reminders or warnings. He knew they wouldn't debate about, argue with, or vote on his instructions. If there were any persons among them who were inclined to take issue with him, Paul's positive expectation gently led them to conform to what they knew they should do, not how they were tempted to act.

A technique for effective letter writing even today is to express appreciation in advance for what you want someone to do. Ending a letter by saying you thank someone for his attention to the matter you have raised, or by saying you appreciate her timely response, is a courteous but powerful way of prompting the best reaction to your writing.

People in general respond better to positive expectations than to negative attitudes. Children reared by parents who encourage them are overwhelmingly better behaved than those reared with threats and anger as tools of discipline. Every pastor knows that church members respond better when praised than when browbeaten, and pastors themselves are more effective leaders when lifted up by church members than when ground down by them. The bottom line is that if you expect the best, a few people will disappoint you, but if you assume the worst, most people will give it to you. Expect the best!

Father, as you saw us worth saving, may we see in others what they can be, and encourage them in becoming it. Amen.

December 5 **Scripture Reading: 1 John 4:1**

Beloved, believe not every spirit, but try the spirits whether they are of God: because many false prophets are gone out into the world.

Knowing what to believe

A story circulated a few years ago that the real reason Nikita Kruschev was deposed as premier of the Soviet Union was that he had become a Christian. According to this account, during a Christian event at a Black Sea resort Kruschev unexpectedly arrived and gave a testimony about having received Christ. Spies accompanying him reported Kruschev's conversion, and he was quickly deposed. Could he who once said, "I will display on national Soviet television the last living Christian in our country," really have professed faith in Christ? Later publications labeled the story a "Christian urban legend," and wishful thinking. Indeed, the original story was *fifth* hand, and the source was unnamed. Probably the story is false.

Christians sometimes are credulous, perhaps because they want encouraging things to be true and want their faith to be vindicated in this world. We yearn to see the promises of God come true in amazing ways. It is possible for people to believe wrong things for right reasons. Perhaps this is why John warned Christians not to swallow the claims of just anyone who said he was an apostle or Christian teacher. Some were led by spirits opposed to Christ rather than the Spirit of God. The intention of deceiving spirits is to get Christians off track, to involve them in tangential pursuits that divide believers and dilute the gospel.

How do you know which book authors, which popular speakers, which media ministers, even which church leaders are leading straight, and not astray? John tells us to test every spirit, try every story against the principles of Scripture and the life of Christ, and sometimes against common sense and documented fact. Be teachable by all God's true messengers, but take responsibility yourself for what you believe.

Father, while many teach, your Spirit is our ultimate teacher. May we be good students of your truth today. Amen.

Thou art worthy, O Lord, to receive glory and honour and power: for thou hast created all things, and for thy pleasure they are and were created.

A reason to worship

Some people ask why they should worship. In Revelation, John records having heard in his vision the twenty-four elders fall down before God and worship him. Their explanation for his worthiness to be worshiped is extremely rich. It states emphatically that the universe is not the product of random events but the purposeful creation of God. It further says that the world, humanity in particular, owes its continued existence to God's sustenance and his forbearance. God could have allowed the universe to dissolve into nothingness at the first incidence of sin, even as he wreaked great havoc on the early earth by an immense flood because of the ubiquitous rebellion of mankind. Instead, he allowed the world to exist and he continues to watch generations of humanity come and go, patiently revealing himself through the glory of creation, the history of a chosen people, the writings of Scripture, and the person of Jesus Christ.

Why does he do this? He does it because he loves what he made, and purposes to bring joy to as many as will walk in his way. This in turn brings pleasure to God. We should worship because God has allowed us to come into existence, has shown us himself, has offered us eternal life, and has welcomed us who believe into his heavenly family and kingdom. Most earthly troubles that deter us from praise are nothing in comparison to these overarching reasons to worship.

Walk out under the sky on a cloudless night, gaze up into the dots of distant fire, gauge the distance to the dimmest one with the rangefinder of your imagination, and picture yourself as an infinitesimal speck in this magnificent vastness. Say to yourself, "God created me for his pleasure." Then worship him, for he is worthy.

Creator God and Father, my heart, wordless, worships you. May my life bring pleasure to you today. Amen.

He retaineth not his anger for ever, because he delighteth in mercy.

God prefers mercy

The infamous attack on Pearl Harbor, December 7, 1941, awakened the sleeping giant and thrust America into the second global war. The U.S. was committed to the defeat of the empires that threatened freedom around the world, and only after all Axis powers surrendered did World War II end. In true form as the nation founded on godly principles, America led the rebuilding of Germany and Japan. Lasting peace depended on former enemies experiencing the good will of those who had beaten them. Righteous anger did not last forever, only until the will and ability to make war was broken. Then America preferred mercy.

Through the years individuals here and there have continued to find it difficult to remember Pearl Harbor without a tinge of temptation toward bitterness. But America as a nation has continued in its resolve to take the high road, bringing healing after waging war. Again and again, American soldiers have repeated this pattern, acting as much as ministers of mercy as messengers of might.

A nation has always derived its collective will from its people's hearts. Mercy in the hearts of Americans inspires the policy of the nation. Alexis de Tocqueville said, "America is great because America is good, and when she ceases to be good, she will cease to be great." We Christians often call the nation to remember that "righteousness exalts a nation" (Prov. 14:34). But we must never forget that the nation will be only as godly as the people of God are. Do you prefer mercy to anger, forgiveness to bitterness, healing to wrath? Have you learned the secret of God's mercy: to destroy your enemies by turning them into friends?

Merciful God, if you had been angry forever, we would not be thanking you now for mercy. Amen.

The land shall not be sold for ever: for the land is mine; for ye are strangers and sojourners with me.

God's real estate

The term "real estate" came about as a means of distinguishing land from other kinds of property. Other property could die, rot, rust, burn, be stolen or be lost. But land didn't suffer from the same impermanence; therefore, of all a person's estate, land was "real." Many novelists and dramatists have expressed the feeling that even the poorest person needs a little plot of land he can call his own. At the other end of the spectrum are many wealthy persons for whom vast acres of land are the symbols of their affluence. The thirst for real estate echoes the idea that land is the only thing worth fighting or dying for.

Yet the scriptures say that no matter who has a title for it, how much he paid for it, how much of it he or she owns, or how many generations it has been in the family, the land belongs to God. Not only the land of Israel, but "the earth is the Lord's," wrote the Psalmist, "the world, and they that dwell therein." This is no vague generality and no mere technicality. It is a truth that should have the most profound impact on the way we regard our homes, our possessions and our incomes. This truth should shape our goals, our plans and our wills. It should order our priorities of life's pursuits, limit our investment in the world's things, and intensify our good stewardship of resources. For while we call all these things "ours," none of them really is. None of them, even the land, is permanent. We cannot own these things forever. We are just using the things, just borrowing the wealth, just passing through the land. In a few short years, we breathe our last and none of what we see passes over with us into the spiritual realm.

C.T. Studd was inspired by this impermanence of life and material things, and wrote in a poem, "Only one life, 'twill soon be past. Only what's done for Christ will last."

Oh Father, teach us to value spiritual things over anything this world has to offer. Amen.

...Thy people shall be my people, and thy God my God.

A heritage of faith

Many marriage ceremonies have included the famous words of Ruth proclaiming her commitment: "Whither thou goest I will go." She spoke these words to her mother in law, Naomi. After Ruth's husband's death, Naomi urged her to go back to her own family and her own gods. Perhaps prior to this point in her life Ruth had not fully assimilated her family's faith, only cooperated with it. But when the moment of decision came, Ruth was ready to turn her back forever on whatever gods she and her family had served and to seek instead to know and serve the Lord of Israel. From that moment, their God would be her God.

The principle the scripture teaches us is that there comes a time in our lives when we must determine what to do with the truth we have heard. We have heard the words, seen the example of others, and been invited to build our lives on the same truths. What will we do? Whether it is a truth about the wisdom of honesty, the obligation of worship, the destructiveness of immorality, the blessing of giving, or the greatest truth of all—that of the good news of salvation through faith in Jesus Christ—the key question is what our response will be. It is a decision that cannot be put off indefinitely.

Ruth chose not just her mother in law's God, but the only true God. When she did, she became the future great grandmother of King David and an ancestor of Jesus Christ. Her character was written into the script of God's word and her example became part of the teaching that has shaped the people of God for most of three millennia. There was no way she could have known the importance of her decision. Typically, we have little inkling of how far reaching might be the consequences of the things we do. Let us commit ourselves to God's way, wherever it goes.

Father, one step at a time, every step in step with the steps of Christ, is our prayer. Amen.

The priests waited on their offices: the Levites also with instruments of musick of the Lord, which David the king had made to praise the Lord, because his mercy endureth for ever…

The contemplation of praise

The Chronicler says that David invented musical instruments. From concept to design to assembly, these instruments came into being for one reason: to praise God. Even after they were created, someone had to learn how to use them and become proficient on them. The entire process of training persons to play was for the sole purpose of rendering praise to the Lord.

Praising God certainly should be done with feeling, not just form. But we are mistaken if we show disdain for detailed planning and rehearsal. The heart of praise is to be found not only in the enthusiasm of spur-of-the-moment inspiration, but also in the long process of planning and preparation devoted to the high moments of worship in which the final offering is made to the Lord's ear. Praise can be a moment's joyful shout, to be sure. But God is also due the praise that we decide to do, plan to do, and prepare to do. Without the creative process involved in this kind of worship, our efforts would not have the excellence that befits God.

It is this scriptural teaching of the role of planning and discipline in the matter of worship that instructs us to continue to praise God even when we are discouraged or when our spirits are flat and unemotional. Life sometimes renders us confused or spiritless. The appropriate response is not to abandon worship until we "feel like it," on the assumption that if we worshiped without our hearts being fully in what we were doing, we would somehow be hypocrites. Rather, the best response is to continue the discipline and obedience of worship, according to plan, according to the wise design of life. In God's time, if we continue to seek him, he will renew our spirits and revive the enthusiasm we long to have when we praise him.

Father, meet us in our worship so that as our voices sing to you, our hearts will sing because of you. Amen.

For who hath despised the day of small things? for they shall rejoice, and shall see the plummet in the hand of Zerubbabel...

Seeing our place in history

Human beings have a tendency to regard the past as if it were unreal, and to dismiss the future as if it were hypothetical. Christians suffering from this temporal myopia may fail to see how their lives contribute to holy history. The result may be that they neglect to do what fulfills the hopes of their ancestors and enriches the live of their descendants.

The Lord spoke through Zechariah to the Jews who had returned to Jerusalem from Babylon. They were in days of despondency and waning faith. They had returned a century before, but the glory of Israel was not yet restored. The current generation did not grasp either its identity as the people delivered from exile or as a people preparing the way for even greater days. God told them not to despise the day of small things. They were to rejoice in every use of a plumb line (plummet), and every chip of a hammer shaping stone, as the temple was raised, one small step at a time.

We Christians must never lose faith thinking our lives do not matter. Our obedience and faithfulness to God now will become a spiritual foundation for our children and grandchildren and theirs. We must not live only for ourselves, as if history began and ended with our lives. Every word of witness, every demonstration of God's love, is important to those living now and those yet to come. We must be content to contribute humbly to history, even to revel in our privilege to be part of God's plan of the ages. If, as is said in the theater, there are no small parts, only small actors, then let us walk faithfully with God, not insisting on more of the spotlight than he gives us, yet loving him and carrying out our individual roles with all our mind, soul, and strength.

Father, if history is His Story, then it is about Christ, not us. Help us to serve the star of history today. Amen.

We made our prayer unto our God, and set a watch against them day and night.

Watch and pray

During World War II, Chaplain Howell Forgy was aboard the U.S.S. New Orleans during the attack on Pearl Harbor. Urgent to encourage the sailors, he made his way along deck, patting men on the shoulder and saying, "Praise the Lord, and pass the ammunition." The remark was reported widely in a short time, and became a popular way of expressing the commonly held belief that people should trust in God, but not sit on the sidelines while they do.

The truth is rooted firmly in the Bible. Nehemiah described how the Jews rebuilding the wall of Jerusalem were subject to guerilla attacks intended to dissuade them from continuing. In response Nehemiah organized contingents of guards and ordered a two pronged countermove: pray and watch. The verse became the source of the maxim, "Watch and pray."

The Christian must avoid two extremes: ever praying but doing nothing; and doing everything but never praying. Instead, the biblical response to trial, trouble, opposition, persecution, difficulty—in short, to the myriad challenges of our lives—is a combination of prayer with obedience to God's never-changing principles. When you can do much, do it, and pray God will bless it. When you can do some, do it, and pray God will augment it. When you can do little, do it, and pray God will multiply it. But whatever you do in obedience, finish that obedience by praying. Pray that God will guide, sustain, and use your actions. In prayer, articulate your trust—not trust in your actions to be sufficient, but trust in God to work. Pray that God, whether he uses your actions or acts apart from them entirely, will be glorified in your life.

Father, help me meet every challenge today in the strength of the Spirit of Christ, to your glory. Amen.

Because of mine house that is waste, and ye run every man unto his own house. Therefore the heaven over you is stayed from dew, and the earth is stayed from her fruit.

The path back to blessing

The Bible does not offer automatic, one-button solutions to any of the problems believers face, or complete and instantaneous ways to undo the results of our sin or the sins of our culture. However, the Bible does teach that righteousness exalts a nation, and that when God's people turn back to the Lord, he will heal their land. In Haggai's day, God's people were allowing the house of God to lie in waste, while they took care of their own houses without hesitation. Affluence was on the rise, but avarice was, too, and inflation frustrated people's attempt to acquire a secure future. Haggai's message was not simplistic, but it was simple: you are experiencing havoc in your economy, and disappointing harvests as well, because you have neglected worship and have stopped investing yourselves and your resources in spiritual things. Build the temple, give of your time and resources, go back to being a people special to God, and he will restore you.

The principle taught by the first chapter of Haggai translates easily into the modern world. While the term "Christian nation" is probably a misnomer for any country, still God promises blessings for nations whose Christian populations are faithful in godliness. But the application to the individual Christian is even more specific. In their quest for security, Christians sometimes put their priority on work, financial success, and material acquisition. In such a plan, giving to God takes a low place on the checklist. Not a few persons have said, "I don't have enough money to tithe." Perhaps, however, the truth is that they do not have enough money *because* they do not tithe. While tithing does not guarantee instantaneous wealth, God says giving is a necessary part of the path back to his blessing. We cannot wait to give until God floods life with blessing: we must give first, in faith, and then wait for God to supply our need, and much more. He will.

Father, help us to believe you more and worry about our needs less. Amen.

And so will I go in unto the king, which is not according to the law: and if I perish, I perish.

Go for it!

In football, when it's fourth down for a team and they're not near the goal line, typically they punt. Even when close to a first down, they may punt rather than turn the ball over with advantage to the opposing team. But when there may not be time enough left in the game to punt, hold the line four downs, and get the ball back, there may be only one reasonable option: go for the first down. People in the stands, urgent for their team to score a winning touchdown, sometimes can be heard shouting, even when it may not seem judicious, "Go for it!"

Old Testament Esther, whose Jewish identity was not known, became a queen of Persia. When malevolent persons in the royal administration attempted to annihilate the Jewish population, Esther's uncle Mordecai urged her to plead with King Xerxes to change course. Since the law forbade her to approach the king unless bidden, she would risk death if she were to do so. But spurred on by the challenge that she may have come to the kingdom for such a time as this, she told Mordecai to have the Jews begin a three-day fast, after which she would go, uninvited, into the king's presence. If she were to be executed for it, so be it. Go for it.

Sometimes we attempt little for the Lord because we are afraid of failure, embarrassment, or rejection. Rather than go out on a limb, stick our necks out, or put our money where our mouths are, we punt. Whatever metaphors we may use to explain ourselves, we may choose to live with great reserve because we wish to avoid the negative repercussions of boldness. But in escaping the possibility of burden, we may be forfeiting the probability of blessing. It may be later in life than we know; it may be shorter distance to the goal than we realize, and there may be no time to wait for another opportunity to score. Go for it!

Lord, as the apostles did, let us also pray for boldness to speak your word and live for Christ. Amen.

In that day shalt thou not be ashamed for all thy doings, wherein thou hast transgressed against me: for then I will take away out of the midst of thee them that rejoice in thy pride...

The healing of heaven

The prophet Zephaniah preached a powerful message declaring God's judgment on Israel as well as her oppressors. But he said that in the end God's people would not be put to shame for their sins. Instead, God would separate his people from those who are not his, and then purify their hearts and conduct so that they would live without fear in his presence forever.

Some people have contradictory expectations of what comes after this life for the Christian. On the one hand, they acknowledge that the Bible teaches that a person who is saved goes to heaven, and they agree that heaven is a place where there is no death, sorrow, or crying. On the other hand, they have been led to believe that Christians who have frequently lost the struggle with sin will lose much of their spiritual reward and thus will be regretful. How can one feel regret and not be sorrowful?

Perhaps this conflict arises from mistaken assumptions about the "judgment seat of Christ" mentioned by Paul in Romans and 2 Corinthians. Those passages assure us that all people, including Christians, will be held accountable for their faithfulness to Christ or lack of it. But theologians cannot say what will happen at that judgment seat, and Paul did not give any details. Whatever the judgment seat of Christ means, it must not negate the promise of perfect joy. There is an accounting yet to come for the Christian, but it will not result in his being embarrassed to keep company with others in heaven. The certain prospect of being evaluated reminds us to be obedient, but the promise of a paradise of peace and perfection assures us that Jesus bore our sins for us. Perhaps each person's judgment will be a private moment before God in which his life is laid bare, his unrepented sins dealt with, and the peace of God's forgiveness then eliminates both guilt and apprehension forever.

Father, empower us to obey faithfully, and encourage us to hope triumphantly. Amen.

Better is an handful with quietness, than both the hands full with travail and vexation of spirit.

A key to contentment

Having capitalism as an economic system blesses a society in many ways, but it carries the potential to infect people with greed as well. Solomon described this danger when he said that man's achievement comes out of his envy of his neighbor (Eccl. 4:5). Then he offered this maxim for wise living: be content with one handful. Going for all you can get usually means saddling yourself with too much work, and experiencing the futility of acquiring things that you cannot ultimately keep.

Interpreting Ecclesiastes properly requires us to realize that the book is human philosophy, void of the transforming hope that comes from walking with God. Solomon began his reign as king with vast wisdom and a bright future. But he wandered from faithfulness, marrying hundreds of women, keeping a harem of hundreds more, adopting some of their religions, and indulging himself in great riches. As a result, his walk with God suffered greatly. When he wrote Ecclesiastes, he was reflecting on the meaningless of much of what he had pursued. Some of his observations were cynical, and are to be taken not as ultimate truths but as hard-nosed proverbs that illustrate what life is like when you lack a close walk with God.

Solomon's recommendation of how many handfuls to aim for is one of these poignant proverbs. Those strongly motivated by a desire to succeed may not run afoul of the dangers Solomon mentions, but often they do. Therein lies the wisdom of this saying: if you strain for two handfuls, you are playing against the odds. Sacrificing family, friends and enjoyment of life for wealth brings emptiness and wasted life. One handful instead of two may well be a key to contentment for most of us.

Father, strengthen us in godliness, and make us content with your blessings. Amen.

The Lord is good, a strong hold in the day of trouble; and he knoweth them that trust in him.

Security in trust

Nahum is a piece of writing that begins with the rumble of judgment against Nineveh and ends with a vision of how her many victims will rejoice at her fall. Little interrupts Nahum's fulminating prophecy against the wicked oppressor—except this tender promise: the Lord is good, and he cares for those who make him their refuge when they experience trouble. Israel was besieged by Assyria, but even while they were troubled from without, they could experience calm within as they placed their trust in God.

Part of the power of this promise in Nahum comes from the very fact that it is a sparkling gem set amid descriptions of evil plots, vile practices, and dark pronouncements. The book itself illustrates the situation of Christians many times. We live in a world that launches frequent attacks against those who worship God in truth and unrelenting attacks against that truth itself. Individually we often encounter a barrage designed to discourage our hearts and destroy our faith. Yet in the middle of the swirling troubles of our lives our sanctuary is found in the invisible but very real relationship we have with God in Jesus Christ. He who lives in our hearts makes us his temple, and he in turn is our sanctuary. As we turn to him in trust, he cares for us, and while the tempest outside may not immediately abate, the storm inside dissipates.

Experiencing the blessing of refuge in the Lord depends on our trust. When our troubles get the better of us, it may be due to our frantic worrying. Perhaps our prayer needs to be similar to that New Testament man challenged by Jesus to believe. He said, "Lord, I believe. Help thou mine unbelief." When both trust and despair mingle in our hearts, may God supply us grace, that we may trust him more.

Father, when all around our soul gives way, be then all our hope and stay. Amen.

Now the birth of Jesus Christ was on this wise: When as his mother Mary was espoused to Joseph, before they came together, she was found with child of the Holy Ghost.

Good news and bad news

Sometimes what looks at first like bad news turns out to be not so bad, or even downright good. Matthew tells the Christmas story beginning with the discovery that Mary was with child. He uses the passive voice to inform us that Mary "was found" to be pregnant. Matthew doesn't tell us how this fact was found out, just that it was. We know how Mary found out—that much is obvious. We also know that an angel calmed down Joseph *after* he found out, but how did Joseph find out? Did Mary tell him? Would she have talked about as delicate a subject as that? Was her pregnancy rumored among some of the women? We don't know. But Joseph found out, and it seemed like some of the worst news he had ever heard when he first learned it.

Everything changed, however, when he found out from a divine source just what the nature of this child was. Suddenly the bad news was good news, not just for Joseph, but for us. Mary and Joseph's willingness to be the bearers of a strange and misunderstood experience was the way the whole world was blessed with a Savior, Christ the Lord. Who knows what your burdens might do eventually—train you to help others? —equip you to deal with problems? —open the door to a whole new life, because you have been through something not everyone has?

A Christian woman was asked what was the best "bad" thing that had ever happened to her. She said it was when her husband had been laid off his job. He shortly became a consultant in his field, and it vaulted them to greater success than ever before. Bad news may come today, or soon, for any of us. But what is waiting around the corner? Sometimes bad news is good news in disguise.

Father, help us to look for the diamond in the lump of coal. For out of bad news came Jesus. Amen.

Joseph, thou son of David, fear not to take unto thee Mary thy wife: for that which is conceived in her is of the Holy Ghost.

God did it

A father happened in on a sibling feud as brother and sister were down to simple accusations: "She did it! —No I didn't; you did! —I did not!" We are frequently obsessed with assigning blame, or for that matter assuming credit. Most times, we prefer that others get the blame and we get the credit. However, when it comes to the most important single item of business for human life, the matter of knowing God in a saving way, God makes clear to us who gets the credit. Matthew said that an angel kept Joseph from divorcing Mary by telling him in a dream that the child was from the Holy Spirit. He further told Joseph that the Son, to be named Jesus, would save his people from their sins.

When it comes to salvation, let this be clear: God started it, and God did it. Joseph thought Mary's pregnancy was the result of unfaithfulness with some other man. In fact, it was the result of God's faithfulness to his promise to send a redeemer for fallen mankind. In this world of inflated egos and people on the way to the top, there is the tendency more than ever to think, 'If I make it to heaven, I will do it on my own.' Many religions give credit to people for earning their way into heaven, making up for their sin, or deserving the gift of salvation. God says: I did it; I started it; without what I have done, without my initiative, you would have nothing to look forward to.

James reminds us that every good gift comes from the Father. The origin of all good things in God has much to say about what our daily attitudes should be. Instead of going around as if God owed us an easy time and every break in life, we should be thankful every moment for every possible blessing, especially the totally unmerited one of eternal life, which we have if we know Christ personally.

Father, we credit you for the blessing of Jesus Christ. Without him, we would have nothing. Amen.

Then Joseph being raised from sleep did as the angel of the Lord had bidden him, and took unto him his wife.

The importance of the virgin birth

Joseph and Mary were not married at the time of Jesus' birth. Matthew's account says that Joseph "took unto him his wife." But Luke 2:5 says that when Joseph went to Bethlehem with Mary, she was his "espoused wife." Whatever Joseph did prior to going to Bethlehem, something legally kept Mary what we would call his fiancée. They had not consummated their marriage. Sexual union made a marriage complete and official. Matthew explains that Joseph "knew her not till she had brought forth her firstborn son" (1:25).

The scripture is plainly saying that Mary's child was of the Holy Spirit, not the result of sexual union. To further emphasize that fact, Joseph and Mary agreed to put off sexual union and, hence, their true marriage, until after Jesus' birth. It may be that although Joseph "took her unto himself," their living arrangement was known to be separate, indicating to all that they were not sexually husband and wife. If they had begun enjoying the sexual union of married persons months before the birth of Jesus, that fact would have cast doubt on his virginal conception.

Not only was God the progenitor of the world's Savior, but he ensured that the world would have reasonable evidence of this truth. Even so, many people have always disbelieved it. Why? Is it simply because of reluctance to believe in miracles? No. Deep down it is because to confess the virgin birth is to go a long way toward accepting the gospel and all the demands of repentance and the Lordship of Christ that it makes. It is not up to us to determine the truth of the virgin birth, only to accept or reject its implications. Isaiah said, "Behold, the virgin shall conceive and bear a son, and shall call his name 'Immanuel'" —God with us. Christmas means God is with us in Christ. Those who confess the incarnation can know God personally and intimately.

Father, thank you for the evidence of Jesus' heavenly origin in his virgin birth. May we experience him with us today. Amen.

For we have seen his star in the east, and are come to worship him.

The significance of a star

When we dig into the possible meaning of the star of the Magi, we discover some interesting facts. The Magi were astronomers of sorts, mostly astrologers, probably from Babylon, who believed that special stars appeared at the births of great people. Most modern people do not put stock in such ideas. Was there a star of Bethlehem? The Bible says there was. In fact, this is what was unique about it: it really did appear at the birth of a great person. To the Magi, the star's location and movement convinced them of its meaning. Why would God cause a star to appear, and thus seem to verify for pagans a superstitious idea?

Perhaps God wanted to contrast truth with fiction. It was said a star had appeared at the birth of the current Caesar, but nobody knew any details, and no one other than the Roman astronomers who claimed it had seen it. Now, here is this manger-born child, birthed in a stable in a village in a conquered country, and a star—or something that could be described by unscientific men only as a star—actually did appear. Moreover, it moved, leading Magi on a journey, and stopped over a house. Here was this great glowing wonder at the boy Jesus' home, for he was the King of kings. Perhaps the Magi were silently admitting to themselves, "We only thought we had seen special stars before, but this one is real: this must be the real thing—the greatest birth of all." And so it was.

Some people think that the Bible is proprietary—that it belongs to a specific religion that is only one of several or many valid religions. But part of the message of the star of Bethlehem is that God has sent his Living Truth to the whole world, both to those who already believe his word and to those who do not yet know it. Choosing faith in Christ is responding to the self-revelation of the God who made the universe and prepared a special star to herald his Savior.

Father, lead us by your light to the presence of Jesus this Christmas. Amen.

And lo, the star, which they saw in the east, went before them, till it came and stood over where the young child was.

God's leading

The Magi do not appear to have been God's people, but whoever they were—and scholars are by no means unanimous in their opinions—their coming to discover the king born in Bethlehem was a curious journey. They followed a star that led them to the region of Jerusalem and from there to Bethlehem. In a scientific age, we want to know what the star was. Many people think this might have been a planetary conjunction, a nova, a comet, or some other known phenomenon. But these things do not lead people across the desert, or stop over a house in Bethlehem. One of these phenomena could "appear" to stop over a particular place, but it would have to appear to do so to each of these Magi, and it would have to appear to do it only after it had appeared to lead the Magi to Bethlehem, which implies movement. It is much easier to accept the proposition that this was a special, miraculous event that cannot otherwise be explained by astronomers.

The larger point of this fascinating bit of history is that God uses various, often inexplicable means to lead us to truth. He sometimes uses indicators that others may not see at all. By the way, the Bible implies that no one else in this story was aware of any star. Was it even visible to others? Perhaps it was, but it did not make sense to any but those who were supposed to be led by it.

The process of leadership is specialized for us. What is essential is for us to see with our faith and be willing to be led. Otherwise, we may pass up an opportunity we ought to take. Or, we might think our circumstances are merely coincidental, not realizing that God designed them purposely to guide us. If we *will* be led, in the end our "star" will show us the goal of our life's journey, and we will have cause to do as the Magi did: "When they saw the star, they rejoiced."

Father, already you are leading us. May we simply see the stars of your guidance and follow them. Amen.

And it came to pass in those days, that there went out a decree from Caesar Augustus, that all the world should be taxed.

God giveth

The occasion of Joseph and Mary's being in Bethlehem was that Caesar had ordered everyone to be taxed. The gospel writer's first mention of taxation is useful. But he literally bombards us with the disagreeable idea three times in the next four verses. The Greek word translated "tax" is perhaps more accurately "register." But the principal reason for the registration of people was to tax them. Either way you look at it, Luke firmly fixes in our minds the fact that the Empire was exercising one of its favorite powers: taking things away from people.

What a contrast this taxation was, however, to what else was happening! Luke says this taxation came to pass "in those days," meaning the days in which God appeared to Mary, placed his incarnate Son in her womb, and led her and Joseph to the place where Jesus was to be born. While in the world the lord of the realm was about to exercise his right to take things away from people, in the little town of Bethlehem the Lord of heaven was preparing to exercise his grace in giving something to all humanity. While the Roman Empire was demonstrating its power to subjugate nations, God Almighty was demonstrating his power to free humanity. As John would later write, "God so loved the world that he gave his only begotten Son."

Old Testament Job memorably phrased a realistic truth: "The Lord gave, and the Lord hath taken away." When Luke wrote about the nativity, perhaps, if only subtly, he was proposing a similar but contrasting observation: The world taketh away, but the Lord giveth. In the midst of the taxing toil the world demands of us, look at the gracious gift God offers us in Christ. While the world seems to conspire to take away joy, hope and meaning, Jesus holds these things in his hand, reaches out to us, and invites us into life.

Father, thank you for giving us what no one can take away, in your Son and our Savior. Amen.

Glory to God in the highest, and on earth peace, good will toward men.

God's great gift

Perhaps no words in the Bible have been reproduced more than Luke 2:14. The King James phrasing has a majestic ring as it describes the nature of God's act in sending his Son. Translators, however, have been concerned about the misinterpretation of the verse. To some people it suggests that Christ's coming guarantees eventual peace as mankind becomes more benevolent under God's influence. Some assume the verse teaches us that God has forsaken judgment, and will simply express goodwill from now on. Neither idea is strictly biblical.

Part of the problem is that the precise meaning of the Greek words is debatable. Translators have offered various alternatives. Some suggest that God's peace is given to *men* of goodwill. Others think the verse says God's peace comes upon men for whom *he* has goodwill. Both these translations solve the problem prompted by the King James, but each creates its own new problem: Does God offer his peace only to those who already are inclined to be nice to one another? Or does God offer his peace only to some people but not to others? The test of any translation of this verse may be to compare it to the clear words of the angel just moments before: "I bring you good tidings of great joy, which shall be to *all* people."

The point of the verse is not dulled by the problem with its exact translation. Any way you render it, the verse proclaims that God's gift of Jesus Christ brings peace to humanity. We know from Jesus' teaching and the rest of scripture that the angel meant first peace with God, then peace of heart, and finally peace between people. We also know the way to receive God's gift is through placing faith in Jesus Christ and exercising that same faith every day. As Paul says of Jesus in Ephesians 2:14, "He is our peace." One day, Christ will return to remove all conflict. Then his peace and goodwill will reign everywhere, and permeate all his people.

Father, Son, and Spirit, let the Prince of Peace reign in our hearts from this day forward. Amen.

And they came with haste…

Urgency to find Jesus

If we had been with the shepherds outside Bethlehem when angels appeared and announced the birth of a Savior, we would not have thought twice about leaving the flocks with anyone who would agree to tend them, and hurrying across the hillsides into the little town to find the manger bed. When we read that the shepherds came "with haste," it really does not surprise us, and it would not have surprised the first readers of Luke's gospel. Though he did not need to do so, however, Luke applied the adjective to the shepherds' coming. Clearly he meant for us to consider the significance of their speed.

Haste is the natural response to urgency. What we feel must be done immediately because we may not be able to do it later we hasten to do before time is lost. Luke's message in describing the shepherds' hurry is meant to exhort each of us to seek the Lord while he may be found. The gospel is good news that people who have bottomed out on self-effort and self-righteousness and seeking to find themselves can find forgiveness, peace and eternal life in Jesus right now. There is an urgency about responding to this news. Paul told the Corinthian church, "Behold, now is the accepted time; behold, now is the day of salvation" (2 Cor. 6:2).

But the Bible exhorts us who are already Christians to continue to feel urgency about seeking the Lord and knowing Christ. Isaiah wrote to God's people when he said, "Seek ye the Lord while he may be found" (55:6). Hebrews twice enjoins the believer, "Today, if ye will hear his voice, harden not your hearts" (3:15, 4:7). When temptations get the better of us, when failure, hurt, frustration, or trouble begin to affect our fellowship with God, there is no time to lose. To delay is to invite bitterness, defeat, and alienation. God sent Jesus to save us, and we must come with haste to experience his renewal. He promised us success when we hurry to him: "And ye shall seek me, and find me, when ye shall search for me with all your heart" (Jer. 29:13).

Savior, like a shepherd lead us, ever back to you, and ever to know you as Redeemer and Friend. Amen.

If ye then, being evil, know how to give good gifts unto your children, how much more shall your Father which is in heaven give good things to them that ask him?

The gift no one will exchange

In some cultures to refuse a gift is to gravely insult the giver. In American culture, while we seldom refuse gifts directly, we commonly refuse them indirectly: we exchange them for something else. The practice is so common that many people when buying presents for others do not concern themselves with choosing just the right gift, or with what the recipient really wants or needs. Instead, they simply spend a target amount of money, and say, "You can exchange it for what you want." While most of us have adapted to this system, it says something about us that doesn't highly compliment us.

An expectation of exchange doesn't heavily influence giving to children, however. Perhaps because adults do not expect children to go back to stores and do their own shopping, their gifts are more thoughtfully given. The look in children's eyes and the unsuppressed excitement on their faces provide confirmation that a present was just what they wanted or needed.

We are God's children. What he has given us in Christ as our Savior and what he continues to give us through the Spirit of Christ daily is truly good. It is precisely what we need, and as we begin to experience the mind of Christ, it is exactly what we want. We may think sometimes that God has not given us what we needed. We may think we need more of this, less of that, or something someone else has. Many things we think are essential, even some things we think God must want us to have, are not in fact what he knows we really need. When we worry or fret or think God is denying us, we need to hear Jesus' words again: You know how to give your children what is truly good. Do you think God our Father knows less?

Do not be reluctant to pray for what you think you need. But more than that, pray for what God wants you to have. When he opens his hand, you will not wish to exchange the gift.

Father, through our walk with you may we want what you want for us, so our prayers will always be answered. Amen.

And this is love, that we walk after his commandments.

Being nice

Too often when people say, “I’m telling you this in love,” really they are trying to exact revenge or achieve advantage. Other times people decline to confront wrong conduct by others thinking that a loving person will tolerate anything indefinitely. How do we know when we are really doing the loving thing?

A woman came to a four-way stop several seconds before another driver arrived from the opposite direction. She had the right of way, but she kindly waved the other driver through. The second driver motioned for her to go, but she did the same. While they were exchanging gestures, a third driver arrived on the woman’s right, and a fourth pulled up behind her. Meanwhile the second driver decided someone had to go, and he did. The woman then cheerily waved the driver on her right to go as well. Balking, the third driver motioned for her to go, since clearly he didn’t have the right of way. But the woman continued to wave, and finally the third driver threw up his hands and drove on. The fourth driver, waiting in exasperation behind the woman, tooted his horn. The woman, waved hello over her head, then slowly turned and drove away. The fourth driver thought to himself: “Don’t be nice: obey the rules!”

Right-of-way rules were devised to make driving both safe and courteous to all. Ignoring them in favor of one’s own idea of what is “nice” frequently creates aggravating and even dangerous situations. The same is true with God’s law and the command of Christ, but in a much more significant way. Christ commanded us to love one another and John defines loving one another as obeying Christ’s commands. That sounds like simply restating the question, but it isn’t. John is saying that loving each other means doing all the things Jesus taught us were part of a Christlike response: being gracious and patient, being forgiving, helping and encouraging, praying and sacrificing for others, and much more. It isn’t enough to say we love or to have warm feelings. Loving means obeying Christ’s commands.

Lord Jesus, help us learn your character by looking at your life and by letting you rule in us. Amen.

Then I spake unto them of the captivity all the things that the Lord had shewed me.

Recipients and conduits

Ezekiel was the recipient of vivid and often intense revelation from God. His vision of the angelic wheel within a wheel gave him a more profound sense of the holiness of God than most people ever imagine. When the Spirit spoke to him, he heard powerful truths. Ezekiel's walk with God was wonderfully and deeply affected by his private experiences with the Almighty. However, Ezekiel did not keep his experiences private. We know of his visions because he wrote them down. But even before his encounters became a Bible book, they were spoken words. Ezekiel told the captive Israelites everything God had showed him.

When you hear from God, you become a messenger. This principle of learning and then teaching is incorporated into the design of the church. Paul instructed Timothy to take what he had taught him, teach it to selected others, and show them how to do the same. If early Christians had not functioned in this way, the church would not have survived.

God works in your life in a personal way. No one has walked quite the same path you have. God's working is designed to mature you in your knowledge of him, but it is not designed to do so for you alone. As you become a recipient, you become a conduit as well. What has God taught you through a recent experience? What has he shown you in worship? How has he shown himself faithful? How has he uplifted you or even corrected you? You have received these messages, learned these lessons, and seen God work so that you may benefit personally and then share the benefits with others. This is the heart of the meaning of *testimony.* God expects us to share with others what he does in our lives. We should do it with humility, not claiming to be any unique spokesman for God, but we should do it. Someone nearby today may be there because God wants him or her to hear what he has done for you.

Father, make me a blessing to someone today, through something you have done for me. Amen.

And Joseph called the name of the firstborn Manasseh: For God, said he, hath made me forget all my toil, and all my father's house.

Forgetting the pain

Women who give birth often say that when they hold their newborn children in their arms, they quickly forget the pain. Physical pain is often relieved quickly through medicine, surgery or other means, and though we remember that we did feel it, we don't feel it anymore. Emotional or spiritual pain disappears more slowly, but God often ministers to us by bringing us into some new vista that displaces the hurt with a new sense of joy or fulfilment.

Joseph was tormented by his own brothers, attacked, bound, and sold into slavery, being carted off into another country to suffer more privations, false accusations, and imprisonment. But because he remained faithful to God he rose from his difficulties in a mounting wave of victory. The country of his enslavement honored him with power, and God blessed him with a new family. When his first son was born, the pain of his past receded so far into the background of his heart that he said he no more remembered all the hardship that had thrust him into nightmare, and all the alienation from his family that had grieved him. God had replaced the pain with new joy.

When we are traveling rough roads, we may find it difficult to believe that a time will come when the pain we are feeling will be virtually forgotten. But if we are faithful in walking with God, while our minds may retain the facts of our hardships, God will give the peace and healing that makes our hearts forget. How he brings this relief differs infinitely. Sometimes he returns a former blessing; sometimes he provides a new one. Sometimes he launches us from shades of night into plains of light. Sometimes the landscape changes with an avalanche of unexpected change, while other times a new day of joy breaks gradually on the horizons of gentle revolution. But God is faithful, and to those who continue to walk expectantly with him, he brings healing to the heart.

Father, help us see with the eyes of faith, and keep doing your will. Amen.

I am small and despised: yet do not I forget thy precepts.

Little lights

A pastor who began a children's sermon time during his church's worship service took as its theme verse Matthew 5:14, "You are the light of the world," and as its theme song, "This Little Light of Mine." He called those few minutes in the service, "Little Lights," because children who love the Lord have a special place in the kingdom of God, giving light to the world.

David's lengthy Psalm 119 is all about the word of God and how he loved it and wanted to follow it and proclaim it. Yet he realized that his individual contribution was relatively small. He characterized himself as small and despised. But he was glad to say with humility that he had given his corner of the world an example of obedience.

If King David, who ruled Israel in her glory, wrote much of what became scripture, modeled praise and worship for all generations to come, and was called a man after God's own heart, was "small and despised," what does that say for most of us? As famous as any of us may become, is he ever more than one person living for God? And since most of us are never in places of great prominence, never lead nations or people in history-making movements, and never influence more than a few people in our own little worlds, are we not even more small and insignificant than David? Yet each of us is responsible for that little corner of the sinful world in which we live, and each has the duty to be faithful in God's precepts. Each of us is a little light for God, a candlestick for the Light of the world, Jesus Christ. Each of us therefore must say to himself, I am not anybody great to whom the whole world looks, but what example I do have will be one of trust and obedience to God's word. Someone's way may be lit by the life I live today. So, this little light of mine, I'm going to let it shine.

Jesus, Light of the world, brighten the corner where I am by shining through me. Amen.

December 31 **Scripture Reading: Psalm 92:12,14**

The righteous shall flourish like the palm tree… They shall still bring forth fruit in old age.

Continue to bear fruit

Between Christmas and New Year's Day, many people don't know exactly what to do, and they don't feel like doing it. But most think about the possibilities that may lie in a new year. Actually, we don't know that we have a new year, or even one more new day. All we have is today, right now. What God wants us to do is to bear fruit now and keep bearing fruit as long as he gives us life.

The Psalmist said that the righteous will be like palm trees, which even when old, if healthy, still bear fruit. No matter what it looks like in this crazy world, the people of God, the believers, the righteous, will outlast the people of the world, the unbelievers, the wicked. The righteous are not sinless, but they are headed in God's direction, after having been pardoned of their sin by his grace. As the saying goes, Christians are not perfect, just forgiven. Because they have been redeemed by Christ, they have become recipients of the promise that they will be victors along with Christ. Evil and the progress of sinfulness and lunacy in this world will not prevail. Though the church also sometimes seems to be on the way out, it will not prove to be so in the final accounting.

A pecan tree that stood in a family's back yard bore great harvests of nuts. Along the way, however, tree borers got to it, winding their way up the trunk. One could see the holes in a nearly perfect spiral up the tree. Eventually the tree went from every other year crops to every third, then fourth, then finally no crop at all. It was cut down and used for firewood. What a shame that a huge tree should be defeated by bugs no one ever saw.

The false Christian and nominal believer will be like that tree, but never the true believer, the ongoing Christian. He will be like a tree planted by the rivers of water, that bringeth forth his fruit in his season (Ps.1:3). In old age, he will still be faithful, and will get the victory.

Father, forgive my failures past, and keep me faithful today and every day. Amen.

www.ingramcontent.com/pod-product-compliance
Lightning Source LLC
Chambersburg PA
CBHW030936150426
42812CB00064B/2933/J

* 9 7 8 0 9 8 3 4 6 4 2 2 8 *